The BACHELOR PAD YEARS

North / South Divide: Volume 5

Interesting Books...
...Fascinating Subjects!

POSH UP NORTH Publishing

www.poshupnorth.com

Publishing History
"Recreational Ice Hockey 1987-1990" was previously published in North / South Divide –
Volume 2: Ice Hockey & Me in September 2021 by Ice Hockey Review, which is an imprint of
Posh Up North Publishing, Beckenham Road, Wallasey, United Kingdom

This edition published in Great Britain in April 2022 by
Posh Up North Publishing, Beckenham Road, Wallasey, United Kingdom

ISBN-13: 978-1-909643-48-2

Cover Photos
Front Cover:
Top left: Marx Engels Platz in Berlin, May 1990
Top middle: Sightseeing in Lancashire, June 1992
Top right: Polish Czech Border, September 1990
Bottom left: First Car, August 1990
Bottom middle: Wedding Usher, September 1992
Bottom right: Away Match at Sunderland, September 1992
Back Cover: Hoek van Holland Ferry, May 1990

LIST OF CONTENTS

INTRODUCTION

This book has not been written as a serious commercial venture. By that, I mean that I don't expect millions of people all over the world to want to buy it and I am not expecting to make any money out of selling it. But it is, at least, available should somebody somewhere feel that need...

I had a bout of ill health in 2020 and, had things worked out differently, I might not have been here now to write these lines.

Luckily I am - more or less - back to normal now – but the whole experience made me reflect upon the fact that, if anything HAD happened to me, then the whole melange of memories, experiences, interesting stories and other trivia that has been accumulated in my brain over 50 or so years would all be lost.

I thought that would be a bit of a shame so, as a sort of "self healing therapy", I decided to write the more interesting things down for the benefit of future generations.

This book is mainly aimed at friends and family members – ie: people who know me and may remember some of the episodes that I have recounted - and I hope they might find the stories interesting and enjoyable.

If, however, you haven't a clue who I am and still want to read this book, then I hope there is enough general interest information for you to be able to enjoy it as well.

Paul Breeze
Wallasey, April 2022

A Note On Photos:

A lot of the photos in this book are a bit ropey, for which I apologise - but there is not much I can do about it.

As we are looking back at things that happened 30 or 40 years ago in some cases, they are all scanned from old photographic prints and many of those originals are not very good either.

You can take a much better image on your phone these days than was possible with the average amateur family camera back in the old days and you can immediately check whether the shot actually has come out rather than having to wait to finish the film and then send it away to be developed.

The problem with making a high quality digital scan of a poor original image is that it tends to enhance the impurities as well as the basic picture – and there are complicated technical things like colour separations to think about as well.

So, some photos are better than others but they are the only ones I have got and I hope they will serve to illustrate the stories included in this book.

Preamble: Girls At School, Girl Friends and Girlfriends

When I was little, we boys didn't tend to have much to do with girls. We weren't strictly segregated like they had been in Victorian times with separate entrances at school or whatever. We all went to the same schools and sat in the same classrooms – but there was always a bit of a social divide.

Boys liked playing football, and fighting, whereas girls preferred skipping and doing that thing where you throw tennis balls up against the wall in rotation and keep catching them – and the two groups didn't tend to mix, unless they were forced to.

Back then, the only girls I ever had much social contact with, outside school, were the daughter of the next door neighbours – who was older than me – or the sisters of my various friends and these usually fitted into two categories. Either the sisters were older, in which they were snooty, aloof and bossy and no fun, or they were younger, in which case they were annoying, got in the way of things and were no fun.

And, whilst I get on very well with women of all ages these days, would you believe that, in some cases when I was at school, being seated next to a girl was actually viewed as a form of punishment!

In Mrs Hunns' class at Southfields Junior School we were all sat "boy, girl - boy, girl" in pairs around the classroom, presumably to avoid groups of mates forming together who would then have the opportunity to mess about and be disruptive.

I was initially placed next to Sarah Cooke and we got on like a house on fire. In fact, we used to natter so much that, not very long into the term, Mrs Hunns split us up and I was ordered to go and sit next to Joanne Harrison instead.

I always liked Joanne, actually. She was witty, intelligent, did great Paddington stares, could read music and play the piano.

She was by far the cleverest girl in any class she was ever in (with the possible exception of Louise Knighton in specialist science classes later on ...) and, as such, she and I were often in the same teaching groups for various subjects over the years.

Despite being miffed at having to move away from Sarah Cooke, I was quite pleased to be sitting next to Joanne as I was hoping that some of her greatness might rub off on me.

By Way Of Explanation: (Plus A Tale of Three Karens)

In case you are wondering, Sarah Cooke is always "Sarah Cooke" in my head – to distinguish her from Sarah Thompson, who was also in our classes in those days. I realise that she is married now and actually has a different surname in real life - but she has been Sarah Cooke in my mind for the last 50 years and I can't really alter that now.

We only ever had one Joanne in my classes at school so Joanne Harrison has always just been "Joanne" and doesn't need to be separately identified. Joanne Korosi – who I later worked with at Baker Perkins - has always been "Joanne Korosi" as a result. I hope that makes sense - it does to me anyway...).

To take this a step further – and I'm sorry to go off the point a bit but this is relevant if you want to understand my way of thinking about things and how I express them.

We had three "Karen"s in my latter years at school: Karen Robinett, Karen Goodacre and Karen Glover, none of whom I had known from primary school and all of whom became known to me over the same approximate period. This is why I would refer to them by their full names, so as to be able to properly differentiate. There may well have been other Karens around but I didn't necessarily know them.

The three Karens and I all ended I up in the 6th Form together and at that time it was quite a small closed community.

There was a huge amount of socialising that went on pretty much all the time – more so than study work for the most part – and we all went to each other's 18th birthday parties, and did lots of other things together, even if you didn't necessarily like all the others people involved.

Overall, it was a bit of a strange "microcosmic world" for those two academic years 1983 to 1985.

Karen Robinett was good at languages and she studied A level French and Italian - like I did - and she also went on the French exchange to Montpellier – as did Diana Pacocha, in fact.

However Karen was a close friend of Louise's all the way through school and Alan Platt was a good friend of mine and we all used to socialise outside of school and also in later years, whereas I didn't with the others - so I did know Karen Robinett slightly better.

If I was talking to Alan and Louise and mention was made of "Karen", then there would be no doubt at all that we were talking about Karen Robinett.

Interestingly enough after she graduated from University , she ended up temping as a secretary at Baker Perkins for a bit – albeit in a completely separate part of the company to where I was.

So I went off and found her one day and said "hello" - just to be sociable - and we did a couple of things after work as mates but then she got some top job in London and I have never seen her since.

Therefore, for the purposes of my overall life story, she needs to remain as "Karen Robinett", rather than a main "Karen" for reasons that will become clearer later...

So, I gathered all the stuff up out of my desk. In those days, we had the old fashioned desks with a lift-up top where you could store all your books and pens etc beneath.

The desks also had a groove across the top beyond the hinge where you'd lay your writing implements when you weren't using them and an ink well holder in the top right hand corner (which must have been very awkward for left handed people...).

We didn't use ink wells by then – these were just very old desks. The school had been built in the early 1950s so I suppose the desks had been in place ever since then. By the time that I am talking about, everybody used ballpoint pens or cartridge pens so the ink wells had become obsolete and they generally had a collection of pencil sharpenings and bits of grotty old discarded chewing gum in them.

I'd hate to think how long the chewing gum had actually been there as nobody I knew ever chewed gum during class.

I seem to think that I had to change places with Mark Eastwood so he moved his stuff out of his desk and took his place next to Sarah Cooke and I moved in next to Joanne - which was over by the window.

As I recall (although this might be a "false memory" that I have made up in the intervening years to add to the dramatic effect of the story), this was done in the middle of the morning in full view of the rest of the class – like most tellings-off and punishments used to be in those days (no mental health concerns back then...!).

So I got installed next to Joanne and the class of whatever we were learning about at the time recommenced. I distinctly remember turning to her to say something or other - and I daresay she has forgotten this by now, but it is fixed in my memory forever. The very first words that I ever remember Joanne saying to me were:

"SHUT UP!"

Memories to cherish – eh?

First Girl Friend

My first girl friend – that's merely a friend who happens to be a girl, as opposed to a "girlfriend" of the snogging variety... - was Julie Carroll, when we were about 8 or 9.

She was in my class at school in the 3rd year juniors when we had Miss Burgess as a teacher. In that classroom we were seated around tables of four and I sat next to Darren McAulay and Julie Carroll and Sheron Howard sat opposite us.

We had the table in the far corner and it must have been a satisfactory arrangement as I think we stayed together for the whole of the year and nobody ever got moved round.

In fact, the four of us jointly designed the winning entry for the whole of the 3rd years for the "SPIF Competition".

I'll explain this as it is a nugget of interesting social history that, by now, most people will have probably forgotten about.

Our primary school was one of the first in the county to have its own swimming pool in the 1960s. I know they later got one at St John's School as well because I used it a few times during summer playschemes – but that was in the summer holiday when the weather was generally nicer.

Both pools were pretty much the same design: outdoor, not very deep - about 1m and maybe a bit deeper at the other end – and they were always freezing cold!

Ours was round the back of the school – past the bike sheds and dustbins - and, in order to use it, you had to get changed in the toilets in the main building and then rush across the yard with only a towel to keep the driving wind and rain off you.

In our modern enlightened times of sensible practices, child protection and health and safety, this sounds like a complete nightmare but our swimming lessons used to comprise of our regular class teacher standing fully clothed (and wrapped up warm...) by the edge of the pool shouting out instructions as to what we poor sodden and freezing mites ought to be doing.

These swimming lessons came as a big shock to me initially as I couldn't swim – and it turned out that everybody else could! The whole of the rest of the class were splashing about joyfully and swimming around and dipping underwater while I stood down at the other end, not really knowing what to do.

The school had a load of floats – rectangular buoyancy aids that you could use to get started - but people who were using these just made awful splashes in their wake and getting the stinging chlorinated water in my eyes did little to endear me to this newly discovered activity of swimming.

It turned out that most people had already learnt to swim by going to the Lido pool in the town centre, the Jack Hunt School pool on the other side of town or at the Phorpres pool which was at the London Brick Company sports and social club. I imagine that most people went with their parents to these places and this is how they came to learn.

My dad couldn't swim - although he used to take me out into the waves on the Norfolk coast when we were away on holiday at the seaside – and, while my mum COULD swim, she always said it was too cold. In fact, I have only ever seen her swim once in my entire life and that was in the sea off Hunstanton and it must have been the long hot drought summer of 1976.

The Lido pool in Peterborough town centre was – and, I believe it's still there - a 1930s style outdoor pool. It had a big main pool with a deep end and diving boards, a smaller shallower pool for kiddies to paddle in and a large grassy area where you could sunbathe and have picnics.

It was the sort of place where families would go for the whole day – but my family never went, obviously, for the reasons already described above.

I did go once when I was little with a friend and his older sister but didn't really enjoy it as the water was cold, I couldn't swim back then and everybody else was bigger than me....

Having said that, I did go to the Lido pool on several occasions as an adult in the early 1990s, during the hot summer months. A group of us would go together after work and that was a much more pleasurable experience.

I was bigger than everybody else by then – an impressive athletic 6'4" - could swim quite well and the cool water was especially inviting after long hot stuffy days in the office.

In 1976 (I just looked that up...) a big new indoor swimming pool complex was built in Peterborough. This was a full size pool, could host major competitions, had spectator seating, the full array of diving boards and a very deep deep end.

The good thing about this place was that it was indoors and it was warm!

It also had a separate shallow learners' pool that was even warmer and nice to lounge around in if it wasn't too busy.

This was called the "Regional Pool" although we all called it the "new pool" for quite a while after that – and I still do occasionally, even though I understand that it is now due to be pulled down and replaced with a new new pool.

Once the new pool opened, I went a few times with Darren McAuley and John Ludman during the summer. We'd walk into town, have a swim, buy some chips and then get the bus back to Stanground afterwards.

Here again, in later years - once I was able to swim properly - I went to the new pool loads of times with different friends and work colleagues.

I even went a few times with my dad after he suddenly decided that he wanted to have a go at learning to swim.

He didn't get on very well but it was a nice family outing for once as me and my brother went in the pool and my mum watched from the spectator seating, so overall, I have very fond memories of the place.

I didn't actually fully learn to swim properly until I was in the final year at Southfields Junior School in 1978. They had a beginners swimming certificate that everybody got once they had managed to swim a length of our freezing cold pool and also successfully retrieved a brick from the bottom.

These certificates were presented in front of the whole school at morning assembly and there was a drive to ensure that by the time you left the school, everybody ought to be able to swim.

I was in Mr Walker's class that year and somehow it was arranged that once a week - or once a month or whatever it was - we would all go over to the big indoor pool at the Comprehensive School for swimming sessions at lunchtime. I don't know if the other classes did this as well or if it was just ours – you didn't get told things like that in those days.

We all had to take a packed lunch with us for that day and we crossed the main road and walked across the big field up to the other school. I got on a lot better in the warmer water of the big school pool and the extra depth helped with buoyancy. I slowly got the hang of it and eventually managed to doggy paddle my way across the width of the pool – which was the equivalent of a length of the small outdoor pool – to lots of shouts of encouragement from my class mates, which was nice.

I somehow managed to hold my nose, put my head underwater and retrieve the famous brick - and that had me qualified to receive my swimming certificate at the school assembly, which pleased me no end.

NONE of which actually explains the SPIF Competition - so let me get back to that...

At some point, somebody at the junior school must have come to realise that making little kiddies get changed in the school bogs and then run across the yard in full view of any passers-by to get to the swimming pool was not a completely satisfactory situation.

So plans were drawn up to build a block of changing rooms adjacent to the pool and to put a roof around the edge and make it a more pleasant place to swim. I understand that there were also hopes to turn it into a community facility and have it open in the evenings to members of the public on a chargeable basis as well, like the Jack Hunt School indoor pool was.

But all this needed money and thus was born the Swimming Pool Improvement Fund - or SPIF for short.

I daresay there were a load of fundraising measures that went on behind the scenes at county education level with grants and so on but the things that we were actively encouraged to get involved with around the school included "buy a brick" and collecting newspapers.

The "Buy A Brick" scheme allowed for parents, families, local businesses and – presumably - anybody else who wanted to chip in, to pay a sum of money and their names were then put up on brick shaped stickers on a SPIF wall in the school reception area.

I think the total raised was posted up occasionally but can't for the life of me imagine that it ever came anywhere near covering the actual costs involved in what was a major building project.

The newspaper collection was something that everybody could easily get involved with and it made us feel as if we were all doing our bit.

This was back in the days before recycling and most people just threw their old newspapers in the rubbish, or if they had an open fire, used them on there.

There were certain organisations, however, that would pay a certain amount per ton for newspapers that they could recycle and do something with - and our school set up an arrangement with one of those.

So everybody started saving their old newspapers at home and, once they had a big enough bundle, would bring them in. There was a big store cupboard on the outside of the main school building where they were all kept and first thing in the morning the caretaker would open it up – occasionally I remember the headmaster Mr Singleton doing it as well – so that new donations could be deposited. Quite often, parents would arrive with a huge boot full in their cars and it was quite a large scale operation.

Once the store was full, the company would send a lorry round to pick up all the newspapers, presumably weighed the load somewhere and then the process would start all over again.

While this was going on, the school decided to run a competition for the pupils to design posters to help promote the SPIF fund. This was motivating the masses at its very best as there was to be a prize of £1 (a lot of money to a 9/10 year old in those days) for the best entry from each of the 4 year groups, 50p for second place and 25p for third place.

Plus you could draw your posters in your normal art class at school so nobody had an excuse not to have a go.

For reasons that I no longer recall, Darren, Sheron, Julie and I decided to do our poster as a group effort and we ended up with something involving a robot with lots of attachments who was holding a SPIF placard.

To my great surprise, our entry was chosen as the best out of all of the 3rd years but, because there were four of us, we had to split the prize money and got 25p each.

I remember quite distinctly when we went to see Mr Singleton to be congratulated on our winning design and receive our prize money that he joked saying it was a funny old world where the winner ends up getting the same amount as the third place prize!

So back to Julie Carroll, my first girl friend. She basically turned up at my house one day – I think it was a Saturday – completely out of the blue, knocked on the door and asked if I wanted to play.

That was the standard introduction in those days if you went round to a friend's house and their parent answered the door: "Is John playing..." - unless they weren't called John, of course. A lot of us weren't...

I remember this quite distinctly – like the old lady in the Titanic film says: it was 45 years ago but I remember as if it were yesterday (or something like that, anyway...). Ask me what I did last week and I couldn't tell you - but all this old stuff is crystal clear!

She was wearing a shiny pink patterned anorak. One of those where, when you have the hood up, it forms a point sticking up from the back of your head – and when the drawstrings and toggles are tied tightly, your face sticks out like a shining bedraggled beacon.

So she came in and, when the rain had eased off, we played in the back garden for a bit and fiddled with the sand pit and whatever.

We met up and played a few more times after that. I went to tea at her house and met her mum and her younger brother Tony and I also remember watching the West Ham v Fulham FA Cup final at their house.

We didn't become inseparable like they do in films and story books but it was nice to do something different for a change.

In later years, Julie's mum remarried and they went to live in Stilton which meant that she went to a different school and I didn't see her for a number of years.

Strangely enough, Julie reappeared on our A Level French exchange to Montpellier in 1984, where two girls from her school came along with us to make up the correct number.

She had changed her name to Sarah by then and she spent most of the time with Diana* smoking menthol cigarettes and drinking snakebites and generally being very sophisticated - but it was certainly nice to see her again after such a long time.

*(*That's Diana Pacocha, by the way, who was also in my A Level Italian class – not the Roman goddess. I only know one Diana and that is she.)*

Something I Need To Say

Now, there is something that I need to say here. It hadn't really occurred to me before but thinking about all this old stuff has raised this issue with me and, as this is supposed to be a sort of "write yourself right" healing project, I need to get this off my chest.

Julie Carroll's mum became Mrs Darke and, like I said, I knew her from going to her house on numerous occasions.

When I got to the senior school - Stanground Comprehensive – in 1978, Mrs Darke was the office practice and typing teacher there. She was also the tutorial teacher for the James House group that Paul Jinks was in next door to mine.

At our school, we had tutorial first thing every morning and first thing every afternoon. This was basically when the attendance register was taken and I don't think anything "tutorial" as such ever actually got done.

I would quite often see Mrs Darke coming in or out of the tutorial room and she would always say hello to me and ask me how I was.

Now, being a shy typical pre-pubscent 11, 12 or 13 year old – even though I knew her and I liked her and she was only being nice – I always found this cringingly embarrassing in the way that STPP lads do...

And I probably just looked at the floor, muttered something and rushed off.

So that wasn't really polite of me and, while she may not even remember it – or may kindly have just put it down to "boys being boys" - looking back, I now feel extremely bad about it.

I also feel bad about the fact that over all that time – 5 years of going into the same tutorial room twice a day, next door to the room that she was in, I did not once – EVER - ask her how Julie was getting on, despite her having been a good friend of mine in our younger years.

I am not really like that as a person. I wasn't like it then (although I might have come across as such) and I am certainly not like it now.

So, if I ever come face to face with Mrs Darke again, I would love nothing more than to say hello to her – maybe give her a hug – and apologise for my STPP behaviour of my youthful self.

And ask her how Julie / Sarah is doing ...

A Level English class in June 1985. Standing at back (left to right): Mr Forster (teacher), Steven Garratt, PB, John Ludman. Sitting middle row: Annette Piccaver (partial), Clare Barsby, Julia Skelton, Jane Kon, Joanne Harrison, Sarah Cooke. Front: Karen Glover, Karen Goodacre.

April 1984: 6th Form Fancy Dress Social - PB and Sonya as Laurel & Hardy plus a couple of decorative Indian girls.

1984: Literally!

My first girlfriend in the true "snogging" sense of the word (I am sorry if that conjures up distasteful images for you - but we need to call a spade a spade in these matters – and don't worry, we won't be getting any more graphic than that...) was a girl called Sonya.

She was Canadian and she mysteriously appeared (rather like an occurrence in an episode of "Doctor Who" or "Fringe") in the 6th Form midway through my first year there, ie: 1983/4.

She was doing some sort of special fast track course separate to everybody else to enable her to get O Levels in English and Maths so that she would be able to at least have the basic qualifications necessary to get a job over here in England.

Sonya took a shine to me for some reason or other - which was quite nice as anybody who I had even fancied from a distance in the past never seemed to give me a second look.

In fact, even at that tender age, I was already convinced that I was destined to spend my whole life as a wizened old hermit living on my own in some – erm - hermitage at the top of a remote hill somewhere.

So we got on well together and spent most of our free time at school in each other's company – but she never wanted to arrange to meet up after school or at the weekends and this I found a bit odd.

I found out where she lived by looking up her address in the attendance register.

I am sure these days that would amount to a serious data protection breach which could theoretically bring the school a £20million fine from the Information Ombudsman (yes - I have done the GDPR course...!) but, back in those easy, carefree, halcyon days, the 6th Form registers used to be left laying around on the top of a cupboard in the corner of the study room near to the office.

Now we'd had it dinned into our little heads all the way through the various school years in no uncertain terms that the class register was a very serious issue - and an important official legal document - so you may well be asking yourself why they were slung on top of a cupboard and left there for all and sundry to have access to throughout the day. So I will tell you.

In the 6th Form, there was a slightly more relaxed attitude to the daily tutorial time and registration sessions than applied to the rest of the school.

For the first 5 years we had to assemble in a particular classroom every morning and afternoon, names were called out and the register was taken in the traditional manner.

In the 6th Form, the registration groups were much smaller – say only 6 or 7 or people – and most of us when we arrived to start the day made a cup of tea or coffee and congregated around the common room chatting.

The various members of staff who were the nominated tutors for these registration groups – usually armed with a cup of coffee as well – would pick up their registers and casually glance around the room to see who was there and who wasn't and mark the register accordingly.

And that was it until the afternoon registration session, which usually went down in a similarly relaxed manner.

Now, the problem with this system – which worked perfectly well for the rest of the school years - was that, in the 6th Form, not everybody had lessons all the time throughout the day.

While there was a general "official" expectation that everybody should be present in the 6th Form block for the whole duration of the school day - and when they didn't actually have "taught lessons" timetabled, they should treat the rest of the time as "private study periods"- that didn't necessarily happen.

True - we did have our own desk each in the adjacent study room where we could keep our books and folders so we didn't have to keep carrying them back home every night, and where you could peacefully get on with studying or homework. It was also quiet during lesson times in the common room so you could sit on one of the comfy(ish) chairs and settees and read a book.

But, as time went on, a certain amount of laxness crept into the behaviour of a lot of the 6th Formers. Rather like in the John Cleese comedy film "Clockwork" we tended to refer to these "private study periods" as "free periods" - and the long-suffering staff constantly turned a blind eye when people who didn't have a lesson first thing in the morning didn't actually turn up until the mid morning break.

The register is meant to be a record of who is present in the building so that, in case of a fire or other emergency, the staff can easily check that everybody has been safely evacuated and nobody needs rescuing.

Unfortunately, if you have a load of people who turn up after the register has been taken, you don't actually know if they are there or not, so we unofficially started marking ourselves "late" on the register on those occasions – I'm sure there is probably something totally illegal about that, but it's too late to sack anybody now.... - so that it was at least demonstrable that we were actually there.

Getting a load of late marks in the normal school years was bad because it meant you were regularly missing lessons - and kids with continually poor attendance records would get letters sent home to their parents or, in extreme circumstances, have legal action taken against them.

But in terms of 17 or 18 year old 6th Formers who didn't legally have to be at school anymore anyway - and who were only basically arriving "late" for sitting and having a coffee in the common room, the worry about having lots of late marks didn't really apply and nobody seemed in the least bit bothered about them.

The problem then arose about people who had lessons early on in the day and then left before the regulation lunchtime or home time. They would be marked as "present" on the register but might not necessarily be on the premises at the time of the potential incident.

In the end, a board with hooks was put up on the wall in the corner where the registers were kept and there was a metal disc with each 6th former's name on it. Basically, when you were there, you had to have your name visible on the board and when you left, you turned your disc round so that the blank face was showing.

This was a very good idea because it meant that anybody at a glance could immediately see how many students were supposed to be present and who they all were.

We all bought into this new system whole heartedly and stuck to it with great respect. This was because we acknowledged that the tutors were treating us like adults and allowing us to keep the leeway that we had built up – and because they could easily have gone all heavy handed and strictly enforced the formal attendance rules instead!

It also brought an end to the mysterious spree of "late" marks as well.

When I finished the 6th Form, I took the disc with my name on it home and used it as a key fob for the padlock on the shed where I stored my bike - and I kept it for many years afterwards. It never occurred to me that they might have wanted to re-use the discs and stick new names on them for the following year. Sorry, everybody!

One more story about registration and 6th formers and then we'll get back to Sonya....

Throughout my time in the 6th Form, whenever somebody had a birthday - or was leaving to start a job - or it was the end of term, we would walk down to the Whittle Way pub for a celebration drink.

It took about 10/15 minutes to get there so you only had time for one drink – or two if you really rushed it – and then you had just long enough to get back within the lunch hour.

If you were a bit late, it didn't necessarily matter too much so long as you didn't miss any lessons – that was the golden (if unspoken) rule.

One day, however, something went awry and it caused a bit of a fuss. I don't remember the exact occasion but it was a nice sunny spring / summer afternoon and quite a number of us had been to the Whittle Way.

For some reason we were all quite late getting back and this caused quite a stir in the 6th form, so much that Mr Forster was stationed outside the door, holding up his watch and writing down on a list the exact times that everybody arrived back.

It turned out that some people had actually been late back for their classes that day as well – the only time I ever knew it to happen.

The list was subsequently posted on the notice board and everybody who appeared on it had to write a letter of apology to the head of the 6th form for their inconsiderate behaviour in coming back late from lunch - and those who had missed lessons had to write separate letters to their respective teachers to apologise for that.

Nothing more was ever said about the incident but I do recall that people did tighten up on their timekeeping and attendance for a week or two afterwards.

*****

So, as I was saying, I found out where Sonya lived from looking in the register and one Saturday afternoon on the way home from my Saturday job at Colton's bike shop in town, I went round to introduce myself. I figured that if her mum saw how nice and respectable I was, it might help things along a bit.

Needless to say, my unexpected arrival was not very well received. I was, at least, invited in and given a cup of tea but everybody seemed very much on edge.

Sonya's mum was a fierce little Yorkshire woman – don't ask me how she ended up in Canada as I never found out – and it turned out that she was a Jehova's Witness!

Now, my later experiences with Jehovah's Witnesses as an adult were that they were always very welcoming and keen to tell you about their views and try and recruit you. But all Sonya's mum seemed to want to do was get rid of me!

So I had to accept that we wouldn't really see very much of each other outside of school time.

We went on a day trip to Cambridge once with the school on the school coach, although I don't know what the trip was actually for. I imagine some school group had something to go and do in Cambridge and the remaining empty seats were offered to anybody else who wanted a day out. Certainly, all we did all day was have a pub lunch and walk round the shops.

On another occasion we met up in town when the fair was on – she had nominally gone with some of her female JW friends who she was allowed to go out and do things with.

They mentioned that they might all go roller skating at the Wirrina one Saturday evening and then go and see the film "Footloose" at the cinema afterwards. I said I'd be up for the film but not the roller skating and the next thing I heard was they had gone and seen the film without telling me - so I didn't think much to that.

I haven't, in fact, still to this day ever seen "Footloose"...

One event that her mum did let us go to together was the 6th Form fancy dress social in April 1984. She even helped us get the costumes together for it and we went dressed as Laurel and Hardy.

I had hoped that it might represent a new positive step in relationships but it was the one bright moment in an otherwise frosty environment.

Sonya came to my house one afternoon and she popped in to see me at Colton's a few times on Saturdays but that was as far as anything ever got really.

The end of the school year arrived and Sonya left almost as mysteriously as she had arrived and, once school was over, I never saw her again.

And After That. In December 1984, I commenced on what – for the purposes of this reminiscences project - is probably best referred to as "My Judith Phase".

For a variety of reasons, it took me until July 1989 to work through this "Phase" and, as this current book is supposed to be cheerful and uplifting, with light hearted and funny stories, that period doesn't really fit in.

As such, we will leave the "Judith Phase" consigned to the deepest vaults of history for the time being.

I suppose I could always branch out and do a separate volume at some time in the future entitled "Things I Wish I Hadn't Done..."

But for the time being, let's leap joyously forward to what is, after all, supposed to be the "meat and potatoes" of this particular volume: "The Bachelor Pad Years"!

As a guide:
1967-1984: Innocence & Youthfulness
1984-1989: The Judith Phase
1989-1993: The Bachelor Pad Years
1993-1997: The Hanja Period (& "Germany Calling" travels)
1998 - present: The Lucy Era

Younger brother Gary in Dam Square in Amsterdam, September 1989

PB on a canal bridge with the famous Skinny Bridge in the background –
Amsterdam, September 1989.

September 1989: Amsterdam

At the end of July 1989, I finally split up with my girlfriend of 5 years.

It didn't really bother me as she was always a bit troublesome and unsociable anyway and it meant that I could start going out and doing all sorts of "young, free and single" things that I hadn't been able to do previously – like going on work social evenings out, birthdays, leaving dos, squash games etc.

Knowing that the momentous departure was on the cards, I took myself off to visit Alan & Louise in London for the weekend and by the time I got back, she and all her stuff had gone - and I found a lot of mine in the bin – would you believe...?

The first thing that I decided to do with my new found freedom was to go to Amsterdam for a few days. I had never been before and always fancied going – but never had anybody suitable to go with.... so I talked my younger brother Gary into going with me and we booked one of those all-inclusive City breaks.

We decided to go in early September when the kids would be back at school but the weather would still be nice and I seem to think that we went Monday to Friday but can't really remember at this distance in time.

Now, based on my many subsequent trips to Holland - and to the north of Germany via Holland, I would NEVER actually propose taking this route, but the itinerary that we were given by the travel company saw us do the following:

- Late afternoon train from Peterborough to London Kings Cross
- Underground from Kings Cross to Liverpool Street station
- Evening boat train from London to Harwich
- Overnight ferry sailing from Harwich to Hoek van Holland
- Train from Hoek van Holland to Amsterdam

The train from Liverpool Street to Harwich had an electrical failure on board – at least in the carriage we were in - so the lights didn't work. That wasn't so bad when we first left London at 6.30pm or whenever it was but wasn't quite so much fun once it started to get dark. Also the air blower system wasn't working so, being a warm and pleasant day outside, it was incredibly hot and stuffy on the train.

Anyway, the train got to Harwich and we got off – took huge breaths of clean seaside air - and walked through the Ferry terminal and got on the boat.

I subsequently discovered that there was, in fact, a train that went direct from Peterborough to Harwich that connected with the ferry sailing - and there was one back that linked up with the returning boat in the morning. This was a slower, local train and the journey took about 2 or 2½ hours as it stopped at all sorts of places on the way - like Ely and Stowmarket - but at least it was direct and you could just get on with your luggage and remain seated the whole way.

The train actually started from Peterborough as well so you could get there early and find a seat in comfort before everybody else got on just prior to departure - and it was still a lot quicker and easier than going via London – and a lot cheaper as well. So, needless to say, for all my subsequent trips on the Hoek van Holland ferry, I used this local train and found it very handy.

They don't seem to run this particular route anymore and, according to the Train Line .com, you now have to change a couple of times to get from Peterborough to Harwich or, indeed, go via London. I suppose that's progress for you!

Anyway, enough about trains for now – back to the ferry boat.

Although I know it now – I didn't know it then but you could get cabins on this boat and make the crossing in comfort.

Nobody mentioned cabins where we were booking the trip nor, indeed, did anybody mention cabins when we were getting on either.

It turned out that we could have paid a supplement and got a bunk in a cabin of 4 (yuk...) or got a reclining chair somewhere or other (tried those before - useless), but not knowing any of this, we had a fairly uncomfortable night camping down on the sofas in one of the bar areas.

In actual fact - in later years, they clamped down on this and you weren't allowed on the overnight boat unless you booked a cabin or a reclining seat, which I would have been quite happy with even then had I have known. Oh well....

So Gary and I emerged the next morning somewhat uncomfortable and bleary eyed having spent the night on settees in the bar and grabbed some coffee and croissants – or, at least, some stodgy Dutch version of croissants - in the Ferry terminal cafe.

The railway platforms were just outside the exit, which was handy, and they had very regular trains to Amsterdam so we got on the next one and headed off.

I have to say at this point that I don't remember a single thing about this train ride through the Dutch countryside towards the great metropolis. Having been very tired after an uncomfortable night, I may well have dozed off - although I hardly ever usually sleep when I am travelling.

I will say here, though, that I went on to use Dutch trains a lot over the period 1990 to 1997 and I was always very impressed with them. They were always clean, on time and the railway staff were always helpful and courteous. The trains were all a fetching yellow colour and had bright orange seats which were always very comfortable.

I never once had a single negative experience on a Dutch train and the fares were very reasonable – being based purely on how far you were travelling, rather than how important the place was that you were going to.

So we arrived at Amsterdam Central station and got off the train, not knowing quite what to do next.

Luckily there was somebody there to meet us off the train carrying the sign for the travel company that we had booked with and he drove us off in a swish black Mercedes to our hotel.

That was a bit unnerving actually as the road kept crossing over the tram tracks and I was worried that we might hit a tram. However it all seemed quite normal for our driver and, having since lived in Blackpool for 11 years where there are also stretches of road that coincide with tram tracks, I have come to realise that there are systems in place to help avoid any dangerous incidents.

The Hotel we stayed in was the Hotel Rokin and it is still there today. It gets very good reviews on Trip Advisor and I can certainly say that we found it very impressive for a "budget tourist hotel" when we went there in 1989.

Despite being on a main street, it wasn't in the least bit noisy and, even though it was quite full, there were never any problems with the other guests and banging doors or whatever.

The hotel was ideally situated right in the middle of everything so that you could easily walk everywhere.

I can't remember exactly how we spent our time when in Amsterdam but, over the course of our visit, we certainly did the following:

- Spent many happy hours along the main pedestrianised shopping area across from the hotel
- strolled alongside many of the canals

- Saw the famous Skinny Bridge that they have in all the tourist brochures
- Visited Anne Frank's house – which was very moving
- Had some Vlaamse Frites from a stand on the Dam Square which had the obligatory speciality of mayonnaise on top. I wouldn't normally have mayonnaise on top of anything but this was part of the general cultural experience so was OK for a one –off.
- Bought cheesy Delft style pottery souvenirs to take home
- Went on a coach excursion to a working windmill out on the banks of a canal somewhere in the countryside. It was nice to see a bit of the surrounding area and there was a pleasant cafe adjacent for coffees and snacks.

Things we didn't do in Amsterdam:

- Visit Rembrandt's House (I did that on another occasion)
- Take a boat trip (I did that on another occasion as well)
- Visit the Rijksmuseum (I have never been there)
- Visit the Heineken brewery (I have never been there either – you have to get there at some really daft time in the morning like 9.30 to do the tour)
- Visit a prostitute (I have never done that but I DO know somebody who has – although, like Belinda Carlisle and the Fun Boy Three, my lips are sealed...)
- Buy any drugs (never have, never will – I'm high enough on life, thank you very much.)

Flea Market at Waterlooplein

Unlike the average car boot sale which was the big thing in England at that time where you could pick up all sorts of interesting things, this place had stall upon stall of the most bizarre old tat you could possibly imagine.

They had boxes of old springs and screws and nuts and bits of deckchair. Old watches that didn't work, used drill bits and other odd things that your average person would have thrown out ages ago.

In short, it looked like a big, outdoor, public version of my dad's shed.

Now, I can fully appreciate that, if you needed a particular size screw or nut or bolt for some cherished restoration task and couldn't find it anywhere else, then you might in fact resort to coming and having a poke through what they had here.

For all I know there may have been a huge underground "make do and mend" subculture in Amsterdam and this was the heart of it all. It was certainly very busy – mainly with little old blokes – and they were all attentively sorting through these boxes of junk in search of whatever it was they were searching for.

One thing that did interest me - albeit briefly - was a stall that sold second-hand leather jackets. The idea was good but the reality was rather disappointing. Not only were these jackets all horrendously expensive, bearing in mind that they were second-hand - but they were also horrendously horrible.

Let me try and explain. They weren't "motorbike jackets" nor were they the soft leather stylish jackets you might wear for an evening out. They were more like work-wear. Straight cut very solid leather with few refinements – almost like the old donkey jackets like council workers used to wear before health and safety considerations drove them all into wearing bright yellow attire...

It was the sort of thing that I could easily imagine a barge worker wearing while chugging along the canals, with one of those round caps on his head that they always seem to wear in films (Ha! Notice I was going to say "Dutch Cap" then but managed to restrain myself ...!).

So that may very well be what they were – second hand work wear for barge crews and other outdoor workers. But all of these jackets were very gungy to be on sale to anybody.

They either had tears in the leather - or buttons and zips missing - and a lot of them were all messed up and grotty around the collar, which would certainly have put me off wanting to wear one.

So, not really wanting to buy any old watch parts, rusty tools or gungy leather jackets, we managed to emerge from the famous Flea Market bereft of any purchases.

Red Light District (By Day)

Being a bit shy and naive, we thought we ought to go and have a look in daylight and see what it was like before chancing an evening visit.

This was quite an eye opener as, whereas in England, Sex Shops tended to be hidden away in unsavoury locations, here it was big business and there were loads of them all dotted around the place.

Also, in England back then, sex shops had to be all boarded up, with no advertising of wares in the windows and, presumably, controlled entry via a locked door (that's me just guessing as I have never actually been in one..), but in Amsterdam the Sex Shops were all prominent, brash and accessible and open to everybody (over 18) with no such qualms.

We picked one of the shops that didn't have any customers in it and decided to have a quick look round – just to be able to say afterwards that we had been in one. Needless to say, I covered both my eyes and rushed round really quickly so as not to expose myself to anything too unsuitable.

That said, my hands might have slipped from my eyes for a very brief moment.

And I might just have caught a glance of a couple of rather strange "niche market" magazines, which might be worth mentioning at this point, if only to establish my bonafides in this matter.

The one I remember most clearly was called "Knocked Up And Horny". Now, I do appreciate that this might sound like one of those humorous things that I make up from time to time for added literary effect, but I can assure you that this is absolutely true. This was a magazine full of photos of women who were in different stages of pregnancy, wearing little or no clothing, and adopting various postures.

The odd thing about this magazine is that, while I remember quite vividly seeing it in the shop in Amsterdam – and I seem to think there were several different issues, so it wasn't just a one –off – I have NEVER seen mention of it anywhere ever again.

Not that I have been looking for it, mind you, but you can find details of most publications - both modern and historic - somewhere on the internet, and people are always selling old copies of all sorts of weird stuff on Ebay, but this is not mentioned anywhere. Most odd!

It's like a book I came across once in WH Smiths in Peterborough when I was looking for something else entirely, obviously. It was called "Getting In Shape For Sex" and was a book of exercises and fitness plans. Here again, I have never seen this anywhere else and nobody else has ever heard of it.

The other magazine that I remember from the Amsterdam sex shop was a bit more sinister and it involved page upon page of women being tied up and blindfolded. In some photos, they even had electrical wires attached to their nipples by crocodile clips, which I thought was a bit much.

I don't remember what that magazine was called but, there again, there was a whole series of them so there must have been some market for that sort of thing somewhere.

Now, the MODERN me – that's the 21st century independent publisher me, as opposed to the shy 22 year old lad back in 1989 – would be very interested to know what sort of market these magazines were destined for. How often they came out, who printed them, what the length of print run was, how they were advertised and distributed in the pre-internet age, and so on.

The other question that springs to mind - from an editorial content point of view – is how on earth do you keep coming up with new and original material to make people want to buy your next issue...?

Surely, once you have seen one picture of a bondage bird with electrodes on her tits, you don't need any more...?

That image is still seared into my mind over 30 years on and I have no hankering to see anything like it again.

And where do they get a constant stream of different models to feature in these publications? Are there really that many shapely photogenic women in the world who happen to be heavily pregnant and don't mind baring all their bits in a magazine? The mind boggles...

Don't forget - this was a good two years or so before that famous naked picture of Demi Moore seven months pregnant appeared on the front cover of Vanity Fair magazine - and back then it was more usual for women to keep their pregnancies covered under swathes of unflattering clothing. That vogue has now changed and, in the intervening years, there have been hundreds of celebs queuing up to be photographed in their "delicate condition" for the glossy magazines. But for 1989, it was quite an unusual thing for people to want to look at.

Oh - and did I mention "P*ss Party" – a periodical aimed at urolagnics...? Probably best not...

We'll come back to the Red Light District again shortly.

Amsterdam Nightlife

In the meantime, we discovered that the Leidseplein was a good place to go for a pleasant evening. It's a bit like Leicester Square in so much as it is a tree lined square surrounded with bars, restaurants and cafes – nearly all with tables outside.

Interestingly enough, despite being the home of the world famous Heineken Brewery, the majority of the bars and cafes around Amsterdam seemed to major on selling Amstel beer and had large signs for that outside.

The original private Amstel brewery was actually taken over by Heineken in 1968 and it is all now brewed in the same place – but it is interesting that they have kept the brand and promote it as a separate entity.

I preferred Oranjeboom – brewed in Rotterdam - which I had first tried in a Dutch themed bar in London ("De Hems", on the edge of Chinatown. It's still there!), so we gravitated towards a cafe on Leidseplein that was selling that particular brand.

While sitting outside enjoying the Dutch brew, we heard the sounds of pleasant upbeat music coming from a bar a bit further along the square.

Upon closer inspection there was an all-girl group – possibly of Dutch East Indies origin – playing all their own instruments and singing popular songs. We went in and listened for a bit and it was really quite enjoyable. I had the impression that they were all related as they were a variety of different ages (like The Osmonds or The Dooleys) and they all looked very similar to each other.

They sung light poppy songs and ballads - things like "Marina (ti voglio piu presto sposar)" – which would appeal to most visitors to Amsterdam on an evening out - and were very talented.

After a pleasant hour of Dutch beer and music we decided it was time to venture into the Red Light District and see what it was like in darkness.

Now, I don't know what it is like these days – and I couldn't say what it might have been like in the winter, when there might have been fewer tourists – or in the middle of the night – but at the time that we went to the Red Light District, ie about 9.30pm on a warm September evening in 1989, it was actually a very pleasant experience and not in the least bit menacing like you might have expected.

For a start it was packed out with tourists – kids, grannies, families the whole lot. There were even whole coach parties of Japanese and Italian tourists being shown round by guides.

As I remember – and I could be wrong here as it was a long time ago and it's all a bit of a haze – the RLD was centred around a couple of canals in the older part of the city. It was mostly bars and peep shows along the main canal fronts and the brothels were for the most part in the side streets.

The Hard Rock Cafe, Amsterdam, was along there somewhere. We walked past it but couldn't get a table as it was too packed.

Another place that grabbed my attention but we also didn't go into was a bar called "Elephants Mess". This had a huge cartoon sign of an elephant outside, was decorated outside and throughout with camouflage netting and it had the loudest and heaviest rock music you had ever heard being blasted out from speakers all round.

It would have been too loud to go inside even if we had wanted to and it made me wonder what sort of clientele it was actually aimed at.

A few doors along from that was a showbar of some sort that advertised a "real live sex show" - or something like that. There was a doorman outside who was trying to entice people in and he called out to Gary and me:

"Hey, Guys! Sucky sucky. F*cky f*cky!"

And would you believe - that did NOT entice us one bit!

A bit further into the RLD we came across a bar called the Rose Bar or the Vie en Rose - or something like that – and it had topless women serving!

The drinks were more expensive in there but I had to have just one – just so that I could say afterwards that I had been served by a topless woman in Amsterdam. So there you are – it's in black and white. I have now said it!

Just along from this topless bar was another bar where we didn't stay very long either. In fact, after taking about three steps inside, we didn't actually stay at all!

The first person I saw when I got in there was a very blond muscular young guy wearing extremely tight leather black trousers and a much too small black leather vest. On later reflection, they might even have been made out of black rubber but in my unworldly naivety I didn't know that people wore things like that back then so I figured it was leather.

The next thing I saw was a guy with a black leather jacket, a thick bushy moustache and one of those leather caps like the chap out of the Village People used to wear and, at that point, I figured it was probably best if we left.

Now, I'm not in the least bit homophobic and have lots of LGBT friends in Blackpool. Lucy and I used to go along to support the Sunday night cabaret nights at Peek-a-Booze on a regular basis when we lived there and there was a whole mix of different people that went there - so I have no axe to grind on that score.

But – back in 1989, when attitudes were not as developed as they are now – and in the middle of the whole AIDS scare – I figured my mum might probably kill me if she knew that I had taken my 18 year brother into a gay bar in Amsterdam.

So we quickly exited and went to look round the prostitutes sitting in the windows instead – as you do...

Here again, I don't know what it is like there now. But when I went for this first time with Gary in September 1989 – and, indeed, on my subsequent visits to Amsterdam in May 1990 with Jane Barnet and September 1991 with Simes it was still the same – but this is what the brothels were like.

There were row upon row of windows along the side streets, basically like the front room of a narrow old style Dutch house - each lit up with a soft red light. Inside each window a scantily dressed female sat on a stool or a chair – mainly looking completely bored, if I'm being honest – and waiting for customers.

Some waved or beckoned and occasionally they picked somebody out from the crowd of passers-by and tried to catch their eye.

Next to each window was a door and if somebody went in, she would pull a big curtain across the window and, presumably, do the business in the area behind. There were girls of all ages, shapes and sizes and a lot of them looked Asiatic.

There were notices up on all the windows saying "strictly no photography". I don't know how they manage nowadays with everybody having a camera on their phone but, back then, they had aggressive looking doormen guarding the blocks of windows and they immediately sprang into action if anybody tried to take a photo. They also kept an eye out that nobody harassed or upset any of the girls.

So, having had enough of looking at partially naked women for a while, we found a bar at the far end of the RLD which wasn't too full – and had an air of relative normality about it. It was decorated around the walls with lots of different beer mats, wasn't smoky inside and had room to go in and sit down. We went and had a last beer in there and headed back to our hotel for the night.

Interestingly enough, despite Amsterdam being the drugs capital of Europe – especially with its liberalised laws back in those days, I never actually saw any overly obvious signs of drug use around the RLD or anywhere else.

There were occasionally people standing in alleyways whispering out of the corner of their mouths as if trying to catch your attention. I assume they were selling drugs but, as I wasn't interested, they left me well alone.

We also kept away from "Coffee Shops" – as distinct from cafes - because they were apparently allowed to openly sell drugs to the public.

The only time that I actually saw anything particularly unsavoury was when I noticed somebody down a dark back alley off the beaten track doing something with tin foil and flame (that's something drug related, isn't it? Don't expect me to know, I've had a very sheltered existence ...). That made me feel a bit uncomfortable - but he didn't come anywhere near us.

So we had a very nice few days around Amsterdam walking round the sights and the shops during the day and revisiting the nightlife in the evening.

On our last morning, the holiday courier guy picked us up in his car, deposited us back at the railway station and we headed back to Hoek van Holland.

The day crossing on the ferry was much nicer because you could sit out on deck, watch the waves and get plenty of sea air.

We did the tortuous UK rail journey in reverse - via London again – but I did notice while we were waiting on the platform that there was actually a direct local service that went straight to Peterborough - but was departing later - that we could have taken.

As we already had our tickets for London, that train was about to leave and I didn't have time to weigh up the logistics of the comparative journeys at that time, so I figured we'd stick with our official itinerary for now and I'd suss out the direct overland route in more detail for another occasion.

Office Evening Out – Circa 1991 (left to right): Chris Rojek (background), Martin Bond, Paul Hornsby, Simon Moulds, Zahlia Atoun-Fitzjohn, PB, Anne Castellano, Steve Kimber.

1990: Welcome To The Bachelor Pad

If you ever asked me the question, I would tell you that I have never been depressed. I am usually too cheerful and busy and active off doing things to have time to get depressed but there was one particular brief period that could possibly come under that heading.

Having got over the initial euphoria of finally being out of a rather negative 5 year relationship – and, as a result, going on an unseemly laddish binge of getting endless pizzas delivered, having birds round and whatever (although if I was being painfully honest, I'd have to admit that there were infinitely more pizzas than birds....) I then entered a bit of a low phase.

I was rattling around in this 3 bedroom house that was much too big for just me, had unpleasant memories and which I couldn't really afford to keep going on my own.

Also there were lots of little everyday things that began to niggle me – one major one being laundry.

We didn't have a proper washing machine in the property – we had a twin tub that I really did not know how to operate. We had bought it cheaply out of necessity from a second-hand dealer – and I can fully appreciate why they were so cheap – it's because they are a complete pain in the arse and I doubt anybody else wants them.

Anyway, I used to concentrate on doing the more "manly" things around the house - like watching telly and waiting for meals to be served - so the complete concept of rolling this thing out, sorting out the pipes, working out which bit did what and then coping with large amounts of wet washing all about the place was rather outside my capabilities.

I'm not overly proud of this but, in order to NOT have to do any washing, I ended up – for a few weeks at least – wearing the same clothes over again, letting them air a bit in between times. But, in the end, some of them got so grotty that I had to throw them away.

I wasn't my usual cheery self and I had a couple of weeks when I didn't pop into my parents house like I might otherwise normally have done.

Would that be classed these days as being depressed? Back when I was younger, people didn't actually discuss things like depression and feelings and you generally just had to get on with it.

I am fairly sure that I was bounced out of this gloomy phase by the urgent need for clean pants and I finally arranged for my mum to do my washing for me.

(As a happy PS here: I never personally owned a washing machine until I eventually bought one when I was living in Preston in around 1994.

I hasten to add that I am actually very good at doing laundry these days – can separate darks from lights, understand about different temperatures - and am very good at hanging things out on the line. I am still crap at ironing, though...!)

Over the Christmas / New Year period I had a bit of a party and invited a load of friends. I prepared and laid out a cold buffet in the front dining room and everything went well. Not quite everybody came and there was a lot of food left over so I continued to snack on that over the next few days.

About two weeks later, with the buffet still laid out in the dining room - and any remaining leftovers looking rather distinctly unpalatable, I suddenly had an Attila The Stockbroker "Away Day" moment (check out his satirical poem of that name on YouTube) and thought "B*ll*cks to this!" and decided to move out and find somewhere smaller, easier to manage and a lot cheaper to live.

I looked through the local paper, rang a few places and ended up going to see a chap with a house on Williamson Avenue. I'd never heard of this street before but it runs between Midland Road down the side of the hospital and Alderman's Drive. It was handy for getting into town and very close to where I worked.

I met the guy and we got on OK. It turned out that, contrary to what had been said in the advert, this wasn't a typical house share in the normal understanding of the term as he, the owner, wasn't there most of the time.

His name was Binkie Squayles. In fact, to be honest, his name wasn't Binkie Squayles at all but whether or not you know his real name doesn't affect this story in any way and, to save him from any potential embarrassment, we'll stick with that pseudonym.

I always wanted to write a story about somebody with the name Binkie Squayles, anyway, so this is as good an opportunity as any other.

Anyway, Mr Squayles was a director of some sort for a famous Utilities company. He lived somewhere else with his family but he had to attend meetings in Peterborough quite often so he had bought this house as a base for that so he could stop there occasionally if he needed to.

I never thought about this at the time but I suppose his idea in seeking out a tenant was to have somebody sensible in permanent residence at the property so that it didn't appear to be empty for long periods of time and who could keep an eye on anything that cropped up.

Over the months that I lived there, Binkie was very seldom there and if he occasionally stopped it was only ever for one night and he then went again. All of this meant that I was basically paying a "half rent" for a shared house but had practically the run of the whole place for nearly all the time.

So that's how my move to the Bachelor Pad came about.

Let me tell you about the house and its layout.

It was a Victorian brick semi on a quiet residential side street. I don't remember what number it was now but, as I doubt anybody is ever going to want to put a blue plaque up on my behalf, I don't suppose that really matters.

The place was very clean and tidy - nice and warm with its central heating radiators in every room - and it had that "just painted and carpeted" smell, which made me think that Binkie hadn't been in it very long.

It had a small yard out the front – not big enough to do anything in, but a good enough size to set the front of the house away from the pavement.

The front door led into a long narrow entrance hall with the front room on the left as you went in, then the stairs going up and the living room door facing you.

The front room had a bed in it - and not much else as far as I can remember. That was a guest room for if Binkie's wife or other family members came to visit so I hardly ever went in there - unless I needed to peer out of the window for some reason.

I think I only saw his wife once or twice - her name was "Mrs Squayles" and she was pleasant enough in a 50-ish homely wifey sort of way.

His daughter came once as well (18-ish, stroppy...) – they were going to do some sort of sponsored walk one weekend and had to have an early start the next day.

I only saw her for about 5 minutes all together but she completely infuriated me by, firstly, turning the heating off that I'd got set to come on for my usual time in the morning and, then, keeping answering the phone every time it rang, completely insensitive to the fact that the calls might easily have been for me.

So, the living room filled the whole width of the property and it had a window looking into the back garden and a door to the under stairs cupboard. Another door led into a half width "through" dining room and the kitchen was at the back of the property.

As I used to suffer terribly from hayfever during these years, I hardly ever went into the back garden so couldn't really tell you anything about it.

At the top of the stairs, the landing led to the main front bedroom on your left and past the second bedroom on your right (looking out over the yard) and to the bathroom at the back. This bathroom was above the dining room and kitchen and I suppose it had originally been an extra bedroom as back when the house was first built they would all have had "outside facilities".

As it was, the room was much too big for what was in it and there was a vast expanse of carpeting with a toilet and wash basin at the far end on the back wall and a bath in one corner.

There was no shower and no shower fixture on the bath so I lobbied for one to be added. However, Binkie wasn't bothered – well, he wouldn't be as he was hardly ever there - so in the end, I bought one of those plastic things that you put over the taps so that I could wash my hair.

It was quite a fiddle to get the temperature right and it usually ended up spraying all over the bathroom so, instead, I tended to wash my hair under the shower after I had been swimming or played squash - which I normally did twice a week.

I had the front bedroom, which was great as it was the one with the most space. I had my big bed in the corner and there was a big window that looked out onto the street.

I initially had my TV and video player set up in the bedroom and was able to watch TV channels after I bought one of those plug in aerials and found the best place to stand it in the room.

The TV didn't remain in the bedroom very long though as I found myself sitting up late into the night watching all sorts of programmes that I wouldn't normally watch and feeling very tired the following morning.

Once it became apparent that Binkie wasn't going to be there most of the time, I set my TV and video up in the living room and left them there. That meant I could get a better signal using the proper aerial and was able to record things to watch later as well.

Another house facility that I made the most of was the phone. It had an answering machine attached which was handy in case anybody rang for me while I was out. I do appreciate that its main function was for people to be able to leave messages for Binkie but, as far as I can remember, not one message was ever left for him the whole time I was there.

The problem with the phone / answering machine was that they were down in the living room and that the answerphone kicked in after three rings.

So if I was up in my bedroom and the phone rang, I had to drop whatever I was doing and rush down to try and catch it because once the message had started you couldn't stop it and had to wait until it had finished, meaning a caller who didn't know this might think you weren't there.

I resolved this problem by buying an extension phone and connecting cable and ran it up the stairs. The cable wouldn't reach all the way into my room so the phone sat outside on the floor of the landing. I didn't fix the wire properly using cable slips but just shoved it along the edge of the stair carpet.

I realise that doesn't sound very health and safety conscious but there was only me there for most of the time - but it did mean that if any of the Squayles clan were in the house, I could easily dismantle it and put it back the next day after they had gone.

I still had to get to the phone before the third ring but at least it was now at the top of the stairs rather than in the downstairs lounge.

So you will have realised by now that, while this wasn't a formal house share in the true sense of the word, it wasn't really a Bachelor Pad in the true sense of the word either.

I never actually thought of it as a Bachelor Pad and never called it that at the time – it's just a crazy tag that I have just adopted for the purposes of this book!

I couldn't just do whatever I wanted as I could never tell when Binkie might turn up for the night. He didn't appear to have a regular schedule and he never told me what he was doing.

All I'd know was that I'd hear the front door open and I'd then have about 20 seconds to open the under-stairs cupboard door in the living room and frantically throw in all my stuff in that had accumulated around the place since the last time he had been there.

Newspapers, crisp packets, take away boxes, garments, sports equipment – you name it, in it went. At least I always knew where to look for anything I couldn't find.

I'd hardly ever manage to stash everything in the time it took him to come through from the hall - but at least he could see that I was making an effort.

In fact, Binkie fully entered into the spirit of things as well because, if he came home and I wasn't there, he'd chuck all my stuff in the cupboard for me...

So because of this, I never really invited anybody round to the Bachelor Pad. I certainly never had any wild parties or orgies and preferred to keep it as my haven of tranquillity to get away from the rest of the world.

If I did ever have anybody round it was all very civilised and one at a time.

I certainly recall Karen Robinett coming round for tea after work one day and I cooked – or rather heated up – a curry. Simes and Jane Barnet from work will probably have come to pick me up or drop me off after squash or some other social occasion.

The French student Natalie who we had in our office for a few weeks came round a few times as I was detailed to entertain her (you can read more about her in France Actually) and "Sea Dash" will have come round a few times at weekends later in the year as well (she comes up later - just whetting your appetite!).

As I mentioned earlier, the Bachelor Pad was in a great location as it was only 5 or 10 minutes walk from my place of work – Baker Perkins PMC on Westfield Road. In fact, because of the geography of the area, it was actually quicker for me to walk door to door to work than to take my car, park it in the car park round the back and then walk through to the entrance of the offices.

I worked out that I could quite possibly get away with not getting up until 8.30am, throwing some clothes on, splashing some water on my face and still being able to be present at my desk for 9am to start work. I don't think I ever quite did that - but it was reassuring to think that I could do so in an emergency.

I did tend to cut down on the hassle of the early morning routine by not having any breakfast before I went out. Instead, I tended to have a cup of tea or coffee as soon as I got into the office and then, at a convenient moment, walked down to the staff canteen where they did the most wonderful toasted bacon sandwiches – which they served until a certain time in the morning.

On the way back home at lunchtime – if I was popping back – or after work, there were lots of different shops on Mayors Walk – which I had to cross to get there – including a decent Co-Op and a couple of really good take aways, so I was really well off in terms of provisions and catering facilities.

And that – in a nutshell – is the story of how I came to be in the Bachelor Pad.

1990: Caribbean Interlude

During the spring and summer of 1990, in the middle of this young, free and single period, I had a girlfriend of Jamaican heritage called Karen.

I would normally just refer to her as "black" here but, at the time of writing, there is a lot of hoo-haa about calling black things black - even if they actually are literally black - and a whole load of people keep finding things to be offended about and bandying the term "racist" around like confetti.

This means that everybody has to go around walking on egg shells all the time (is that not in itself offensive to eggs – and, by association, chickens...?) - just in case they inadvertently upset somebody.

So, it's probably better if I don't refer to my black girlfriend as black even though there is currently an organisation called "Black Lives Matter" which, if we are not allowed to refer to anybody as black, makes you wonder who they are actually aimed at.

It is all rather confusing, especially when Asian people refer to themselves and each other as "Pakis" quite often and rap singers of Afro-Caribbean heritage are always writing lyrics about - and calling each other - "niggaz" (apparently, if it is spelt wrongly, it's not as offensive as if it is spelt correctly, for some reason or other...). I wonder if that works with "Gingaz" as well...

In all honesty, most of the people who seem to get offended by this sort of thing don't tend to be particularly connected with the offensive tag in the first place and are often muck-stirring doo-gooders who are just looking for something new to complain about.

Anyway, Karen had been working on and off for a temping agency and kept cropping at my place of work in different departments – the stationery store one week, the mail room another week, the spares stores – and so on.

Despite my being a very shy person, we got talking, arranged to meet up for a drink and we got on quite well together.

My chronology is bit off here, but one of the earliest things that I remember about Karen was how on the morning of Alan & Louise's wedding (April 1990), I turned up at her flat with a new shirt that I had just bought from Marks & Spencer and that, as it had just come out of the packet, desperately needed ironing.

I'd like to think that the "modern-day me" wouldn't do that as I am a lot more mature and chivalrous than I was back then - plus I now have 24 hour access to an iron and ironing board and do – in theory at least - know how to use them. But in the heat of the moment and under the correct pressing circumstances (excuse the pun...), who knows...?

Anyway, my mum was out at work - so she couldn't do it - and I really couldn't turn up at the wedding wearing a shirt that had obviously just been unwrapped. So, in a bit of a panic - and with the clock ticking - I rushed round to Karen's and, to my great surprise and relief, she ironed it for me - even though I wasn't even taking her to the wedding!

Karen had three sisters and two brothers. She may even have had more than that - but those were the ones that I met. They had all been born in this country after their parents had come over from Jamaica.

What I found fascinating was that, even though she spoke just like me the rest of the time, when she was with her sisters, they all suddenly slipped into this odd sort of Caribbean patois like it was special code among themselves. They'd say "innit" instead of "aren't we", "didn't you", "won't they..." etc rather like in the French where the coverall phrase is "n'est-ce pas" irrespective of the context.

They'd also say "aks", instead of "ask". They'd refer to the white population as "inglish peeple", and use lots of other slang words that I'd never heard before.

They also occasionally pronounced the odd everyday word in a slightly different manner in normal conversation with me, which often threw me. I remember once getting caught out when Karen said "realistic" but, because of the intonation she used, it sounded more like "really STICK", which needed explaining as it didn't make sense.

One of her sisters was older – I'm sorry, I can't remember her name – and she lived quite close by so Karen used to go and visit her a lot. She was married and had a couple of kids and her husband was African, as opposed to Caribbean.

I was told that there were/are a lot of cultural and character differences between people from the West Indies and people from Africa and that mixed marriages like that often encounter problems, but that wasn't the case with Karen's sister. I was also told that you can usually tell if somebody is of African or West Indian descent from their names as well.

Most West Indians tend to have anglicised names like, for example, John Barnes the England footballer who was born in Jamaica - and then there is another England footballer Ugo Ehiogu whose family were from Nigeria, to give an example of an African name.

They had a family friend called Eric. He was a retired chap - white (can I call him "white" without upsetting anybody...?) and I imagine that he lived on his own as he used to sit in Karen's sister's living room all day long colouring in pictures in colouring books to pass the time. He was very pleasant and chatty and he was always willing to give the family members a lift in his car if they needed to go anywhere.

Karen only had a small one bedroomed flat but she had two other girls sharing with her – illegally subletting most probably, but who's counting.

One was a rather overweight blonde girl and the other was an incredibly young looking waif-like creature who apparently used to keep getting pregnant and having abortions.

I never fully got to the bottom of where everybody found room to sleep and I got the distinct impression that Karen usually cleared them out of the way when I was going round.

One very pleasant afternoon that I remember – and I can tell you the date of this – 22nd April 1990 – as it was the day of the British Ice hockey championship final at Wembley and it was live on BBC1's Grandstand on the Sunday afternoon.

The game was a draw after 60 minutes and went to a sudden death penalty shoot out and it took an incredible 23 penalty shots before Cardiff were crowned the winners over Murrayfield.

So that was great fun to watch and afterwards Karen cooked a Jamaican dish of dumplings with spicy mince.

There used to be a club of sort – at the bottom end of Lincoln Road in Peterborough near to – or possibly opposite - the Chilli Hut where you could pay £1 to go in and they carried on serving alcohol later after the general closing time (this was back when the pubs all used to close at 11pm on Saturdays and 10.30pm on Sundays).

I don't remember what it was called – or, indeed, exactly where it was - but it was upstairs above a shop and Karen and I went there one Saturday evening to watch Simon & Rosie's band playing.

We also went to Shanghai Sam's one night and that was the occasion when I did something that I had never done before or since (don't worry, mother - it's nothing rude...).

You know in films where they have the scene of James Bond - or Jean Paul Belmondo - or somebody else like that, walking home in the early dawn light...?

Usually in a deserted street in Paris, with just a street sweeper for company – with his evening wear still on and his tie hanging loosely around his neck...?

Well, I DID THAT! Just the once, walking home from this night out at Shanghai Sam's. It probably won't have had quite the same effect – walking down Midland Road past the hospital heading to my Bachelor Pad on Williamson Avenue – but it's a memory that is very clearly fixed in my mind.

We also went to The Gables night club in Peterborough once - to meet up with Karen's friend Ann who was white and pregnant – and Ann's (black) boyfriend, whose name I have forgotten.

This is a completely different Ann, by the way, to the Anne I used to work with at Baker Perkins. I have called this "Gables Ann" Ann (without an E) instead of Anne so that you can differentiate between the two, although I have no idea of how her name was actually spelt.

On the way in, I noticed that this Ann was fiddling around on the roof of the car with something that looked like mixed herbs for cooking.

The only time I had ever knowingly seen anybody with drugs in the past was once in the 6th form when some prat who I knew but didn't really like went round one day showing off a little bag with some chopped up weeds in, trying to make out that he was some sort of Narcotics Crime Lord.

As far as I could tell, he wasn't selling them but just making a pathetic attempt at trying to impress people.

I should point out that, back in those youthful, innocent days nobody knew much about drugs – nobody that I was involved with anyway – and we all thought that even smoking a cigarette was incredibly naughty.

Leaping forward in time a bit: Lucy and I did end up getting unintentionally exposed to somebody smoking "wacky baccy" one evening when we were out with my brother Gary and my school friend Steven in Ramsey where Gary was living at the time as it was handy for where he was working. We were sitting in a pub and a rather strange tobacco smell wafted across the room (this was back in the days when smoking in public places and enclosed spaces was still legal...).

Steve said that it smelt like – (whatever it was) – and that he had come across it before when he was doing his student year in America – so we quickly left and went somewhere less unhealthy.

When we got home, we neither of us could get to sleep and we both lay there wide awake for hours, which I can only assume was the effect of this substance that we had unwittingly inhaled. It was not a very nice feeling and I really can't understand why people would actually choose to want to do that to themselves.

I don't even like taking aspirins or any prescribed medication - but at least with those you have the name of the manufacturer on the packet, a list of ingredients and a certain amount of comeback if anything goes wrong.

But buying some strange substance in a car park or pub toilet from a dubious person you don't know, having no idea what is in it or where it came from, and then smoking, ingesting or injecting it for "FUN" is a completely alien concept to me.

Anyway, the mixed herbs that this Ann was fiddling around with looked vaguely similar to the stuff that the 6th Form Narcotics Crime Lord had been showing off several years beforehand.

It also looked just like a packet of mixed herbs that you could easily buy in any supermarket, to be honest, but I didn't see any particularly valid reason why somebody would be taking some paper twists of oregano and basil into a night club - so this did raise some suspicions.

I whispered to Karen that it looked as if Ann had some drugs with her and surely that wasn't a very good idea if she was pregnant. And the next thing I knew, Karen rushed back over to Ann, shouted something at her, grabbed the mixed herbs and threw them across the car park.

One of Karen's brothers was a police detective so I imagine she must have heard plenty of stories about the negative side of drugs, and, therefore, had a very sensible attitude to that sort of thing.

So - that made me "Mister Popular" for the rest of the evening – but I was the sort of über honest person who used to report people at school for pushing in the dinner queue as well, so was quite accustomed to being badly thought of - for a good enough reason.

Apparently, after I had gone home, this Ann, her boyfriend and a couple of others all turned up at Karen's flat in the middle of the night and they had a huge row about this. Luckily it wasn't actually me who had chucked the oregano and basil away, otherwise there might have been some sort of underworld contract put on my head.

I think the fact that Karen's brother was a policeman - and that she had the fearsome podgy blonde and the serial aborter there in their dressing gowns sticking up for her – meant that the "drugs posse" departed peaceably enough. But I was rather glad that I had opted for an early night!

I don't really know how I came to split up with Karen. In fact we never actually formally "split up" as such - and we certainly never had a terrible argument or a big falling out.

For all I know, she might think we are still going out together and I have just been out for a very long time fetching some milk - who knows...?

Seriously though - it just fizzled out over time really. I was away with work and busy with overseas customers a lot during that period and she changed jobs - as the temping wasn't regular enough - and ended up working for a firm of Gangmasters.

That entailed being picked up early in the morning with a load of others in a van and being taken to wherever they needed unskilled labour on any given day.

One day it might have been packing mushrooms, another day working in a warehouse. During the summer there would have been lots of agricultural work and, with there being so much farming industry for miles and miles all round Peterborough, it could sometimes be quite a long way away.

This meant that she was never sure what time she would finish and get home on any given day and, often being really tired afterwards, it was difficult to plan things.

But, there you go – it was fun while it lasted!

Trendy friends at The Millionaire nightclub in Peterborough, late 1980s.
Paul Jinks, Mark Eastwood & PB.

21st April 1990: PB wearing the famous "ironed shirt" at Alan & Louise's wedding in Stanground. Peterborough United were playing local rivals Cambridge at London Road the same afternoon and you could hear the roar of the crowd tantalisingly wafting across the fields. They lost 1-2 so we didn't miss much. Also in photo (left to right): David Gilding, John Ludman and Steven Garratt.

The main entrance to the Drupa Exhibition in Düsseldorf, 1990

1990: DRUPA Exhibition

During April and May 1990 I spent time in Düsseldorf in Germany working for Baker Perkins PMC – or Rockwell Graphic Systems as they were then known – at the huge international Drupa print and paper exhibition.

As far as I can remember, there used to be major international exhibitions every year for the printing and allied trades with the main ones being on a four year rotation so you'd have Drupa in Düsseldorf in 1986 and 1990, Ipex at the NEC in Birmingham in 1988 and 1992 and so on, with the others in Italy (Grafitalia) and Chicago (GraphExpo).

I was working in the fitting shop office in early 1986 when some of the fitters had to go to Düsseldorf to install the equipment on the Baker Perkins PMC stand for the 1986 exhibition and I heard all their stories about what a great place it was with huge exhibition halls, loads of people from all over the world and all the nightlife around the town.

I went to see the Ipex exhibition at the NEC for a day when it was on in 1988 because by then I was working in the sales / contacts department so I already had an idea of what a major trade exhibition was like, so when I was given the opportunity to go and work on the stand at Drupa 1990, I grabbed it.

From what I remember, the flight from LHR to Düsseldorf went OK (I travelled on my own for some reason) and I got a taxi to the hotel.

Upon arrival, I discovered that I wasn't in the same hotel as everybody else, which miffed me a bit. They were all in the luxurious Penta with all its facilities, whereas I was in the "second choice" hotel along with the late bookings and the smaller exhibitors. I COULD tell you why this was but then I'd have to kill you (as they say in films...).

Not that I minded, to be honest, as it was nice to be slightly apart from the people who you were going to be working with all day long.

This was a pleasant bed and breakfast type place and they did do nice filling breakfasts, and had an evening bar but no restaurant so you had to go out for main meals.

So I wasn't really sure what to do next – I was there for work, after all.

I called the telephone number of the exhibition stand and that didn't work so I tried a few of the other numbers that I had been issued with for BP people at the exhibition. I very quickly learnt the meaning of the German Telecom's recorded "kein Anschluß unter dieser Nummer" message here, I can tell you.

I eventually managed to get hold of Keith Dalton who was one of the sales managers and asked him what I ought to do next. He told me that a group of the salesmen were going out into town for dinner later and if I got myself to their hotel reception for 7.30 I could go with them.

That was pretty decent of him as he didn't have to do that - and I doubt that they particularly wanted to go out with me anymore than I did with them. Whilst I got on OK with them all in a working office environment, we didn't tend to socialise between groups to that extent.

I asked what to wear and he said "smart casual" but, not really knowing what sales managers wore to be smart casual, I erred a little more on the smart side just to be sure.

As it turned out, the evening was very pleasant. Had you told me before I flew out to Germany that I would go out on the town with Keith Dalton (UK Sales Manager), Nick Collins (France, Italy & Spain Sales Manager), Steve Fox (UK, Benelux and Scandinavia sales) and Keith Amos (UK Sales) plus the somewhat scary Sales Director Ian Mackay - and managed to enjoy it - I would never have believed you.

Ian Mackay was a very charismatic character with a loud bombastic personality and most people - including me - were frightened to death of him.

To be completely fair to him, away from the workplace Mr Mackay was a lot less gruff and pretty good company. I later sat in on a visitors' lunch with a Spanish customer back in Peterborough and he was charm personified throughout.

So I imagine - a bit like teachers in the classroom (and me in my Exam Invigilating sessions at the post 16 college in more recent years in Birkenhead...) - he may have put on a bit of a front for work purposes.

They wanted to go to the "Zum Schiffchen" in the Altstadt - which is still there today and described as an "historic tavern for robust German dishes like pork knuckle, served with house-brewed beers." Unfortunately, everybody else seemed to have the same idea and the place was packed to bursting so we ended up at a Churrasco Mexican steak house instead.

Although they were all very friendly and welcoming - and perfectly happy to include me, I felt a bit out of my comfort zone with these guys so I just sat quietly in the corner, spoke when spoken to and ate and drank at the appropriate moments.

But, we had a nice evening overall and some good food and I then got a taxi back to my hotel - and they got a separate one back to theirs - ready to prepare for the first day of the exhibition on the morrow.

Once the exhibition started in earnest I got into quite a good routine. I'd get up, get showered and have breakfast at my hotel and then get a taxi in to the Messe Park, which was huge.

I had my Sony Walkman with me (that's a pocket-sized cassette player with headphones) that I always had with me when I travelled anywhere as it helped pass the time, and I had a particular home-compiled tape in it that I played every morning on the way in to Drupa.

This wasn't by design - it just happened to be the one that was in the machine on the first day that I sat down in the taxi and I stuck with it after that.

The first songs on the tape were "Anchorage" by Michelle Shocked, "My Blue Heaven" by The Pogues and "Summer of 69" by Bryan Adams and, depending on the amount of traffic on the way in, Bryan was normally just kicking in when I arrived at the Messehalle and walked through to our stand.

I can't begin to tell you what a great feeling it was to be driving through an exciting city in the morning sunshine looking forward to meeting up with lots of interesting people from all over the world.

So I'd listen to the rest of the tape on the way back in the evening – that usually took longer because the traffic was very unpredictable and there was often a queue for taxis because most of the exhibitors finished at a similar time – and then I'd rewind it to start with "Anchorage" again the next morning.

Even now, over 30 years later, if it's a crisp bright sunny morning and I hear any of those three songs, it takes me right back to the feeling of sitting in the taxi heading in to the exhibition, tingling with anticipation for the day ahead.

The Exhibition Stand

As a major player in the production of printing presses at the time – even more so since Baker Perkins had become part of the Rockwell Graphic Systems (RGS) group, alongside other brands such as Goss and Hantscho - we had a very sizable stand at the exhibition.

The merger between Baker Perkins and RGS was still in its infancy so there were different "factions" all with their own diverse sales and admin people stationed on the stand and, and just to complicate things, the area was divided into two distinct sections.

We - that's the sales, marketing and admin people from Baker Perkins PMC, Peterborough, plus the people from our German sales office in Offenbach – had the right hand side of the stand (looking outwards).

The other RGS entities – off the top of my head, that's people from:

The Goss factory in Preston,
The Creusot Loire factory in Nantes
The RGS sales and marketing office in Hounslow
The RGS Paris sales office
The RGS German sales office in Obershausen
had the left hand side of the stand (looking outwards.)

Each side had its own reception desk and these were at a 90 degree angle to each other so that, if you saw one as you approached the stand, you wouldn't see the other one and we actually spent half of our time redirecting visitors around the corner to the other desk.

I can't speak for the RGS side of the stand – although I imagine that both halves were probably constructed in a symmetrical fashion – but our portion had a large display area with various pieces of machinery set up and tastefully illuminated.

I don't actually remember what machinery we had on display now – which is rather remiss of me – but there must have been a freestanding print unit there, with its innards slowly rotating, as I distinctly recall at one point explaining the concept of the CUIM roller mechanism (that's short for "Continuously Undulating Inking Module", by the way) to one of the Goss sales guys.

There were also display boards and TV monitors showing videos of our product range.

We had a discreetly closed off hospitality area where invited guests and other important people could sit in comfy chairs and have drinks and snacks - and I think there might have been a quiet private room for meetings.

Then there was a sizable storage area around the back where the office supplies and equipment and whatever was all kept and where we, the staff, could leave our stuff and go and relax for breaks.

The reception desk had all the sales brochures neatly arranged on displays behind it. This was so that we or the sales people could give them out to any seriously interested parties but they were sufficiently out of the way to avoid any old body just grabbing a handful for the sake of it.

A lot of the other exhibitors gave away printed samples of posters, maps, etc on their stands so there were a lot of general sightseers who used to go round gathering up freebies.

Bearing this in mind, RGS produced a handy size tubular bag made out of throw away plastic with a drawstring top and the RGS group companies' logos on so that people could carry all these giveaway posters around in them - and these were very popular with the passing crowds.

As far as I can remember - and I apologise if I have missed anybody out but this was quite a long time ago, plus people rotated over time – the PMC side of the stand was manned by:

Marketing Department: David Stamp, Joanne Korosi, Cristina Rivas.

Sales Department: Ian Mackay, Keith Dalton, Nick Collins, Steve Fox, Keith Amos & Spiros Doukas.

German (Offenbach) Sales Office: Michael Mandel, Gabriele Cordes.

Commercial / Sales Admin: Paul Breeze, Anne Castellano.

Plus 3 agency hostesses (more about them later...).

The RGS side of the stand – as far as I could work out - as we were never all properly introduced to each other, was overseen by the RGS Hounslow marketing people – that was a guy called Matti Hindrekus and a girl called Fiona.

They also had all the sales people from the other offices in the UK, Germany and France who I got to know more about later on after the exhibition.

These were, among others: Heike Heck & Franz Sengpiel (Obershausen), Claude Mercier and Michel Carpentier (Paris), Michel Foing and Nathalie (Nantes) and Peter Selby, David Renshaw, Paul Feeney & Mike McCarthy (Preston / Hounslow).

There was a tall very smart lady from the Chicago office called Barb Gora who was there for a lot of the time and some other Americans who we knew like Pat Cassidy, Al Laudage and Tim Mercy who came and went as it suited them.

A lot of technical people from the various offices and factories all came over for a day or two at a time as well so we met up with quite a lot of colleagues old and new over the course of the exhibition.

Above: PB with Gabriele Cordes on the reception desk on the RGS Baker Perkins PMC stand at the Drupa 90 exhibition in Düsseldorf.

Above left: Anne Castellano at the Drupa exhibition. The man in the background is carrying one of the RGS poster bags. Above right: Stand hostess Valerie Ghiglione.

Agents' Reception

As well as our own permanently employed sales people, our company had a network of sales agents in most countries around the world and they often came to the stand with various customers to hold sales discussions.

At the end of the first day of the exhibition, there was a special reception held off site somewhere or other for all of our sales agents to be able to meet up together.

A coach was laid on to take everybody to the venue and there were cakes and tea and coffee and, I think - champagne, set out in an elegant dining room.

Ian Mackay gave a brief speech welcoming all the agents to the exhibition and thanking them for all the hard work that they were putting on the company's behalf.

I had seen some of the agents in our Peterborough office from time to time when they were visiting - like Phillipe Langzam from Ofmag (Paris), Lars Adolfsson (Sweden) and Paoli Bormann (Finland) but this was the first time that I had met Ferdinando Facchini and Milva Arnoldi from the Italian agents (although I had spoken to them on the phone a lot in the past), Ken Rendell from Australia and Gilbert Verstraat from Belgium.

There were people from far flung places such as India and Korea as well, although I didn't get the chance to talk to everybody – plus I was still rather shy at that time.

Drupa Nightlife

The majority of people who were at the exhibition headed for the Düsseldorf Altstadt (Old Town) overlooking the picturesque River Rhine in the evenings .

The weather was unseasonably warm that year, with bright sunny days and mild evenings throughout our stay, meaning that you could go out without needing to be weighed down with heavy coats and jackets - and it was just right for wandering from bar to bar.

The whole place was packed with food outlets of all types from bratty stands to exquisite restaurants and everybody was out for a good time.

The Gypsy Kings (Spanish / Italian - ish guitar band) were popular at the time and there was a bar that just played their music all evening long - and so many other great places it is really hard to remember them all now.

The traditional local brew in Düsseldorf is a dark beer called Altbier and that was very popular among the visitors – including me.

Despite covering quite a large area and being full of visitors from all over the world, you'd quite often bump into people that you knew from work so it was a really great atmosphere all round.

I don't know how it came about but I remember eating out with Steve Lee (that's he of IGPM fame – see "France Actually" for more details...) and some of the designers from the drawing office one evening.

I also did a bit of bar trawling with Anne Castellano - who was my colleague and fellow language expert from the commercial office – bumped into Joanne and Cristina one evening and also the visiting Jane Barnet, about whom you'll hear more later.

Hostesses & Cinema

As I have already mentioned in passing, on the exhibition stand we had three locally hired hostesses. By that I mean decorative agency staff who were employed to brighten the place up and serve drinks to visitors and clear away afterwards so that the sales people could concentrate on the nitty gritty of actual selling

One of them was a professional model (although presumably just "between modelling jobs" at that time...) and she wouldn't even let me take a photo of her working on the stand. She did have her modelling card with her, though – citing her height and vital statistics – just in case anybody might discover her, and she did at least let me have one of those.

I can't remember anything about the second girl but the third one was much more down to earth and normal and she was called Valerie.

When I mentioned that I didn't have anything arranged for a particular evening after work she immediately invited me to go with her and boyfriend to the cinema, where they were going to see Driving Miss Daisy or "Miss Daisy und ihr Chauffeur" as it was called in German.

I seem to think that I met them outside the cinema at the agreed time - so I must have gone back to my hotel, freshened up and taken a taxi to get there.

We went in and saw the film and it was very enjoyable, although my German was rotten at the time and I hardly understood any of the dialogue. If you've ever seen that film you'll know that it is nearly all dialogue and no action so this left me at a bit of a disadvantage.

But it was nice to go to a German cinema for the first time ever and to be in pleasant company.

Now – if you or I arranged to meet somebody to go to the cinema, you'd perhaps have a drink beforehand – or something to eat, or go for a drink afterwards - but you need to understand a bit of the German mentality here.

If they say a particular thing, they mean that particular thing. If you are meeting up to go to the cinema, that is exactly what you are going to do. No beating about the bush – nothing more, nothing less.

Another example of this: if you say, for example, "we'll have to get together sometime for a meal / drink /coffee", while your common or garden English person will say "yeah, right, whatever..." and not necessarily give it a second thought, your average Teuton will feel very aggrieved if you don't then follow up with a fixed invitation for said meal, drink or coffee.

So, I had my first experience of this German exactness when we emerged from the pictures, with me rather peckish by this time, Valerie and her bloke abruptly sad goodnight, mounted two-up on his pushbike and off they went.

Undaunted by this slightly odd behaviour, I took myself to a snack stand further down the road and had a couple of bratwursts and some chips and then got a taxi back to the hotel.

I wasn't put off by any of this, by the way, you just need to appreciate the cultural differences and know how people are.

We did the exact same thing the following week and went to see "Kuck Mal Wer Da Spricht" (Look Who's Talking) which, as there was a lot more visual comedy involved, I found a lot easier to understand.

Dinner at Penta Hotel

One evening I finally managed to get further than the reception at the Penta Hotel as Gabriele Cordes very kindly invited me to meet her for dinner.

This was nice as, although we had spent each day together working on the stand - and I had seen her when she came on a visit to the Peterborough office in the past, there was never much time for chit chat so we hadn't really talked socially before.

She said she'd meet me in the bar at a particular time so I went and sat down and ordered myself a drink.

It was a very swish place. There was a rotunda bar in the middle of the room, subdued lighting all round and discrete booths around the walls. There was a pianist playing nice background music on a white grand piano in one corner and I think there may have been a small dance floor.

The restaurant was similarly tastefully laid out and it had a balcony with views overlooking the swimming pool.

I don't remember what we had to eat now or what we talked about but it was a fun evening and I really enjoyed it.

One thing that has stuck in my mind from that occasion which was quite amusing was that Joanne Korosi came past with a book under her arm at one point and said hello.

We invited her to join us but she made a big thing about scuttling off again and "leaving us alone" (nod, nod - wink, wink) – although quite what she thought was going to happen, I have no idea - it wasn't "that" sort of dinner!

Drupa Party Night

Over the middle weekend, the organisers held a massive party night for all the exhibitors to be able to let their hair down.

This was held in a different area of the Messe Park and was set out across a range of interconnecting halls all with different themes, to reflect the international mix of all the visitors.

They had, for example, a Mexican Hall where a band was playing Tijuana brass music and all the food and drink was Tex-Mex orientated. And there will have been a traditional German room with an oom-pah band and sausages and beers - and so on and so on.

No expense was spared for this event and they even had a full Scottish pipe band marching around the corridors!

The party covered such a big area that they issued everybody with a map so that they could find their way round.

*****

So, there you are. Two weeks' wall to wall fun (more or less) at the Drupa exhibition in Düsseldorf and getting paid for it as well!

What could I possibly do for an encore?

How about a weekend in Berlin...

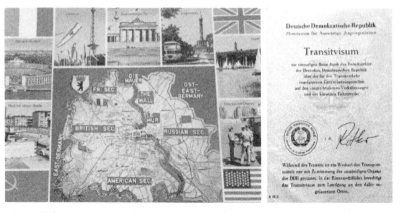

Above left: Berlin postcard showing the Allied occupation zones still technically in place in May 1990. Above right: DDR Transit Visa allowing train travel across East German territory to Berlin.

May 1990: Berlin

My biggest problem about going to Berlin after the exhibition had finished was finding somebody to go with as, whilst I was desperate to go, I didn't really fancy going on my own.

The difficulty arose when asking around for potential travel mates was that, after two weeks of being away at the exhibition, most people had families and homes to maintain and all wanted to get back home so they could catch up on their washing etc over the weekend before returning to work on the Monday.

It just so happened that one of the women from the technical department called Jane Barnet was also keen on all things German and a bit more free spirited than some of the others. She spoke German better than I did at the time - and I knew her from when she helped out when we had German customer visitors.

She was actually married to somebody or other but seemed very independent – and was always going off on her own to do things.

And it turned out that the idea of going on a platonic weekend with me to East Berlin didn't appear to phase her one bit. So, at least I didn't have to go on my own!

I know that in these enlightened modern times, everybody is cynical and suspicious and is quick to believe the worst of people, but I can categorically state that I never had any romantic involvement with Jane Barnet and anything that we did together was perfectly innocent and amicable.

Luckily we both had regular British Airways air tickets through work – rather than the cheap bucket shop tickets that you might have booked yourself for a holiday trip to save money – so it was fairly easy to ring up the BA desk at the airport and change our return flight reservations to Sunday tea time.

Most of the others who were heading home after the exhibition would have been booked on flights on Friday or early Saturday morning so it wasn't too busy for the Sunday.

On the following pages, you will see an account of our trip to Berlin that I wrote quite a few years ago – in the mid 1990s while I was at work in Preston and probably ought to have been doing something else entirely...

Anyway, the benefit of this is that this account is much more detailed than it would be if I was to try and write it all now completely from memory – and I hope you find it as interesting to read now and I have done in re-reading again!

Having safely arrived at the main railway station in Dusseldorf with ten minutes to go until the train left, we were met by a stony face at the ticket desk who refused to take a credit card in payment and insisted that we go all the way to the far end of the foyer to the exchange counter.

We eventually lunged on to the train just before it was due to pull out and took our places in an unreserved compartment.

Apart from a few others the train was actually quite empty, although many of the seats were reserved from places further along the route. There didn't seem to be a buffet car of any sort and we were both feeling a bit peckish. We sat looking out of the window watching the countryside go by.

The platform at Hanover was full of people waiting for the train, large rucksacks seemed to bobble along the platform supported only by little legs, grandmothers hugged unwilling grandchildren and, most importantly, a catering trolley was brought on board.

We were quite lucky to avoid the groups of noisy schoolchildren and smoking studenty types. The first person to enter our compartment was an oldish woman with greyish black hair tied back and wearing an old blue mac.

She pointed out quite severely that one of our bags was on **her** seat and didn't show the least appreciation when I smilingly moved it for her.

It later transpired that she was East German which probably explained her attitude. Having later seen some of what had been East Germany, I think I would been ratty too if I'd lived there for 40 years.

The mood was lightened slightly when a young boy/man came in and asked very politely (in German) whether one of the seats was free, to which I motioned that it was.

He had a huge sports bag from which during the journey he took all sorts of little treasures. He had a Walkman with a never-ending supply of tapes. He had a lunchbox with quite yummy looking sandwiches. He had a little plastic bag with hard boiled eggs in.

He had a supply of napkins to collect the discarded egg shells in and he even had salt and pepper pots to season his ever growing feast. I didn't spot any lashings of ginger beer but I wouldn't have been surprised.

Our hunger for food was finally satisfied when the food trolley finally arrived in our carriage, although the choice of fare was limited to bockwurst with mustard and cans of beer and Fanta. The sausages went down very well actually but I avoided the beer – just to be on the safe side.

The border crossing at Marienborn was marked with flags and a few customs people only - a far cry from the mirrors under the train and full scale searches that had been there before the fall of the wall.

As the train pulled away into Eastern Europe we were confronted by an East German guard who wanted to see our passports. He was unshaven, overweight and rather shodily dressed and, in my opinion, typified everything that had been wrong with communism - lack of pride or ambition.

The old woman handed over a blue passport which he purely stamped and handed back. The young lad was given a fancy folded document with a flourishing crest on it for which he had to pay 15 DM.

In comparison I was rather disappointed with the little transit visas that we were given but the disappointment soon went and I still have mine as a souvenir to this day.

The weather began to deteriorate and I wasn't relishing the thought of it raining the whole time that we were in Berlin.

The first major place that we encountered in East Germany was Magdeburg, which I had heard of, but nothing more. It was very interesting to see a Russian (Soviet Union at that time) army base in the forest just to the west of the city, with soldiers and tanks and whatever else. Unfortunately, the train passed too quickly for me to get a photo of it, although if I had, I would have probably been shot for spying.

It was pouring with rain by the time we pulled into Magdeburg. The train stopped but, due to transit corridor regulations that were still in place at that time, no-one was allowed to get on or off, except the East German passport control people.

At one of the other platforms stood a Deutsche Reichsbahn train from the East German railway which looked as if it were probably a local commuter train.

We all looked out in awe at the train, trying to catch a glimpse of these poor people who had been terrorised for so long by an oppressive regime. I thought that for some reason they might be looking out at us in envy at our western freedoms and wealth but, on reflection, I suppose they weren't in the least bit interested in us, having seen thousands of western tourists over the years.

As we pulled away from Magdeburg station, I got my first real view of an Eastern European town. There were a lot of tall grey blocks of flats, grey cobbled streets, drab walls with very few posters or colour of any sort and all the cars were those horrible little Trabants. Admittedly, in heavy rain anywhere can look dull but this place really had a despairing look about it.

From then on we didn't really see much sign of life until we got to Berlin. The train passed almost exclusively through beautiful rolling countryside, seemingly untouched by modern life. If it hadn't have been such bad weather, it would have been even nicer.

As the afternoon wore on the weather got better until there were blue skies and bright sunshine as we entered the outer suburbs of Berlin. The excitement mounted on the train and people congregated in the corridors to get a better view out of the windows of this intriguing city. One man, who looked American, stood with a video camera pointed outside, filming the arrival.

The young German lad enquired of the old lady whether it was allowed to do that or not, the "of course you can" reply seemed a little too emphatic considering that it would only have been a very recent luxury.

First Impressions

We got off the train at Berlin Zoo Station in West Berlin, waiting a while to avoid the European rush, and tried to decide how to get to the hotel that I had booked.

I had been told that it was close to the Hansaplatz U-Bahn station so we bought tickets and, after a considerable amount of indecision and jostling, got onto the right train.

Hansaplatz turned out to be in the middle of a quiet residential area with wide pavements and cleanly fronted houses. We spent what seemed like an age traipsing around in the early evening sun trying to find the right street. I wasn't dressed particularly warmly but felt very warm indeed under the weight of all the baggage that I was carrying.

We eventually found the place - it was a large, plain looking building without even a hint of a hotel sign or any publicity boards whatsoever. I was about to go up to the front door when it was opened from the inside and a very old and frail looking nun stepped out.

This, somewhat naturally, came as a bit of a surprise to both of us and I started fumbling in my pocket to check the address of the hotel. As the door swung closed I noticed a small sign inside with the words "Hotel Reception" so I cautiously popped my head round the door.

The whole place looked a bit like the recreation room in a hospital which, had I thought it through, wasn't particularly surprising as it was a B&B run by the Kaiserwerther Verband – a charitable religious group.

With some scepticism, I approached the reception to announce our presence and found myself hoping that it wouldn't be staffed by another elderly nun.

The receptionist turned out to be a cheery, plumpish civilian and she pointed us up to our rooms on the second floor. Having been rather put off by the sterility of everything that we had seen so far, I was pleasantly surprised at the rooms themselves.

Mine was very large for one person, bright and airy with a nice big window looking out onto the main street below. To one side was a wide coffee table and two wicker chairs, there was a colour television in the corner of the room and twin beds with bedside tables.

There was a radio alarm clock and telephone on one of the tables and lots of wardrobe space to the left of the bed.

The en-suite bathroom was also large with a huge shower cubicle with aqua blue wave pattern tiling and a large mirror opposite.

Jane had never been to Berlin before either so we were unsure where to go for the evening. We decided to take the U-Bahn to Tiergarten and decided to walk for a bit and see where we ended up.

It was just beginning to get dark and the Siegessaule monument to a victory over Napoleon looked very impressive - tall and shining gold - standing in the middle of a large roundabout.

As it was early evening, there was a lot of traffic about so we decided to walk through the park, which was huge. In the distance behind the trees we could see Belleville palace which, we later learnt, was the residence of the German president.

Emerging from the woods a little further down the road we noticed a little area a bit further down where quite a few people were congregating taking photos.

It was a wide, straight road (with about 6 lanes, the middle two of which were used for car and coach parking) which led down to the Brandenburg gate. The sight of this sent my blood running and I grabbed Jane by the hand and we marched off towards it. As we approached the people a couple of motorcyclists with English plates drew up and joined the throng.

What they were all looking at was a huge stepped area with cannons and flowers, the centre piece of which was a tall monument with a grey statue of a soldier atop.

It was immediately obvious that this was a Russian monument because there was a large hammer & sickle on the front of the construction surrounded by cyrillic lettering and two **real** armed Russian soldiers who stood to attention at its base.

The whole area was cordoned off by a low chain fence patrolled by two German police to stop anybody approaching. The ensemble was finished off by two full size Russian tanks, one at each end, positioned on plinths and facing outwards.

This was, to say the least, quite an impressive sight unfortunately it was already too dark to take photos so we resolved to return the next day in better light.

We proceeded down the road towards the Brandenburg gate. This area that we had seen so recently on TV with thousand of partying Berliners hugging each other and hammering at bits of wall was now totally devoid of wall altogether.

It had been replaced by crowd barriers with an opening which was manned by an East German guard checking passports and visas. We decided to save our foray into the East until the next day to be able to make a day of it.

Beneath the trees along here were a couple of strange looking people selling East German and Red Army bits and pieces - belts, buckles, badges etc (at this stage all the merchandise seemed individual and genuine as opposed to all the profiteers that one can find there now with their mass produced plastic rubbish).

After lots of deliberation I decided to buy a hammer & sickle belt buckle from one and a DDR rank badge from another. There were also a few E German officers' caps and some Red Army furry hats which I thought to be too corny for the occasion but, on reflection, I often think that the DDR cap might have been a good investment.

From here we walked along a quiet deserted, yet very wide road which passed behind what turned out to be the Reichstag.

This was intersected by another equally wide road which had originally passed into the eastern sector but which had for the past 30 years gone nowhere at all.

It was such an eerie sensation to see the high blocks on the eastern side which came to an abrupt end where the border had been. It must have been awful for the people living there to be able to see into the west but never be able to go there.

The whole area was littered with dust and rubble from the recent dismantling of the section of wall which had probably stood there. There was a grassy strip between the road and the buildings that had previously been in East Germany - this had probably been part of the "death zone" which had been so fiercely covered by the border guards and where so many people had previously lost their lives.

The road ended at the side of the river which snaked past the Reichstag building. From our side of the river it was still possible to see the wall across the other side.

A little further up stream was a black metal bridge that spanned the river. This was obviously on the Eastern side as there was barbed wire and fencing beneath it and below the waterline to prevent people passing under it.

The deathly silence was deafening in this area which, in its hey-day, would certainly have been very lively. It was almost dark and the final sight of the evening we were not prepared for. Positioned between the Reichstag and the area where the wall had been were a series of crosses bearing the names of those who had been killed trying to cross the wall.

Even more poignant were those crosses which just bore the date of the death and the legend "unbekannt" (unknown) where someone had obviously recently come across and handwritten the name of the victim underneath. Some of these had had to wait since the early sixties to be named, which was particularly moving.

Having spent a moment heads bowed in memory of the dead, our thoughts to turned to food and how we hadn't had any since the sausages on the train. Not fancying retracing our steps back through the woods in the dark to the U-Bahn, it was quite fortuitous that a bus came along and stopped at the Reichstag - its eventual destination being the Kurfürstendamm.

It turned out that our 24 hour U-Bahn passes that we had bought earlier were also valid for use of the bus so we took our places, rested our legs and watched Berlin life whizz by for a while. The bus passed by the Zoo and we resolved that we would come back here tomorrow and look around it.

Upon arrival at the Kurfürstendamm we neither of us had any idea where to head for and so just went straight to the first Chinese restaurant that we came to. It turned out to be on the third floor of a tall building and our table by the window afforded magnificent views of the bright lights and hustle and bustle down below.

From there we took the U-Bahn back to Zoo station - which was only a couple of stops away - where we had to change to get the right line to go back to the hotel.

The area around the station was very lively with many cafes, takeaways, souvenir shops etc.

The March Eastwards

The rain that we had worried might spoil the day was not in evidence as I looked out of the window onto a bright Berlin Saturday morning ready to go out.

I had managed to find a British Forces radio programme on the radio which kept me informed of the line ups for the FA Cup final between Manchester United & Crystal Palace - to be played that afternoon.

Breakfast passed without particular incident and was neither spectacularly good nor spectacularly bad.

We left the hotel and went straight to the U-Bahn, having decided that the famous Friedrichstrasse in the east would be our destination.

The train snaked over ground past many tall buildings, many of which were being cleaned up or rebuilt. We passed by some woodland and the station "Belleville" suggested that we were close to the wall sector. As we pulled out again into open countryside it was possible to see the open grassland and, beyond it, the Reichstag building.

In the foreground was the plain, white painted Berlin Wall and before it a wide strip of nothingness where hardly even any grass was growing. In the middle stood one guards tower - now empty and lifeless but previously keeping watch over the death-strip.

I have always regretted not having taken a photo of this particular sight but it came and went so quickly and I didn't really expect it all to have gone before my next visit.

As we pulled into Friedrichstrasse station and heard the command that all Westerners had to get off and go through Passport control, my sense of adventure heightened considerably. I was about to personally step foot in the former diehard Communist bastion of East Germany. A long time ambition fulfilled at last.

Everybody was directed into a large hall way and had to queue to pass through "immigration". The whole place looked very drab and uninviting as did the passport control people. Unimaginative black and white signs that looked as if they dated from the sixties pointed to separate queues for DDR, Communist Bloc or Western passport holders and consequently, practically everybody from the train had to queue up to squeeze through one little gateway.

Despite the fact that their little empire was crumbling around them, the East German immigration people were still living very much in the cold war. Each person passing through had to squeeze through a gap and into a sort of wooden cabin where the passport window was. The cabin had a ceiling mirrored at angles, to the side of the place was something which looked very much like a two way mirror.

Every now and again there came a flash as if a photograph had been taken of the person passing through.

The controller seemed to take an age looking through everybody's passport before officiously filling out a temporary entry visa and stamping it. This was a wonderful A5 official-looking document with the DDR crest embossed in swirling colours across it. I was very loathe to give it up as we later left the Eastern Sector but didn't really fancy the more permanent alternative.

Having safely negotiated the immigration procedure we found ourselves in the main station hall. The whole place looked amazingly grey and drab. All the signs were in black or grey and there was no advertising or colour of any type. The ticket windows blandly offered domestic or international tickets and the bank where we went to get some Ostmarks was very reminiscent of an early sixties black & white spy film.

Armed with our tin-like and practically worthless O-Marks, we stepped out into the fresh air again.

It was at this point where my advanced planning had fallen down somewhat in so much as I didn't have a tourist map or guidebook with me and such things were yet to be thought of in the Eastern sector.

We walked south along Friedrichstrasse for a while, stopping briefly by a pretty grassy area with flowers where there was a stand selling Bratwurst. Elevenses time.

There was also a sort of a map showing the places of interest (East side only) which suggested that we were heading in more or less the right direction.

It is very hard to put into words the feeling that I felt walking along Friedrichstrasse that bright May day at the end of the cold war. On one hand there was the sheer exhilaration of being there and being able to feel the shadow of the old régime hovering over the place.

On the other there was the grey gloom and despair of a failed system. Many of the tall, drab, grey buildings were in a bad state of disrepair.

Some even still had bullet holes left over from the last days of the Second World War when the battle for Berlin was still raging. Parts of the roads, even the main roads still had cobbled surfaces, as they probably had in the twenties when this street had been alive with colour and decadence.

In order to avoid a premature arrival at Checkpoint Charlie and the gateway back to the West, we took a left turn and ended up in some semi-residential area. The pavements were wide and empty and were lined with tall blocks of flats whose coloured window boxes did little to alleviate the uniformity of the place.

Many of the shops were closed as it was Saturday afternoon. I must admit that from the goods offered in the windows, I didn't feel that I was missing out on very much. There weren't many fancy goods shops - at least not in this street. It was mainly necessity shopping - groceries and knitting wool.

We tried to gain access to a supermarket which appeared to still be open, just for a look around really. The man on the door stopped us entering. At the time I figured it was probably because we were obviously foreigners but, on reflection, it was probably because they were about to close. Here again, the fare in the windows looked very bland and was packaged in plain boxes with very little or no brand names on show.

By now, the thick city air had taken its toll and we were in need of a drink. At the bottom of one of these high rise towers was a bar with a terrace.

It looked like the sort of place you'd have tried to avoid in an English inner city concrete shopping centre back in the 70s but, as there didn't seem to be anyone much about, about from two, very "East German" looking women (badly dressed, short hair, overweight, unattractive, no makeup etc), we decided it was worth a try, to experience some normal everyday Communist life if nothing else.

I ordered a beer and Jane an apple juice. They didn't have apple juice so she got orange juice.

After just one sip of East German beer I made up my mind to have a coke next time. The round of drinks came to some mysterious amount such as 2 marks 55 or something similar - quite strange as drinks in the west were always costed in Marks or -50s and the total cost of this beer and juice came to something like 30p altogether.

I later learned that prices for necessities and household items in East Germany hadn't been increased since the early 50s and that these items were often produced at a loss just to ensure that the population didn't starve.

The beer tasted rather nasty and I didn't feel that I could finish it. This left me in a bit of a dilemma. I couldn't decide whether I should offer it to the two women who were sitting there looking very depressed on the terrace.

As in many East European countries, beer may have been a bit of a luxury which, even at such comparatively low prices, may not have been easily affordable for most people, If that was the case here, I did not want to upset anybody by wasting such a valuable commodity and showing myself to be a fickle western tourist, just there to make fun of their predicament.

Similarly, I didn't want to go too far to the other extreme being over-charitable and embarrass them by offering them a half drunk beer which they could easily afford themselves.

The dilemma eventually resolved itself as the two women got up and left. Feeling a little better about it, I also got up and left, leaving the beer in plain view on the table for anyone who may have wanted it.

We headed off into what was a very deserted residential area and it left one wondering where everyone might be on a Saturday lunchtime - perhaps there was a law stating that they all had to eat at a certain time.

The road that we were following ended up in a sort of square cum playground which was in reality a vast area of concrete with a few trees, some unexciting modern art work and little else.

Not wishing to waste any further time in such a non-descript area and also, wanting to make sure that we didn't lost in the faceless, characterless zones beyond, we quickly decided to head off in a direction which would bring us back to the main tourist trail.

We walked along a pathway which had a river or canal on one side and a slightly more picturesque block of concrete flats on the other. All the flats looked identical from the outside - not very big and with a little balcony as a token gesture.

The road was cobbled and led to small wooden bridge. On the other side of the river was the plain dark wall of a factory building of some sort. Beside the road and in back alleys was parked the odd eastern european car - all painted in awful garish, old fashioned colours, as if to try and provide some distraction from the grim realities of life. There wasn't a sound to be heard and no movement at all except for the advance of two western tourists in awe of their current surroundings.

We eventually found ourselves in the very militantly named "Marx-Engels Platz" which was a large square and seemed to be a sort of focal point. Behind us was a wide building with walls in a bronzy mirrored material which, from the right angle, beautifully reflected the building across the other side of the square (another once-in-a-lifetime photo opportunity wasted! it was cloudy anyway....).

In the centre of this mirrored building was a large DDR crest. We later learnt that this was the government building Palast der Republik that housed the Volkskammer – the DDR national parliament. The middle area of the Platz was being used as a car park for lots of Trabants and Ladas painted in a horrible blue colour. I did remark at the time that the entire road surface around there also resembled that of a car park.

Not my photo, unfortunately, I don't appear to have taken one of the iconic "Palast der Republik". This is a view of the square and the building from 1977 by Istvan (Wikipedia (CC BY-SA 3.0)

According to Wikipedia: "The Palast was completed in 1976 to house the Volkskammer, also serving various cultural purposes including two large auditoria, art galleries, a theatre, a cinema, 13 restaurants, 5 beer halls, a bowling alley, 4 pool rooms, a billiards room, a rooftop skating rink, a private gym with spa, a casino, medical station, a post office, a police station with an underground cellblock, an indoor basketball court, an indoor swimming pool, barbershops and salons, public and private restrooms and a discothèque."

Approaching the Palast building we found that on the outside ground floor to one side of the main entrance was a cafe terrace which was full of people all being waited upon by waistcoat clad waiters.

This was a total contrast from the dull forlorn bar that we had seen earlier. In fact, here it was impossible to get a table.

There was music coming from inside the bar and, in a sort of surreal irony considering the political situation, the radio was playing "World Outside Your Window" by Tanita Tikaram.

It was, by now, well past lunchtime and my stomach began to inform me of this with several loud rumbles.

The tour of the rest of Marx-Engels Platz was cut short - particularly as I still didn't have a guidebook and could, by consequence, do nothing more than hazard a wild guess at the names and functions of the old looking, domed, cathedral type building and the wide, knocked about place with columns set back in its own grounds.

Heading back towards the western sector we crossed a rather ornate stone bridge with statues along the parapets. Alongside the river was an outdoor cafe which seemed quite popular. We were about to go and sit there when we noticed another set of tables outside the museum building where there seemed to be a bit more room and fewer Americans.

Lunch And Afternoon

My first experience of Eastern European cuisine was interesting to say the least. For the grand sum of £1.50 or thereabouts, we were to receive a well balanced platter of meat and two veg.

Unfortunately, the average East German idea of meat fell somewhat below my own and although edible, I wasn't really able to tell what genre of "meat" I was actually eating. The vegetables in some respects proved how good the much maligned school dinners of the past had been.

The watery potato mixture wasn't horrible, but wasn't good. The carrot had been boiled for too long and had lost any flavour that it may have had. The sauerkraut wasn't too bad (for sauerkraut at least, and I didn't particularly like sauerkraut at that time...).

The cutlery was mis-matched and rather old and the crockery would even have been rejected by a factory canteen. This dissuaded me from trying the tap water and I ended up with an East German cola – the price 1m 50 printed permanently on the label.

I do not particularly seek to ridicule or put down this attempt at fine cuisine as it was quite nice to be able to sit outside in a capital city and be waited on with local fare. Where in the west could you get a main course so cheaply? It was a very meaningful cultural experience for me and one that I am pleased not to have missed out on.

Unfortunately, as we were dining, the weather changed again and dark clouds began to appear, making the air sticky and uncomfortable.

It became a bit cold sitting there by the river so we paid our bill and walked on a little down the famous Unter Den Linden.

The museum where we had dined appeared to be staging an Exhibition about the "fall of the wall" the previous November which I would have liked to have seen but didn't really have the time.

Just as we were deciding against the exhibition, a sort of a procession could be seen coming towards us. It turned out to be a march and drive past by the East Berlin "feuerwehr" (Fire Brigade). No particular reason was obvious but the sight of their equipment made me feel reassured that we were stopping in West Berlin.

A little further down the road we came across a large amount of people with cameras etc who were crowding around to look at something.

It was a plain, square building with columns at the entrance which was being guarded by East German soldiers. Obviously, something interesting was scheduled to happen so we pushed through to the front to get a good view.

As we did so a roll of drums came from somewhere around the corner behind the crowd and some more soldiers came marching along. Obviously this was to be a "changing of the guard" ceremony.

A rather young looking officer barked out instructions and the relief guards goose-stepped to the beat of the drum to face the two guards who were about to be relieved.

12th May 1990: Changing the guard at the Tomb of the Unknown Soldier in East Berlin.

After a few showings and shoulderings of arms, the new guards took position and the relieved pair were marched off with the officer and drummer.

The soldiers were wearing the field-green uniforms of the East German army with light grey helmets of a shape made famous by old photos of the border guards from the sixties. They had the name of their regiment on a cuff band around their right arm and were very smartly done out, in stark comparison to the rest of the East German officialdom that we had seen thus far.

The spectacle over, we decided to follow some of the other onlookers into the building to see what all the pomp and ceremony was for.

The interior was a large dark circular room with a high ceiling. In the centre was an "eternal flame" and draped around the walls were DDR flags and banners.

There was a single inscription across the wall - "Dedicated To The Victims Of Fascism" (or something like that...) in German.

We departed this dim remnant of the communist past (it was too dark to photograph) and continued our march west along the Unter Den Linden towards the Brandenburg Gate. Just before it intersected with Friedrichstrasse stood the Humboldt University which looked very old and grand but a bit shabby.

From here on, the road was tree lined along both sides and large, bright looking shops and offices lined the pavements. There were also people in cars who had come from the West and were selling fresh fruit, drinks etc from their boots.

The clouds had cleared again and it was quite warm and sunny - very thirsty work being a tourist. We bought some melon slices and pigged them hungrily - obviously the meat and 2 veg hadn't been as filling as it looked.

The road opened up into a sort of a square which led up to the Brandenburg Gate.

Amongst the crowds of people standing around or sitting on the benches, I noticed a Russian soldier -probably an officer - sitting and talking to somebody. He was wearing a smart green uniform with high boots and crisp cavalry trousers and a wide cap with a red band - very cavalry looking.

Having passed the large and ornately decorated Russian Embassy a little earlier, I assumed this to be a common sight in the East but, surprisingly, didn't see another Russian soldier anywhere in Berlin.

There was still a lot of wall skirting around the tall buildings to the left set back behind lawns and trees (the same buildings that we had observed from the other side the previous evening) but nothing left to suggest that the wall had ever been across the Gate, apart from the line of crowd barriers.

The Gate itself was covered in scaffolding, unfortunately, which meant that the photo opportunity was spoilt somewhat.

Around the square were dotted around a few stalls selling postcards, souvenirs and bits of grey painted concrete pertaining to be parts of the wall. We bought some postcards but held back on the wall souvenirs, deciding to obtain our own somehow instead.

We decided that we had had enough Eastern culture for the time being and decided to sample the pleasures of West Berlin for a while. We returned to Friedrichstrasse and took up again the route that we had started earlier that morning heading towards the famous Checkpoint Charlie.

Storm clouds gathered as we walked along the grim street with its tall grey buildings and tacky, depressing little shops with nothing in them gave way to faceless offices.

We still had quite a few Ostmarks left and, not wanting to waste them, Jane had the idea of stopping off at the uncharacteristically pleasant and elegant looking Grand Hotel with its ornate gold lamp fittings and covered terrace. This looked particularly welcoming as it was about to start raining.

Unfortunately, the only thing on the menu that looked even half appetizing after our previous experience of local cuisine was Ice Cream so we found ourselves eating a large ice cream sundae in the Grand Hotel, Berlin, in the middle of East Germany, in the middle of a rainstorm.

From there, it was just a short dash to the border checkpoint. We stopped briefly at a bank to ask whether they bought Ost-Marks (stupid question - of course they didn't!) and then went on into the passport control area.

The East German side of the border was very official looking and intimidating. There was a big covered area with five separate lanes for motor vehicles - rather like the customs hall at a major port.

Even in these days of openness they were still stopping every car. The westerners queue to exit the DDR moved a little quicker than the entry queue at Friedrichstrasse (perhaps they just wanted to eject us all out into the pouring rain sooner) although the building itself was very dour and gloomy. The rain was absolutely pouring down now and the heavy grey clouds overhead made the border crossing point look even less inviting.

Whilst we were sheltering from the worst of the storm, I took advantage of the situation to take a few photos of the border post (quite risky at the best of times and, on reflection, probably illegal in most liberal minded Western countries, let alone somewhere like East Germany).

In years to come I was happy that I did so, however, as soon after the unification of the two Germanys, this security- intensive crossing point became an open air car park.

The formalities were soon over with, and my beautifully ornate temporary visa was handed back to become a statistic compiled by some bureaucrat somewhere within a paranoid and dying system.

Back In The West - The Zoo

We crossed the neutral zone at a swift canter because the rain hadn't let off at all and we didn't want to waste the rest of the day standing and looking out at it.

Checkpoint Charlie turned out to be a white wooden hut in the middle of the road some fifty yards away from the DDR checkpoint and its widespread fame as a symbol of freedom and democracy far outstripped its impressiveness as a sight to look at.

The flags of the three occupation allies (Britain, America and France) were on show and each country seemed to be represented by one incumbent of the hut.

No immigration procedure was required and the post seemed to be more of a place to ask for directions than anything else.

Checkpoint Charlie,
Koch Strasse,
Berlin. 12th May 1990

Top photo:
The East German
border control post

Middle photo:
View of the western
check point and
famous mutilingual
sign

Bottom photo:
PB at Checkpoint
Charlie – in torrential
rain!

Top left: PB next to
East Berlin tourist map.

Top right: PB in Marx
Engels Platz

Middle: PB next to the
River Spree with the Berlin
Wall intact in the
background on the
Eastern side

Bottom: PB at the
Reichstag building before
it had its replacement
glass dome fitted.

PB on the western side of the Berlin Wall, 12th May 1990

We braved the rain for a quick photo session beside the hut and also under the famous sign stating that "You Are Leaving The American Sector" in English, French & Russian.

After the endeavours of the day thus far, a cup of warm, relaxing, western tea was in order. Unfortunately these two westerners who had been so rich in the East suddenly found themselves to be rather penniless in the west as we had run out of D-marks. The barperson at the cafe near Checkpoint Charlie told me that the nearest Bureau De Change was at zoo station. Unfortunately we didn't have any money left for the U-Bahn fare.

Not knowing how to walk to the Zoo, and the continued rainstorm, soon made our minds up that it was time to break the law and travel without a ticket. Experience had shown that there were no ticket barriers on the U-bahn and ticket checks were very rare.

This short journey seemed to last a lifetime but we managed to get to Zoo station without being apprehended.

Out of remorse for my inexcusable criminal behaviour, I later gave a street beggar the equivalent change of the train fare to clear my conscience.

As we emerged from the semi-darkness of the underground we found that the rain had stopped and that the sun had, thankfully come out again in full force.

The Bureau de Change was just on the outside of the main station building and we went in and joined the queue. Outside was an incredible sight (which I later saw in many Easter European countries) as many people, obviously from the east, were trying to buy D-Marks from the tourists in exchange for dubious amounts of Eastern currency. Most of these people were unkempt looking and didn't look particularly trustworthy and so seemed to be avoided by most people.

With wallets fully replenished with wads of negotiable currency, we went to a burger bar in the station complex.

The need for a cup of tea had been replaced by the odd hunger pang. Following this we decided to make the most of the good weather and have a quick walk around the zoo.

A "quick look" around wasn't in fact possible as Berlin Zoo is in fact a huge place with many different themed areas all individually landscape.

It was very well laid out, with picturesque pathways between zones, lots of grassy areas and well signposted. The animals looked to be clean and well looked after and, for the most part, happy. The exception was in the big cats house where one lion was rather annoyed at being in a separate cage to a fine looking lioness.

He began to roar rather loudly, the noise deafening as it resounded around the bright and sunny block. Then another of the lions joined in as if vying for attention and neither would be pacified until the keeper climbed into the cage and gave each one a bit of a cuddle.

There were also tigers in another cage who were, unfortunately, asleep although how they managed through all the noise I don't know. Perhaps it was a common occurrence.

Our tired legs had covered probably only 50% of the zoo's expanse when, mercifully, it closed at 18.00. This prompted us to continue with our plans to revisit the Reichstag crosses and Russian monument to get photos in better light. Luckily the rain clouds of earlier gave no hint of a return and the early evening sun shone down from blue cloudless skies.

We took the U-Bahn back to Belleville Park and then walked across the great expanse of lawn leading up to the Reichstag that we had seen earlier on through the train window. It seemed a lot further on foot than it had by train and we broke the walk up a little by stopping for photos at half distance with the great symbol of German unity in the background.

The sun was just starting to set by the time we got back to the memorial crosses but the light was still sufficient for souvenir piccys of the occasion.

Just a little way away where the path was intersected by the river, some sections of the wall were still standing, although access was denied by a wire fence.

This fence had been pushed aside slightly and a little bit further around the corner two scruffy looking kids were chipping away at the wall with a little hammer, obviously planning to sell the pieces.

I had waited too long and come too far to allow a spot of minor trespassing to come between myself and a piece of the Berlin Wall. Anyway, I'd broken the law once that day already. Fate seemed to play into my hands at that moment as a couple of mild mannered (for once...) West German policemen who had been wandering slowly around for a while came into view and the pair of urchins scuttled away. They had obviously been warned away before.

Once the policemen were on their way again I seized my chance and we stepped through the gap in the fence and disappeared around the corner. We were on a sort of a wide path which was lined by the wall on one side and a grassy bank down to the river on the other. The path led off towards the previously described bridge and, in pre-Wall times, would have continued into the east of the city.

The wall was still standing strongly here although it had several holes bashed in it and the other side could be clearly seen if you stooped down to look. On the other side was a large building (as they all were around there). It would probably have looked quite impressive in its heyday but had now fallen to ruin.

Laying around on the floor were a few tiny bits of the wall and lots of dust which had obviously been produced during people's hammering, but nothing that one would consider worth taking as a souvenir. By a stroke of luck, the two kids had left their little hammer behind in their rush to avoid the attention of the police.

Feeling quite decadent and daring by this point, I picked it up and took a joyous swing at a hitherto untouched section of the wall. There was a bit of a noise, a little dust and nothing more.

Feeling that time was against us, I decided to have another go at part of the wall that had already been breached. Several chunks fell away this time and were quickly pocketed.

We took a couple of photos to authenticate our souvenirs. I took up what I considered to be a very symbolic pose, leaning against the wall with my arm bent through to the other side - in a sense, the single handed reunification of this country stricken by forty years of subjugation and division by totalitarianism. At this point the two kids returned and did not look amused at our having used their hammer. I just dropped it to the ground and walked off past them nonchalantly.

I couldn't help feeling that "our" section of wall didn't seem to have as much graffiti as other parts. A quick search of pockets showed that nobody was carrying a pen of any description.

Undeterred, I dashed back to the main pathway and quickly borrowed a blue ballpoint pen from a surprised passer-by.

I would expect that she was even more surprised to see her nice pen being used to scrawl a message "All the best from Peterborough - 12.5.90" on the hard, gritty concrete. The message also photographed for posterity and the pen returned to its owner, we returned to the main pathway again before the policemen came past again. Quite whether they noticed our suspicious behaviour or were in the least bit interested was never ascertained.

Still glowing inwardly with some considerable pride at having achieved another of my longtime ambitions, we retraced our steps of the previous evening in reverse past the Brandenburg gate and back to the Russian monument. The light was just sufficient to allow a couple of photos of Russians, columns, tanks etc

Throbbing feet and grumbling tummies signalled the end of the day's sightseeing. We returned to Zoo station as we had decided earlier in the day to do, to look at the souvenir stalls there (I had to get a Berlin saucer for my mum!).

Not fancying the trek to the K'damm, we chose to partake our evening meal in an Italian/Turkish take away cum café where they had reasonably priced, and reasonably tasting pasta.

A quick bout of souvenir shopping was swiftly followed by a U-Bahn journey back to the hotel.

The Journey Home

We had a frantic start the next morning as we had to catch the 8.00 am train in order to meet our plane in Düsseldorf. We got up and packed quickly and raced down to catch the first serving of breakfast.

Jane went back up to her room to perform whatever ablutions it is that women perform when you're in a hurry to go somewhere whilst I tried to square the bill.

This wasn't easy as the reception wasn't open. The round and vaguely friendly-looking breakfast cook cum waitress cum cleaner told me it would be open at 8.30.

When I explained in my not-so-fluent-at-that-time German that we had to go **now**, she managed to find our names on the list and proceeded to make up a bill.

This got rather complicated when I, being very honest, owned up to having made a telephone call. This threw her into total disarray as she couldn't get into the computer to bring up the cost of the call.

I finally managed to convince her that it had only been a short local call (I had rung British Airways, Berlin, to confirm my return flight was still there - with some relief I was told that I was confirmed on the flight) and she eventually agreed to accept 10 DM to cover it.

By this time we had no chance of getting to the station on time by U-Bahn, particularly as it was a Sunday morning and they would, no doubt, be running a reduced service.

The friendly, but by now somewhat irate at the number of breakfastees waiting to be served, kitchen hand patiently rang for a taxi to take us to the station.

The taxi-person on the other end of the phone didn't seem to recognise the hotel name and she had to repeat it several times, after all, it was in reality a Red Cross hostel in a residential backwater.

My fears began to mount as we found ourselves standing outside the hotel some 10 minutes later with still no taxi to be seen. It was a glorious sunny day as we stood surrounded by luggage out by the roadside, the vast sweeping lawn of the "hotel" recently cut and birds singing cheerfully high up in the surrounding trees. The majority of the local population had not yet stirred and slept peacefully, unaware of our plight.

Finally a yellow Mercedes swung leisurely around the corner as if out on a Sunday picnic and the driver peered out at us as if to enquire whether it was us who had ordered the taxi.

There was no time for pleasantries as we quickly stashed our bags in the boot and leapt into the back of the car.

By some strange quirk of fate, probably down to the fact that it was early on a Sunday morning, there was hardly any traffic on the roads and we actually got to the station before the train arrived.

Once safely on the train we had time to relax a little. The weather was beautiful as the warm spring sun shone down from cloudless skies across green fields and untouched woodland.

On more than one occasion we passed areas of what one might call in England allotments. In many big cities people had these and went there at weekends to relax. Many had built little huts which even had television aerials. It was quite a sight to see the funny little Trabant cars parked next to these little places.

We managed to keep the compartment all to ourselves for most of the journey apart from a youngish, grey haired looking gentleman who joined us between Helmstedt and Hannover.

The twin towered cathedral at Magdeburg proved to be an ideal photo subject as we had a perfect view from our window during the stop there. No passengers were allowed to alight so I assume the stop was to let the DR caterers off before the border. Au revoir to their bland tasting cola and plain bread, even though it was cheap.

As we drew into the Ruhrgebiet the weather seemed to turn again and by the time we were snaking through Düsseldorf's suburbs there were thick dark clouds overhead - perfect flying weather!

The flight passed without incident although it was a little too turbulent for my liking. In stark contrast, and typical of the whole weekend, we touched down at Heathrow in bright sunlight. The tube trip across London was quite calm and relaxing and we tea-ed on a Casey Jones burger at the BR station before taking the train home to Peterborough.

Above left: PB with children from Rostock and Güstrow on Summer Camp at Budišov nad Budišovkou in the Czech Republic in summer 1996. Above right: PB with fellow youth leaders who were all DDR born and bred.

Post Script (2022):

Since the time that I wrote this account of the visit to Berlin, I have had the opportunity of spending a lot more time in the eastern part of Germany.

During the summers of 1996, 1997 and 1998, I visited the city of Rostock on the Baltic coast and worked as a volunteer youth leader for groups of children from that area on summer camps.

You can read more about my involvement in the summer camps in "North / South Divide - Volume 3 : Cricket & Baseball" - and there will be a lot more about my various trips to Germany coming up in "German Calling" as well - but the point I that want to make here is that this experience allowed me to meet lots of people who had been brought up during the DDR period.

From listening to their stories of their respective childhoods, I can now appreciate that, contrary to what we had been told in the west, it wasn't all bad - there were a lot of very positive aspects - and so long as you weren't actually a political dissident, most people could have a happy, healthy life growing up behind the Iron Curtain.

Therefore, some of the critical observations that I made in my mid-1990s account would not necessarily be as relevant if I were writing it from scratch today.

AMSTERDAM

May 1990: Amsterdam 2

One good thing about the place that I worked – Baker Perkins as it was originally and then APV Baker and then Rockwell PMC after a series of mergers and takeovers – was that, as well as the number of holiday days that you got to take when you wanted to – you also got the week off between Christmas and New Year - and a week over Whitsun, following the late May bank holiday.

Whilst the factory was closed, the offices were still technically open even though most people were off. What they did do was operate a skeleton staff, with just one person in each office to answer the phone, fire-fight any problems that came up as best you could and take messages as necessary.

The person who did this got holiday days off in lieu and the atmosphere during the shut-down was very relaxed. You could wear casual clothing and have the radio on and I picked up on the merit of volunteering to do this quite early on as I didn't have any family stuff that I wanted to go off and do.

Anyway, having quite enjoyed my trip to Amsterdam with my brother in August 1989, I quite fancied going again and, following on from the successful trip to Berlin that I had shared with Jane Barnet, I was wondering if I could further impose on her goodwill and get her to go to Amsterdam for a few days.

She quite fancied the idea of going to Amsterdam – but didn't seem overly keen on going with me, which was a bit of a shame (too much of a good thing, and all that – I suppose...). But, she did eventually manage to rope in another girl – Kath Simmonds - to go along as well, so the trip was on!

I worked two days in the office – having a good time and not doing very much - and then we took the train on Thursday morning to catch the day sailing from Harwich.

I won't go into minute blow by blow details, of this trip because, basically if you've been once to Amsterdam, then you've been to Amsterdam.

We did pretty much the same things that I had done when I went with Gary the previous year – ambled around the shops, lazed by the canal sides, looked at all the sights and hung around the Leidseplein and Red Light District in the evenings.

Now, before you start berating me for chauvanistically dragging a pair of intelligent upstanding women around the Red Light District of Amsterdam, I will just reiterate what I said before.

At the height of the tourist season, the RLD is one of the busiest and most popular tourist attractions in the city.

You don't HAVE to go and use the prostitutes. You don't HAVE to look round the sex shops. You don't HAVE to go and see a live sex show on stage - and you don't HAVE to take any drugs. You can just walk around, take in the atmosphere and have a drink in a cafe without doing any of these.

I managed to get away with not doing any of those things on three separate visits.

Well, I might admit to glancing around the odd sex shop (just out of curiosity) - but I certainly never partook of the other three. So 3 out of 4 ain't bad, as Mr Meat Loaf says.

And it's not wholly populated by stag parties and pervy blokes getting off on looking for ladies of the night, either.

There were just as many women as men there when we went in 1990 and most of them were in family groups. And, for the record, Kath and Jane Barnet found our mooch round just as entertaining as I did.

We went and saw the Anne Frank House (again, in my case) because I thought it was important for the girls to see it - and we also saw around Rembrandt's House.

We also took a boat trip along the canals and out into the Amsterdam harbour. That was interesting as you got to see sights from a different perspective. They talked about the city's history of merchant shipping and also explained that Amsterdam Centraal railway station was built on stilts over the water and how it was achieved.

If I recall correctly we helped pass the 6 hours ferry sailing in each direction by going to the on-board cinema. I seem to think that we watched "Sea of Love" – a murder mystery about a serial killer starring Al Pacino and Ellen Barkin - on the way out and "War Of The Roses" – a black comedy about feuding spouses starring Michael Douglas and Kathleen Turner - on the way back.

The cinema on these Stena Line ferries was very good and they always had up to date film releases. There was usually a choice of two or three films to choose from all, starting at staggered times.

During the 1990s, I travelled by that route on numerous occasions and always went to watch a film to help pass the time.

I even saw a world premier of the "Chaplin" film starring Robert Downey Jr on a crossing once!

Photo by Peterborough Images.com

23rd May 1990: Belinda Carlisle

Belinda Carlisle played at the Mallard Park venue in Peterborough on 23rd May 1990 and I was there!

She was a huge internationally acclaimed artist at that time, it was the very first date of her Runaway Horses world tour, and the announcement of the concert had generated a huge amount of excitement across the city.

Back when I was growing in the 1980s, major artists hardly ever played in Peterborough because they didn't have a suitable venue. A lot of the big names had played in the 60s – like the Beatles - at the Embassy Theatre but that huge auditorium was then converted into a 3-screen cinema and the large capacity venue was lost.

Many well known punk bands played at the Wirrina in the late 70s and there were a lot of Northern Soul events going around but these were not high class venues with comfortable facilities and, therefore, couldn't really attract bigger name acts on a regular basis.

To see anybody who was really well known and mainstream, you had to travel to the famous venues in London or to go to the De Montford Hall in Leicester or the Corn Exchange in Cambridge which both featured more readily on the established tour circuits.

So when the Court tennis centre started staging 4000 capacity concerts featuring big name stars, this was quite an exciting development.

Peterborough Images describe the venue much better than I could when they say: *"The short lived Court Hotel, Badminton and Tennis Centre at Bretton which popped up in the 1980s and vanished after a fire in the 1990s. For a time it hosted international tennis indoor tournaments as well as several major pop concerts."*

It was located on the industrial estate at North Bretton on Mallard Road round behind the ice rink and across from the snooker centre. It had a huge hall which I seem to think started off as an indoor tennis centre and then got used for other things — which was where the concerts were staged.

Certainly at the time of the Erasure gig it was known as the "Court Exhibition Centre" and the venue was later re-christened the Mallard Park Hotel.

Over time it hosted such big names as Erasure, David Lee Roth, Chris Rea, Level 42, Vanilla Ice, Wet Wet Wet and Status Quo.

Finding myself temporarily single at the time of the concert — despite having obtained two tickets in the hope that it might make me appear particularly "eligible" - I was lucky enough to get Jane Barnet from work to go along with me, and she also gave me a lift in her car - which was handy because I didn't have a car at the time and Bretton wasn't especially easy to get to from my Bachelor Pad.

The evening is a bit of a haze to me now. I remember standing in a huge queue of people outside waiting to get in and seeing lots of people I knew so I was glad to not be standing there on my own looking like a "Norman No Mates".

It really was a great show – as you might expect from a world class performer. She had a full backing band and two backing singers and, to my mind, the live performance had so much more oomph to it than the studio album recordings.

It was a lot more punchy and rocky and, interestingly enough I recently saw a re-run of Top Of The Pops from 1990 when she appeared live with the same backing ensemble and this confirmed how I had remembered it.

According to setlist.fm, the playlist for the evening was: Runaway Horses, Summer Rain, (We Want) The Same Thing, Mad About You, Circle in the Sand, Nobody Owns Me, I Get Weak, Valentine, La Luna, Vision of You, Leave a Light On, Heaven Is a Place on Earth and the encore was: Our Lips Are Sealed(Go Gos), We Got the Beat (Go Gos), Shades of Michaelangelo.

I seem to think that we missed the very last song so as not to get stuck in 4000 people's worth of traffic on the way out but, as it turns out, I didn't know that one anyway so didn't really miss much.

I actually had the chance to see Belinda again when she came to Blackpool – where Lucy and I were by then living - in March 2011 doing a "close up and intimate" acoustic tour of smaller venues.

Rather ironically, the self same weekend we had already arranged to go to Colne to watch Blackpool boxer Jeff Thomas's professional bout at the Colne Municipal Hall and couldn't be in two places at once. We had arranged to spend the weekend in East Lancashire and do a few other things as well so it wasn't just a matter of popping across.

We had interviewed Jeff for our radio show on 103.2 Preston FM and had been plugging the boxing evening. We had also been given media access and VIP seats to the event, so couldn't really not turn up.

We covered quite a few local sports people in our shows back then and also met up with and interviewed other Blackpool based boxers such as Brian Rose - who went on to be British and WBA Intercontinental Light Middleweight champion - and Matty Askin, who became British Cruiserweight champion.

Rather bizarrely, Belinda Carlisle's acoustic tour took her to Colne a couple of weeks later but, having just been there once, it wasn't really practical for us to go back again quite so soon after.

Erasure with Mark Eastwood - 10th August 1988

I had already been to a concert at the Mallard Park before – back when it was still called the Court – when Erasure played there on 10th August 1988.

I hadn't planned on going, but one evening I was outside my mum's house and Mark Eastwood pulled up and said he had a spare ticket and did I want to go?

Now, Erasure were a huge act at the time and, with lead singer Andy Bell coming from Peterborough, there was a lot of excitement about this concert so I thought I really ought to say yes – especially as it had been handed to me on a plate. So I did say yes.

The band had expressed a desire for an up-and-coming local band to play as their support so there was a "battle of the bands" type competition at the Fleet centre in Fletton a few weeks beforehand to select the lucky group.

This was held on a Friday night and I went along with Alan and Louise and whoever else of the lads might have wanted to go.

There were 4 or 5 bands playing - none of which I had actually heard of before - but Ian (Nobby) Clarke from Chapel Street – who had been in our year at school - was in Big Blue World, so it was nice to see them play.

The competition was won by a band called "Two The Dark" and they went on to support Erasure in front of 4000 music fans at the Mallard Park gig.

The day of the Erasure gig was red hot and sunny. We decided not to take Mark's car as, with so many people going, there might be problems parking so instead we both went on my motorbike.

The bike I had at the time was an old Honda CD175 – not even very glamorous in its heyday, a sort of old bloke's going to work bike – and mine was very shabby and bashed about.

I'd had to buy it in an emergency when my own bike - a CB125 twin that I'd had for ages - suddenly developed a serious engine fault that wasn't worth repairing, leaving me without transport and unable to get to work easily.

My mum had rung up the motorcycle dealer in Ramsey where we had bought my first bike back in 1983 – and who knew my grandmother for some mysterious reason – and he took pity on us and sold me this bike for about £80 because nobody wanted it.

It was mechanically sound – came with MOT and tax for a year and got me out of a hole, so I was quite grateful.

Because it was already quite old, over the time I had the bike, the vinyl covering on the seat got worn and split and, despite attempts at repairing it with tape or covering it with an assortment of plastic bags, the foam inside got wet and was difficult to dry out.

Therefore you'd often emerge from a ride on the bike with a wet behind, whether it was actually raining at the time or not.

I do appreciate that this is very bad for your health but, when you're a 20 year old lad, you don't tend to worry about that sort of thing.

The bike also used to backfire for no apparent reason from time to time and it was always amusing to see the reactions of people around when that happened.

So we went on my motorbike and Mark had obviously dressed ready for the stuffy environment inside the venue rather than for the ride there. I don't remember what I was wearing but I vividly recall what he had on.

He wore a blue and white striped vest – in a nautical / Breton style – light grey cotton jeans cropped and elasticated at the calf and light deck shoe loafers.

He used to have quite poncey hair at the time – this was the 80s, after all – and one chap who we used to see occasionally down at the Carpenters Arms in Stanground where Mark, Paul Jinks and I used to go for a regular Friday evening pint once said he "just looked more trendy every time you saw him..."

So you get the idea. He was always slimmer than me, so clothes always looked better on him, and on this occasion he looked as if he had just walked out of a Wham or Duran Duran music video.

Now, I am not trying to cast any nasturtiums here but Erasure had a big gay following – and singer Andy Bell really played up to that in his stage shows.

When he introduced the song River Deep Mountain High at this gig, for example, he started off by saying: "When I was a little girl.... I told my mummy – when I grow up, I want to be a homosexual ..." so that is the tone we are looking at here.

Also the huge backdrop at the back of the stage had ERASURE written in the same style and colours as the Mars Bar logo – so there may well have been a hidden message there, although I wouldn't know what.

There were a lot of cars parked all around so it was the right idea to come on the bike. As it was an industrial site, there were plenty of concrete areas where I could stand it – and it's not as if anybody was going to want to nick it!

As we were walking towards the venue, this young male rushed to catch up with us and he started talking animatedly to Mark about looking forward to the gig. I figured from the way that he was chatting on that he must have known him from somewhere or other, although I didn't know him from Adam.

It turned out that Mark didn't actually know him either and he had just turned up, out of nowhere.

He talked to Mark all the way along to the Mallard Park – completely ignoring me – and we only managed to get rid of him once we were mingling among the crowds by the entrance.

I didn't dare say anything but, thinking about it afterwards, I had the distinct impression that, from the point of view of Mark's George Michael -esque attire, this lad must have thought he was gay and was trying to hit on him!

According to setlist.fm, Erasure played the following songs on the night: Phantom Bride, Heart of Stone, Hideaway, Yahoo!, A Little Respect, It Doesn't Have to Be, Ship of Fools, The Circus, Witch in the Ditch, Who Needs Love Like That, Oh l'Amour, Hallowed Ground, Say What, Chains of Love, Victim of Love, Sometimes, River Deep, Mountain High & Spiralling.

I didn't know all of the songs but was familiar enough with the chart hits so fully enjoyed the performance. As I have already said, big artists didn't tend to play in Peterborough very often so it was a great event to be part of and an unforgettable experience.

STEVE JASON ENTERTAINMENTS BY ARRANGEMENT WITH SOLO
proudly present

THE STRANGLERS
+ SPECIAL GUESTS

WIRRINA STADIUM   BISHOP'S ROAD
PETERBOROUGH

WEDNESDAY 25th MARCH, 1987

Ticket £6 (subject to booking fee)

DOORS OPEN 6.30pm - SHOW STARTS 7.30pm

MANAGEMENT RESERVES THE RIGHT TO REFUSE ADMISSION.

25th March 1987: The Stranglers at Peterborough Wirrina

Going back a bit further, I saw the Stranglers play at the Wirrina leisure complex in Peterborough on 25th March 1987. This was good because the band still had their original line up at the time as it was before lead singer Hugh Cornwell left to do other things.

I would imagine that everybody who ever lived in Peterborough during the 1970s and 80s must have gone to the Wirrina at least once in their lives as it used to host all sorts of different events and activities

After it had been pulled down, the Peterborough Evening Telegraph described the Wirrina as follows:

"It opened in 1968 and was used for a variety of events including a youth club, a rollerskating rink, a ballroom and a wrestling venue. It was also famous for its Northern Soul all-nighters and became a popular live music venue particularly during the punk era when the likes of the Clash, Elvis Costello and The Attractions played there."

"It fell into disrepair and despite several attempts to redevelop it, including a plan to turn it into a hotel, it was demolished in October 2010."

The Tropicana night club was there for while, although I never actually went - but I did go there for a beer festival once and I also remember seeing a "Lennie The Lion" children's show there when I was little.

I went to the Stranglers gig with Alan and Louise - and probably a few others as well. By this time, the band had mellowed slightly. They were no longer the fearsome razor-edgy punks of ten years earlier and much of their audience had matured with them.

Plus they'd had a lot of mainstream chart success in recent years including the huge - but definitely un-punk - hit "Golden Brown".

As such there was a very eclectic mix of people in the audience – a lot of them I recognised as regulars from the Glasshouse (see below) and others from the Tech College. It was basically a "who's who" of the local Peterborough music scene at the time.

The support band were called Hurrah! and, while they were OK as warm up entertainment, I couldn't tell you much about them or what they played.

Wikipedia describes Hurrah! as "a British jangle pop band formed in the early 1980s and active until 1991. Two band members traded off lead vocals on track-by-track basis, giving the band two distinctly different sounds." They were the regular support for the Stranglers on this 1987 Dreamtime Tour and apparently, they also supported U2 and David Bowie at one time or other.

To my mind, Hurrah!'s other main claim to fame was that one of their posters appeared on a wall in the background of the market scenes on EastEnders for a long period of time.

Having keenly followed The Stranglers – on record at least, if not in person, it was great to be able to finally get to see them live.

Their set list for the evening was as follows: No More Heroes, Was It You?, Down in the Sewer, Nice in Nice, Punch and Judy, Souls, Always the Sun, Strange Little Girl, Golden Brown, North Winds, Big in America, Nice 'n' Sleazy, Who Wants the World?, (Get a) Grip (on

Yourself), Bring On the Nubiles, Shakin' Like a Leaf, Uptown Tank, Toiler on the Sea, Encore: 5 Minutes, Duchess, London Lady.

They played most of their punk classics as well as a selection of songs from their new Dreamtime album - which the tour had been organised to promote, so there was something to please everybody.

In later years, I met up with both Steve Drewett of the Newtown Neurotics (above left with PB) and Attila The Stockbroker (above right) to do interviews for our "Paul & Lucy's Best Kept Secrets" radio shows on 103.2 Preston FM and they both said how much they fondly remembered appearing at the Glasshouse Sunday sessions.

The Glasshouse – Key Theatre, Peterborough

"The Glasshouse" was a Sunday lunchtime music club held in the bar area at the Key Theatre in Peterborough. It was so called because the bar had huge windows all the way round which gave great views of the River Nene embankment and across to the city centre.

It had been going for quite a few years before I started going – probably since the theatre opened in the 1970s - and was a great showcase for local singers, artists and bands as well as better known performers.

The Glasshouse was organised, if I remember correctly, by Ann Johnson who had fingers in numerous pies in the Peterborough music scene.

It cost something ridiculously minimal like 50p to get in and you could sign up for a membership for 25p that gave you a further reduced admission.

I'm afraid that I don't recall any particular dates here but Alan and I went most Sundays while we were in the 6th form - ie from 1983 to 1985 - and afterwards during the holidays when he was home from university. We'd have a pint of lager and a packet of scampi fries and then have proper lunch once we had got back home afterwards.

There used to be a regular crowd who I would recognise by sight even if I didn't actually know who they were, and most people used to go for the social side irrespective of whether they were interested in the band that were playing,

Obviously, different artists would also bring their own followers with them so there was always a good mix of people and a nice atmosphere.

There was a group of bikers who used to go every week – and they would always drink bottles of Newcastle Brown. A few people who I knew from work went occasionally and a few other friends and acquaintances but I only ever went when Alan was there as it was "our thing" that we used to do together.

The bigger name artists that I recall seeing at the Glasshouse include John Otway, The Newtown Neurotics and Attila The Stockbroker.

There was also American band Timbuk3 – who had a couple of chart hits with "The Future's So Bright I Gotta Wear Shades" (1986...?) and "Radio Africa" and we saw them live shortly before they appeared on Top Of The Pops.

In between the bigger names there would be opportunities for local acts to appear and there was a great mixture of styles and genres from week to week.

Some of the local bands that I remember seeing are The Frantix, The Sixx, Lloyd Watson, March to the Grave, G-Men, The Pleasure Heads – which had Graham Hill's cousin as a member, Watt The Fox and Tree House (who were The Sixx but minus the drummer...)

And there were novelty acts such as Ritzen Ritzan Rotzen and 4 Million Telephones.

There will have been loads of others as well but, over time, I have forgotten quite a lot of them - but I certainly have many nice memories of Sunday lunchtimes in the mid 1980s at the Glasshouse.

ⒶⒷⒸ PETERBOROUGH Licensed Bar
TEL 3504

WEDNESDAY, DECEMBER 8. One performance at 7.30

ON THE STAGE

THE

WURZELS

"COMBINE HARVESTER"   "CIDER DRINKER"

with

WICHITA LINEMEN

Compere MIKE DELANEY

Stalls or circle £2.00, £1.50, £1.00. Advance booking opens Monday, November 15 at 11 am. No telephone bookings. Cheques, P/Os payable to ABC Theatre and SAE with order. Box office open daily 11 am to 8 pm.

"OOH ARH — OOH ARH!"

8th December 1976: The Wurzels at Peterborough ABC Theatre

I suppose that the first live band that I ever saw in concert was The Wurzels when they played at the ABC Theatre (previously the Embassy) in Peterborough on 8th December 1976.

Technically, the first band I ever saw would have been the support act who were, apparently, called Wichita Linemen - but that's just me being picky.

The Wurzels were at the height of their fame at this point. They did humorous agricultural-related songs and had a huge number 1 hit in 1976 with a "I've Got A Brand New Combine Harvester" – which was a bit of a parody of the 1971 "Brand New Key" song by Melanie.

They also did "I Am A Cider Drinker" to the tune of "Una Paloma Blanca" and other tittersome compositions.

They were very much in the public eye at the time and you couldn't watch a family TV show without them appearing on it at some point.

Now, only being 9 at the time, I couldn't go on my own to watch the concert so my long-suffering dad went with me to this.

Although my mum and dad both liked music, they were never concert-goers as far as I could work out – not even before they got lumbered with kids.

One of my mum's cousins once told me that my mum and dad used to have great bottle parties at their house - and the best collection of rock n roll records – but that's a side of them that I can't really relate to, unfortunately.

I have been going through old family photos recently and there is a photo of my mum aged 25 sitting on Ryde seafront on the Isle of Wight, illuminated by car headlights at midnight having some sort of holiday picnic with a group of friends.

Now, I have never in my entire life known my mum to do anything at midnight – not even on New Year's Eve - so this was quite an eye opener.

But anyway, there are no family stories that have been passed down about when they went to see Marty Wilde or Georgie Fame in the 60s or whatever, although apparently my dad did once bump into Long John Baldry coming out of the toilet in a pub in Warboys, if that rates as a claim to fame at all.

So – he saw The Wurzels in Peterborough in December 1976 and so did I.

A lot of punk bands played at the Wirrina in Peterborough in the late 1970s – The Clash, The Damned, The Stranglers, Stiff Little Fingers, Elvis Costello – you name it they played there, but I was too young to go to any of those and the first proper gig that I went to – on my own - was in October 1982 when Darren McAulay and I went to see Vice Squad in Cambridge.

Vice Squad in Cambridge, 28th October 1982 (Thursday)

I first got into Vice Squad when I heard "Living On Dreams" off the "Last Rockers EP" being played on the John Peel show on BBC Radio 1 one night when I probably should have been going to sleep ready for school the next day.

That came out in 1981 so it was probably late-ish in that year that I went into town after football on the Saturday afternoon and bought the EP from Andy's Records. I also loved the title track "Last Rockers" as well as "Latex Love" - which was a bit on the rude side - and started keeping a look out for other material by the band.

I bought their "Stand Strong Stand Proud" album when it came out in early 1982 and played it to death and when we discovered that they were coming to Cambridge on tour, my friend Darren McAulay from school and I decided that we would have to go and see them live.

The train times to Cambridge did not fit in with the timings of the concert so we travelled down on a regular service bus after school and my dad came and picked us up afterwards.

I don't know how he managed to find the venue in the dark on his own but he used to be a lorry driver in the 1950s and 60s back when roads and communications were poor so he must have developed some sort of sixth sense for navigating.

Despite loving all of their music, I didn't get to see Vice Squad again until 2010 when they were playing at the Rebellion weekend festival in Blackpool, where I was now living.

Although they had played the annual festival numerous times before, this was the first time that I was able to go on the day and time that they were on so I was determined to go and see them.

I wrote a review of the performance for our "Paul & Lucy's Best Kept Secrets" news and review website and, as that is the most concise and contemporaneous account, here it is in full:

Vice Squad at Rebellion Festival, Blackpool - 7th August 2010

It is actually 28 years since I last saw Vice Squad play live - October (ish...) 1982: Sea Cadets Hall Cambridge. Absolutely Brilliant! The support was a local band called Flowers of the Past. It was particularly memorable as there were no trains or buses back to Peterborough afterwards so my dad had to drive all the way to Cambridge - find the place - and then drive me and Darren McAulay home afterwards, ready for school the next day.

It was just after the "State of the Nation" EP had been released so they played all the songs off that, plus all the songs from the "Strand Strong Stand Proud" LP (which I absolutely loved and still do). They didn't play "Saviour Machine" but did do a version of the Pistols' classic "EMI" so that was alright - plus I bumped into Shane coming out of the toilet...!

So, as Vice Squad are my FAVORITEST BAND EVER - why did it take 28 years before I got to see them again ? Well, you know - the usual things, I had work.... and, well, stuff..... Of course it didn't help that Beki left the band to form Ligotage ("Crime and Passion" - great song!) and I never really took to the "Lia incarnation" of the group.

Fast forward now to 7th August 2010 and I'm Back - finally! Having seen the long queues of people trying to get into the Arena stage to see Peter & The Test Tube Babies, I immediately made my way to the Olympia stage to make sure of a place and found a safe place with a decent view leaning on a pillar.

The room filled up and tension mounted. The band came on and started with a song I didn't know..! Oh dear, hadn't thought of that... "Punx United" though - good rousing tune - then another "new" song. Oh well, I couldn't really expect them to play 30 year old songs JUST to suit me, could I..?

But then came "Living On Dreams" from the Last Rockers EP -the very first Vice Squad song I ever heard – back on John Peel's Radio 1 show – and everything was all right.

Apart, that is, from probably the only bloke taller than me in the room who didn't appear remotely interested in what was happening on stage, standing right in front of me and chatting and laughing with his entourage. I moved from my cosy pillar and went to a side wall - better view of the stage, slightly closer, more "personal space" around me and the 50/50 nature of the set continued.

We got "Scarred for Life" and "Citizen" from the "State Of the Nation EP", "Latex Love", "Out Of Reach" and (my favourite...) "Rock n Roll Massacre" from "Stand Strong..." mixed with newer material such as "Defiant", "Goodnight England" and others that I can't quite remember after just one hearing.

They signed off with the great anthem "Stand Strong Stand Proud" and then a spine tingling rendition of "Last Rockers" that made me feel as if it was 1982 all over again.

So there you go: Beki's back, I'm back, Vice Squad are still brilliant and the Rebellion Festival is a great opportunity to catch up on all those bands you've seen and loved / not seen for ages... only let's not leave it another 28 years, eh guys...?

From 2009 to 2014 Lucy and I had a radio show on 103.2 Preston FM community radio and in November 2011 we broadcast a special one hour show to celebrate the release of Vice Squad's "Punk Rock Radio" album.

We had exclusive interviews with both Beki and Paul and played a selection of tracks from the new CD.

Shortly after our radio show, the band played at Blackpool Cricket Club so we went along and met up with them. The "Best Kept Secrets" website report from that event can be seen here:

PB with Beki Bondage and Lucy with Paul Rooney at the Vice Squad gig at Blackpool Cricket Club, December 2011

Vice Squad at Blackpool Cricket Club - 17th December 2011

We went to a terrific evening of punk at Blackpool Cricket Club on Saturday evening featuring Litterbug, Pink Hearse, One Way System and my favourite band Vice Squad.

The cricket club are trying out different types of events - music nights featuring different genres, beer festivals etc - in a bid to maximise the use of their facilities and attract different revenue streams and are to be encouraged if you look at the amount of new people that Saturday's event brought in to the clubhouse.

Although Litterbug and Pink Hearse are both well known locally, I hadn't heard either of them play before so it was a great opportunity to do some catching up.

I first heard of One Way System back in 1981 when I bought the 12" vinyl compilation "A Country Fit For Heroes" which had their track "Jerusalem" on it and, here again, I had never seen them play live before so it was nice to finally do so (after only 30 years....).

They finished with "Jerusalem" and also played the Blitzkrieg song "The Future Must Be Ours" that I also remembered from the same album...

All credit to the 3 local bands who played very well and received lots of support but obviously, the highlight for us was the performance by Vice Squad who we had featured in a one hour interview special in our radio show on Preston FM a few weeks ago.

Having first heard of Vice Squad back in 1981 when I heard "Living On Dreams" on the John Peel Show, this really has been a 30 year love affair with their music for me and I was not disappointed as they played a nice mixture of old and new favourites.
In no particular order - well, not the order they were played in, anyway...:

From the "Stand Strong Stand Proud" album they played "Rock n' Roll Massacre", "Latex Love" and "Out of Reach" and we also had "Scarred For Life" that I originally heard at the Cambridge Sea Cadets Hall as part of the State Of The Nation Tour back in October 1982.

They played "Living On Dreams" and then from the "Defiant" album, the title track, "Fast Forward" and "Voice Of The People". From "London Underground" we had "Sniffing Glue" and my own favourite (and Beki's apparently...) "Ordinary Girl".

Vice Squad have a brand new album out called "Punk Rock Radio" which I would heartily recommend to fans new and old alike. From this album they played "Stuck in Reverse", "Punk Rock Is The Blues" and "Are You Looking At Me?" and then finished in rousing fashion with a couple of old favourites: "Stand Strong, Stand Proud" and "Last Rockers".

It was a thrilling, energetic performance that we enjoyed from beginning to end. Do go and see Vice Squad play live if you get the chance - we are sure you won't be disappointed.

Vice Squad really do represent the true spirit of authentic punk rock.

They manage themselves - organise all their own merchadise (Beki was there selling t-shirts on the sales stand), organise their own gigs and produce their own CDs.

As well as thanking Vice Squad, who made the journey up north in awful weather, Lucy wanted to say thank you to everyone who took part - the audience, Spider Man, the sound engineer and the staff at Blackpool Cricket Club - for a really fantastic evening.

She was inspired by Pink Hearse and encouraged by Lee and his friends to finish her latest song that she had been working on.

We both saw Vice Squad perform again – and also their acoustic alter-egos "The Dirty Folkers" – at the 2012 Rebellion Festival while we there gathering interviews and material for our radio shows.

23rd October 1984: The Gun Club at Nottingham Rock City

During the October half term break when we were in the 6th Form, I went to see the Gun Club play at Nottingham's Rock City with Darren McAulay and Richard Ellis.

They weren't actually a band that I knew much about – apart from the fact that they had featured on John Peel's late night show on Radio One quite often and they were a bit like The Cramps, who I liked.

I think somebody else was supposed to be going to this gig and had dropped out so I was offered the spare ticket at the last minute.

We went in Darren McAulay's car. He hadn't long passed his test so this was quite an adventure for us all to drive to Nottingham to try and find a place that none of us had actually been to before.

Despite being a well-known and respected venue that had hosted many big name bands over the years, Rock City is situated down a pokey back street and, when we went in 1984, entry was via one of those funny little doors where they open up a spy-hatch first to see who you are before they let you in.

It has probably changed a lot in the intervening years but the interior, as I remember it, was also a lot different to what I had expected. The stage and lighting were pretty good but there was a traditional wooden dance floor area in front of the stage – not very big – and much of the rest of the space was taken up with comfy settees and soft lighting. It felt more like a night club or a wine bar than a rock venue.

I had an argument with a friend at work one day when I mentioned having witnessed this rather strange interior at Rock City and, although he hadn't actually been himself, he simply would not accept the fact that it could be anything other than a big empty concert space with a bar and merch tables and not much else.

He did go to Rock City himself to see a band on a later occasion and had to acknowledge that it was different inside to what he had expected.

I doubt most people today will have heard of The Gun Club but their Wikipedia page describes them as "one of the first bands in the punk rock subculture to incorporate influences from blues, rockabilly, and country music. The Gun Club has been called a "tribal psychobilly blues" band, as well as initiators of the punk blues sound cowpunk."

Apparently there was a support band called The Scientists who were originally from Australia but relocated to London in 1984 and they obviously managed to get taken on as warm up act for this Gun Club tour.

As we had set off from Peterborough in really good time, we arrived at the venue really early – so early, in fact that we were able to park up right outside on the other side of the road. As such, we must have seen the Scientists play first but I'm afraid that I have no memory of them whatsoever.

The Gun Club were ok – although I didn't know any of their songs, but it was a great experience to have gone to the famous Rock City and seen an unusual American "John Peel" band on tour.

We got back to Peterborough very late and I was quite pleased that it was half term and there were no lessons the next day.

I doubt that anybody other than dead keen Gun Club afficianados would know any of these songs, but apparently their set list for the night was: Walkin' With the Beast, Sex Beat, Moonlight Motel, Eternally Is Here, Bad America, Stranger in Our Town, Preaching the Blues, Fire of Love, Black Train, Sleeping in Blood City, Goodbye Johnny, Encore: A Love Supreme

freemans ROCK SPECTACULAR

Starring:

★ **BOB GELDOF** and
THE BOOMTOWN RATS
★ ★ ★ ★ ★
The Bluebells ★ Hard Rain
Conspiracy

The organisers accept no responsibility for loss or damage to property or accident or injury to persons however caused.

№ 0458

31st August 1985: Boomtown Rats

The Boomtown Rats gig was held, as I recall, in the marquee on Peterborough Embankment that had been used for the Country & Western Festival a week earlier.

There's a newspaper cutting with a report from this gig in the Peterborough Standard dated Thursday 5th September 1985 so that would suggest that it must have taken place on Saturday 31st August – the bank holiday weekend having been the week before.

I seem to remember that it was charity gig with a % of the takings going to the Mayor Of Peterborough's charity fund, which that year was supporting the Bradford Fire Disaster.

I went with Alan & Louise and, with it being on a Saturday evening, it took some military style planning to make sure we were able get there!

Although I had just started working full time at Baker Perkins in the middle of July, I was still helping out in Colton's bike shop in town on Saturdays as well as I quite enjoyed it.

Louise was working Saturdays at Marks & Spencer's at the time - before heading off to start at University in September - and, if she had got the bus home afterwards like she normally did, it would have made everybody very late. So we came up with a cunning plan whereby I would finish work and zip into the main town centre on my motorbike, pick Louise up and take her straight to her house so she could get ready.

Alan would then go round and fetch her – I imagine he travelled in on the bus from Farcet – or came on his bike, I never asked - and they would then come round to mine ready to walk to the Embankment as our house was on the way.

Despite the odd niggling doubts in the back of my mind as to whether Louise had ever actually ridden on the back of a motorbike before, and also as to how long I might be able to get away with sitting parked up in the main shopping bus stop layby at a peak time, everything passed off as planned.

Fortune was on our side. I didn't get held up leaving off work – and nor did she. By the time I had got down to M&S through the Saturday traffic, Louise had already had time to pull her jeans on over her working stuff and was standing there waiting - so off we went.

Ha ha - in 7 seven years of being at school together - and lots of years as friends after that as well – that's the only time Louise ever put her arms around me!

So we zigzagged through the traffic jams and I managed to get her home so she was able to have some tea and then get ready for the evening out. I dropped her off and rushed home myself and we managed to get to the river bank in plenty of time for the show.

The venue was supposed to hold 5000 but apparently only about 1700 went to this so there was plenty of room and we managed to find seats on the wooden benches that were along the back so as to get a very good view of the stage.

I remember that, on the way in, there was somebody from the West Country who was selling strong traditional cider in gallon canisters. My guess is that he had probably been there for the C&W festival and stayed on for the extra few days in the hope of some extra business.

So, we bought one of those between us and shared swigs throughout the evening, which saved having to keep queuing for the bar.

The evening was very enjoyable overall. The Bluebells, who were supposed to be the main support band, suddenly split up shortly beforehand and didn't appear. That's they who had hit singles with "Young At Heart" and "Falling In Love Again", so we didn't see them – which was a shame as they were very well known at the time.

According to the newspaper report, a Norfolk band from Dereham called Harlequin were drafted in at the last minute to play as another band Beltane Fire didn't turn up either. I'm afraid that with the passage of time, I don't really remember anything about them nor the other band Hard Rain, who also played.

The other support act, Conspiracy, were bumped up to main support and they were very good. I couldn't tell you much about them but I do remember that they had a very pleasant lady singer and she sang "My Favourite Waste of Time" – which became a big chart hit for Owen Paul the summer after. Bette Midler had recorded a version of the song in 1983 and, listening to it now on YouTube, that sounds very similar to the version that Conspiracy performed and certainly much more so than the Marshall Crenshaw original.

It was great to finally see the Boomtown Rats live as I had liked them since the late 70s when I had enjoyed their chart hits such as "She's So Modern" and "Like Clockwork".

In fact, when a group of friends and I briefly set up our own punk band in Stewart Johnson's bedroom in the summer of 1978 – called The Stink Bombs – my punk name was "Boomtown Breezy".

The other members were "Stinking Stewart" (drums), "Rotten Richard" (vocals) and "Wailing Wiggy" (keyboards).

We recorded two songs, in one single take each, on a home cassette player: "Come On Ye People (We're Up Against The Queen)" - penned by Wiggy and sung by Richard – and then "Chop Off His Head, Fred" which I sang and made up the words to as we went along, as I insisted that we HAD to have a B side!

I strummed very enthusiastically but badly on an un-tuned guitar and the whole thing sounded particularly awful – but that was the whole point of it, after all!

A follow up single - "Do We Want Cars? No, No, No!" also composed by Wiggy, never made it as far as the makeshift recording studio.

I had the only copy of this historic cassette recording of the two songs in my possession for many years but it ultimately got chewed up - as these things often did in those pre-digital days (by the cassette player itself, that is – not by a dog or person...) and it is thus now, sadly, completely lost to the world.

Bob Geldof had actually lived in Peterborough for a while. He used to come over from Ireland as a student for the summer holidays in the late 1960s to earn money and he mentioned on stage about how he had worked long hours in the Smedleys Pea Factory and "lived in a sh*thole on Cromwell Road...!"

Anyway, this was a special one-off concert for them rather than being part of an album promotion tour so I seem to remember they played all of their old famous songs rather than focusing on tracks from the latest LP release, which a lot of casual fans might not have known - so it was very enjoyable throughout.

The Pogues & Me

I saw The Pogues live for the first time with Alan Platt in December 1985.

We had got into their music when we were in the 6th Form as somebody had brought their debut album to play on the communal record player – it might have been Alan himself but I seem to remember Richard Ellis giving it his stamp of approval as well.

I remember the date of the concert - 10th December - as it was my mum's birthday and she was a bit miffed that I was buggering off rather than stopping at home to celebrate, but there you go.

Mr Platt was away at Reading University and the band were playing at their SU Christmas party so he got me a ticket and invited me to go.

I took the train to London, and then got another one from Paddington to Reading and he met me and took me back to his accommodation.

Although I was a bit tired after working all day since 7.30am and then travelling on the train, it was a great evening and I really enjoyed the show.

It was still the original band line up at that time, with Cait O'Riordan on bass, which looking back over time makes it all the more special.

I stopped overnight in Alan's pokey student room – sleeping on the floor, if I remember rightly, and dived onto his bed when he got up and went out for a bit the next morning.

Then we both got the train into London – as he was free that day – and we went to Imperial College to see Louise as that's where she was studying sciency things.

Graham Hill was studying there as well, doing mechanical engineering, although we didn't see him on this particular occasion.

We braved the crowds and had a look round Harrods (as you do) and also went and had a look round Carnaby Street. Then Alan went back to Reading and I got the train from Kings Cross back to Peterborough.

London – July 1987

The next time I saw The Pogues was when they played a Picnic In the Park in London's Finsbury Park on 18th July 1987

I travelled down on the train with Wiggy and we met up with Alan and Louise at Finsbury Park station.

Don't ask me how we managed to coordinate to meet up in those pre-mobile phone days, but we somehow seemed to cope with things like that much better in my youth.

We went to the famous Sir George Robey pub on nearby Seven Sisters Road which had been named after the musical hall star and which had in itself been a popular music and entertainment venue over the years.

According to various useful online resources, the set list for the Pogues that day was: Intro, The Irish Rover, Streams Of Whiskey, Rake At The Gates Of Hell, Medley (The Recruiting Sergeant, The Rocky Road To Dublin, The Galway Races), The Ballinalee, Body Of An American, If I Should Fall From Grace With God, Lullaby Of London, South Australia, Turkish Song Of The Damned, The Sick Bed Of Cuchulainn, The Broad Majestic Shannon, Metropolis, Dark Streets Of London, Dirty Old Town, Sally MacLennane, Greenland

Whale Fisheries, Jesse James, Fiesta, Boys From The County Hell, A Pair Of Brown Eyes, Waxie's Dargle, And The Band Played Waltzing Matilda, The Wild Rover

which, if you know your Pogues music at all, you'll agree was damn' good show. "All killer, no filler " as they say in the music biz.

The other artists on the bill that day were The Proclaimers (just before they became famous), the Potato Five (who never became famous) and some people called "Head" apparently – who I do remember as being an instrumental group but couldn't really say much about else about them...

The only problem with this lovely summer's afternoon event in the idyllic surroundings of Finsbury Park was that it absolutely chucked it down with rain all day and the marquee concert venue became a mud bath.

By the end of the event, a lot of silly people were throwing mud at each other but we managed to avoid getting splattered - and the showers - and get safely back to the station.

Leicester – February 1988

I next saw the The Pogues at the De Montford Hall in Leicester on 23rd February 1988.

Simon and I went to this together and we went on a Steve Jason coach package that included the ticket and transport.

Steve Jason was a local DJ and music promoter in Peterborough. At one time he had a specialist ticket agency in the Westgate Arcade where you could buy tickets for all sorts of concerts right across the country.

For the more popular ones, he organised and sold coach travel - and this was one of those.

This was a really great show and I thoroughly enjoyed it. Having the coach drop you right outside the venue and pick you up outside afterwards was so much easier and you could leave your coats on board rather than having to cart them around inside.

We stood on the main floor quite close to the stage and had really good view. The Pogues were superb – as they always are.

The playlist for the evening was: The Battle March Medley, The Broad Majestic Shannon, Medley, If I Should Fall From Grace With God, Wild Cats of Kilkenny, Lullaby of London, South Australia, Bottle of Smoke, Metropolis, Kitty, Thousands Are Sailing, Turkish Song of the Damned, Streets of Sorrow / Birmingham Six, A Rainy Night in Soho, Fiesta, Dirty Old Town, Sally MacLennane, The Sick Bed of Cúchulainn, Jesse James, A Pair of Brown Eyes, The Irish Rover, Greenland Whale Fisheries.

As a post script to this - Simon and I later went to see The Dubliners play at the Cresset in Peterborough on 5th May 1988

Cambridge - November 1991

In the autumn of 1991, The Pogues were on tour again and I went to see them at the Corn Exchange in Cambridge on Friday 29th November with Graham Hill. He was living in Cambridge at that time and I went over there a few times, once I had got my car, for evenings out or to watch football matches.

He went and got the tickets for this and they were good seats up on the - more refined - balcony away from the moshers on the main floor.

This Pogues tour was very important because the lead vocalist Shane MacGowan had left the band to do his own thing and Joe Strummer – formerly of The Clash - was singing lead vocals instead.

Strummer had guested with The Pogues in the past and sung the odd song but this was the first time (and the only time, in fact) that he ever did a full tour with them as the main lead singer.

They started off in the US and Canada in September and then did France and Germany in October and November.

The dates at Cambridge were their first UK dates of the tour and they played elsewhere around the country before finishing off in Ireland – and then going to Japan and Australia in the new year.

The setlist for the Cambridge gig was: If I Should Fall From Grace With God, Sayonara, Cotton Fields, Young Ned of the Hill, Rain Street, Repeal of the Licensing Laws, Tombstone, Turkish Song of the Damned, Rainbow Man, London Calling, Thousands Are Sailing, The Sunnyside of the Street, Straight to Hell, Medley, Dirty Old Town, The Sick Bed of Cúchulainn, Yeah, Yeah, Yeah, Yeah, Yeah, Star of the County Down, I Fought the Law, Brand New Cadillac, Fiesta.

Not all of the songs suited well to Joe Strummer's voice but it was a real treat to see live him - and also singing Clash classics such as London Calling, Straight To Hell and I Fought The Law.

Joe Strummer died in 2002 aged 50 and, since then, has achieved a sort of mythical cult status so I consider myself very lucky to have seen him perform once in the flesh.

Preston, 25th June 1993

The last time that I saw The Pogues play live was at the Heineken Music Festival in Preston's Avenham Park in June 1993. These were big free festivals that were staged in various cities across the UK over the summer for couple of years and they had a great mix of less known and well known artists.

This worked out well because Hanja was visiting for a few weeks before she came to start at University in the September and although she liked the Pogues, she had never seen them live before.

As I recall, the year after, we got to see Doctor and The Medics, The Christians and Ruby Turner as well.

PB outside Coneygree Road with the sporty yellow Datsun, September 1990

August 1990: Paul Gets A Car!

My life changed dramatically (for the better) in August 1990 when, despite having been able to drive perfectly well for several years already, I finally got around to taking my test and getting a car licence.

Most people that I knew took driving lessons and passed their test as soon as they were 17.

That certainly happened with contemporaries of mine when I was in the 6th Form and I distinctly remember that quite a few used to have driving lessons during their private study / "free" periods and their instructors used to pick them up and drop them off again right outside the 6th Form block.

Once people had passed their tests, they often started borrowing their parents' cars – or, if they were lucky, got one of their own, obviously a rather old one to start with - and several of them used to drive into school (rather like an American high school movie – albeit in gloomier weather and surroundings).

There may well have been others, but the students that I remember driving cars to school regularly during that period included Richard Ellis, Darren McAulay, Jane Kon and Joanne Harrison.

In fact, they ended up taking over a whole corner of the big playground round the front of the school (that nobody ever actually "played" on by the way – we were 80s teenagers, after all) because it was handy for getting to the 6th Form Block, and turned it into an unofficial sixth form car park.

I left my motorbike over the road with Mr & Mrs Clark, where I had previously parked my bike for a number of years.

So, as I had a motorbike to get around on – and had passed my test so that I could carry passengers (11th March 1985 – according to my driving licence), I didn't see any immediate need to get involved in all this car owning mullarkey and associated expense.

Admittedly, it was a bit inconvenient for getting dressed up and going places – and you often got cold and wet when the weather was bad but, having had a bike since I was 16, I was used to all that and worked round it.

Also, there was no point in me trying to have a trendy hair style as it just got flattened down underneath the crash helmet. Indeed, if you look at any photos of me from 1983 to 1990, my hair is always poorly styled and a bit of a mess.

Plus, "only" having a motorbike as your main form of transport wasn't really very good for pulling birds, if I'm completely honest.

I could – theoretically - have attempted to woo a "biker chick".

She would, at least, have been immune to the discomforts and vagaries of the weather and crash helmets – but I always found them rather scary, to be honest.

Having said that, I did actually know one quite well and she was always very friendly and chatty with me. She was a year or two older than me, the cousin of one of my school friends and a friend of my original "Ex". Her mother had been a dinner lady at our junior school and we actually went to her wedding when she married a fellow biker.

The thing is, of course, that biker chicks only fancy proper bikers – with long hair and powerful bikes and, for all I know, Hell's Angel tendencies - so the likelihood of any of them taking a shine to a quiet and shy office worker riding a 250 Superdream with a luggage top box was rather remote.

My previous girlfriend (84-89) had her own car and she always drove everywhere, which suited me fine as I could drink on a night out without worrying about it. I'd driven her car with L Plates on before and also my mum's car so was already quite proficient by the time I came to do my test.

In fact, the Ex had a rather odd attitude towards me learning to drive. She didn't mind me driving her car on Ls but she went completely loopy when I announced that I was going to have driving lessons and get my licence.

I never really understood this – I always thought that the more people who knew how to drive the better - but we had several blazing rows over it and, in the end, I gave up on the idea.

So fast forward now to the - happily – young, free and single Bachelor Pad me of 1990.

I'd had car lessons before and, apart from "hill starts" - which were quite difficult to practice in Peterborough because it was so flat everywhere, I was quite a capable driver and figured that I could already drive just as well as most people I was related to.

Oddly enough, the catalyst – when it came - for making me finally get round to getting my licence wasn't anything to do with birds at all, as it happens.

My younger brother Gary – who was 4 years younger than me – ie 18/19 at the time, had been having lessons and he passed his test earlier in the summer of 1990. He started borrowing my mum's car to go out and about in and then got his own second-hand Austin Allegro.

And that really bloody annoyed me!

So I thought "Sod This!" – as you do if you are me and you are really bloody annoyed about something - especially if it's something that you could easily have sorted out ages ago and just didn't – even more so if your little brother has gone and done it before you and made you feel like a total and utter PRAT - and I got hold of his driving instructor and asked him to give me some refresher lessons.

On the first day out, he told me I should put in for my test straight away as I was easily ready to take it – and they took a few weeks to come through. So that's what I did.

In the intervening period we went round all the routes that they use for the actual tests – that's the benefit of going with a proper instructor, they know all this – and we practiced emergency stops and three point turns in the very places that they were likely to want to do them on the test itself.

The night before my test, I walked down to the nearby pub, sat quietly in a corner with a pint and re-read through the Highway Code.

I already knew things like road signs and level crossings off by heart as I remember taking a great interest in those when I was little and my mum was learning to drive many years before – but I especially needed to mug up on braking and stopping distances.

Funnily enough, when I was little, I was always worried about the road sign for riverside and quayside (pictured left) and I kept a somewhat manic look out for it whenever we were out in the car as family.

This probably stemmed from the fact that I couldn't swim and often used to have nightmares about finding myself trapped next to huge bodies of water.

It also didn't help that the car pictured in the sign looked exactly the same shape as the Austin 1100 that we had at the time.

The fact that my dad was a sensible adult, used to drive for a living and knew exactly where he was going cut no ice with me at all and I felt I needed to be extra vigilant – like when I made up a "Fire Precautions" poster at home during the 1977 firemen's strike and stuck it up on the airing cupboard door.

When we used to go and visit my grandparents in Ramsey on a Sunday afternoon, we would sometimes go the back way via Ramsey St Mary's and that necessitated driving along the river for a bit – so that always made me feel very uneasy.

And my friend from work in later years, Anne Castellano, actually lost control of her car once when driving alongside the River Nene on the back road between Peterborough and Whittlesey and she ended up in the drink and had to swim to safety.

That happened before I knew her but I was aware of the story and, even though I could swim from the age of 11 onwards, I was still very wary about going along that stretch of road as well.

Fortunately , I am happy to report that since moving to the Wirral in 2015, I have driven along the docks and open quays in Birkenhead many many times and can safely say that I no longer have the nagging fear of being near water that I used to have!

Anyway, the day of the test came – 7th August 1990 - and it was a gorgeous bright sunny day with blue skies and not a cloud in sight.

There was a nice light wind so it wasn't too hot and it was exactly the sort of day that I like for going out and doing exciting things. Conditions were just perfect for me to do my test and get my driving licence.

I was secretly hoping to get a female examiner – don't ask me why I'm just like that... - but I had been told that they only had one female test examiner at the Peterborough Test Centre so was a bit crestfallen when she came out first and took somebody else.

Some of the other test candidates were then called and went off with their respective examiners and - would you believe it - another lady came out of the office and called my name. I was overjoyed – what a positive sign!

The test went very well. We took one of the routes that I had been practicing and I was confident that I knew what to do in every eventuality.

However, we hit a snag when I was approaching a bend, with crosshatching in the middle of the road that you needed to keep out of, but with a very slow cyclist holding me and the following traffic up.

If you have local knowledge of that area, it was going along Mayor's Walk in the direction of Bourges Boulevard, coming off the bridge over the railway line and approaching the bend just as you come up to the Royal Mail Sorting office. If you don't know the grand metropolis of Peterborough at all, that won't mean a thing to you - but you can always check it out on "Google Maps".

I had to make a split second decision whether to overtake the cyclist – and thus "make progress" albeit by edging onto the hatching on the approach to the bend - or just sit there and hold everybody up.

I'm going to leave you in suspenders here by not actually telling you what I did but, luckily, I must have made the right choice because I passed the test with flying colours.

When I discussed it all with my instructor afterwards, he told me that he had heard that one of the other examiners had been taken ill that day and this lady (who he had never come across before) had been brought in from somewhere else to cover for him. So that really was my lucky day!

So I started borrowing my mum's car – a blue Morris Marina estate at the time – to get used to driving on my own and, over the next few weeks, had a look round the local car dealers for something affordable that I could get started off with.

I saw a bright orange VW Beetle that would have looked great with the Peterborough Pirates "P" logo painted on the doors, but the engine smoked rather badly when it was started up so we ignored that one.

Then there was a white MK1 escort but that was left hand drive and wouldn't be good for a beginner – and a sporty metallic lime coloured Lancia, but there was something not right about that either.

There was also a 70s Ford Cortina – a yellow one with the black vinyl roof - that seemed OK at first but I noticed that all the seats had been stitched up and badly repaired and it made me wonder what else might have been bodged elsewhere - so that was out as well.

There were several used car dealers based on the fields along Fletton Avenue on the way into the town centre and I often used to cruise by slowly and see if there was anything that grabbed my attention.

One day I spotted this bright yellow car – the colour made it stand out from all the reds and silvers that were there - so I stopped and had a look at it.

It was quite old by then – 12 years or so - but looked in pretty good condition considering.

I got my dad to go back and have a proper look with me and he looked at the engine, started it up and it seemed OK.

It was only £300 so you couldn't really expect much more than "seeming OK " for that price and I decided to buy it. It was an S-registered - ie 1977/78 - Datsun Cherry 120 F11 Coupe, apparently. I just checked that on the internet now – as far as I was concerned back then, it was just "a car...".

The guy who owned the yard was somebody who I vaguely recognised from school although he was older than me and I didn't know his name. But the deal was done, and I went back to pick the car up a few days later.

And the rest - as they say – is history!

Being able to drive certainly meant that I was able to be more independent when I started travelling to and working in Preston in later years.

On the social front it meant that I could pick people up, give people lifts and return the favours of many years. It also meant that I could appeal to a better class of woman (sorry, biker chicks – don't take that the wrong way...), could cart more stuff about with me and generally do more.

I certainly think I'd have got on better with my ice hockey training and playing had I taken my car test a lot sooner – but it is easy to say these things with hindsight.

And I got there eventually.

Motorbikes That I Have Owned:

Left to right: PB with the Puch Monza in the yard at Cleverleys shop in Fletton, Summer 1983 - PB on the Honda MB5, 1983 - Alan and Louise elaborately draped across my Honda CB125TDC in the car park at The Whittle Way, Summer 1985.

1983: Puch Monza 4 GP

1983-84: Honda MB5

1984-86: Honda CB125 twin

1986-88: Honda CD 175 (above left)

You can read my description of this bike in the Erasure concert write up.

1988-93: Honda CB 250N Superdream - AEG 979Y (above right)

The photo isn't actually of my own Honda Superdream as I sadly don't appear to have any pictures with it in. I found this image on a website where the bike was being sold recently for an incredible £1100!

This is the same year, model and colour that mine was. Mine had a luggage rack and white box on the back and full length fairing and screen on the front - so that it looked a bit like a police motorbike.

It had a Laser 2-into-1 exhaust that made a wonderful rasping sound and annoyed all the neighbours if you revved the engine - and also a six speed gearbox.

However, once I got accustomed to the relative comfort of driving my car – and was then was up in Preston most of the time for work, my bike got a bit overlooked and I hardly ever used it after that.

My mum very thoughtfully sold it for me to help pay off a huge telephone bill that I had somehow managed to run up during 1992 and 1993 making international calls.

Honda XL 185 (1991-93)

I also had an XL 185 for a while. I bought it on a whim while I was back at my parents and had a bit of spare cash. I had always wanted to own a trail bike and the opportunity came up. Unfortunately, there seemed to be something wrong with – it kept losing compression and generally didn't service very well.

I was by no means technically minded – not like Mr Hill who used to very capably do running repairs on his British classic bikes by the side of the road - and couldn't be bothered messing with it so I never really used it very much.

The XL went as part of the "not tied down assets selling off" frenzy at the same time as the CB250 Superdream.

Cars That I Owned Or Drove During The Bachelor Pad Years

1990-92: Datsun 120 Cherry F11 Coupe - S Reg (See previous)

1992-93: Citroen BX16 TGS Meteor estate (company car)

This had been Steve Pressley's company car, who worked in the IT department at Baker Perkins / Rockwell PMC and I was given it to use for my year in Preston after he had left (read The Bachelor Pad Mk2 for more about that...).

I had actually been in it before as Paul Hornsby and I travelled up to Middlesbrough with Steve to see Peterborough United in the League Cup quarter final replay in February 1992, so it was a strange coincidence to be allocated the same car shortly afterwards.

1993: Ford Escort – X Reg

Once my year at the expense of the company expired in Preston and I became a normal employee, I needed to get my own car. Neil Cook - who worked in my office - was really into cars and he used to change his every 6 months or so and get something different.

He knew everything there was to know about every different variation of every make and model and he was kind enough to go round with me when I started looking around for vehicles.

I had originally planned to buy his Fiesta XR2 off him but it was a 2.2 litre engine and I couldn't get insurance for Hanja to drive it as she was under 21.

It turned out that one of Neil's friends had this silver Escort that he wanted to sell so I got it for something like £600 and it kept me going until I found something more suitable.

My mum had this Escort after me – and I lost track of what happened to it after that.

PB with the Vauxhall Cavalier in Preston, 1993 (post Bachelor Pad photo)

1993 – 97: Vauxhall Cavalier Commander 1.6i estate - C72 EFR

The Cavalier also came from one of Neil's friends and it was a good size and fit for me.

Having only paid £1200 for it, I was very pleased with how it coped with my usage, driving back down to Peterborough on a regular basis, heading off to football matches in far flung locations, and going across to Germany during the holidays.

It finally gave up the ghost and went to the "parking lot in the sky" in the spring of 1997 and was replaced by the loan of Hanja's mum's Nissan Bluebird which I kept hold of until February 1998 when I was in Luxembourg (more on all that another time...).

September 1990: Polish Pursuits 1 – Trip To Zakopane

Please note that this account was account was written in the mid 1990s – probably when I was at work supposed to be doing something else.... As such the memories were fresher in my mind at the time of writing, enabling me to go into more detail than for some of my other reminiscences which have been written much longer after the event.

My first ever visit to Poland was in the late summer/early autumn of 1990. The Solidarity government had been in power for a year or so following the first free elections for decades and the economy was in a state of expansion.

I hadn't specifically set out to arrange a visit there but had been strangely enchanted by the images and descriptions in the holiday brochure and became inquisitive to see more. Besides, it was cheap.

Having decided that I wanted to go, I decided that I didn't want to go on my own. Poland didn't really have the reputation of being one of the great tourist haunts so this would probably not have been easy, except for the fact that I had an old school friend in Graham Hill who, like me, wasn't so bothered about sun and beaches.

It took a bit of coercion but he eventually agreed to go with me – although he had to get permission from his employers first because he was working in the aeronautical industry at the time and, as Poland was still an Eastern Bloc country, there was always the fear that he might get kidnapped by Russian spies.

I had no idea what to expect – so I imagined it might be like East Berlin had been - but with a mountain or two thrown in.

Our destination was the mountain resort of Zakopane in the extreme south of the country encircled by the High Tatra Mountains.

Dover etc

The booking was made direct by me with the operators in Birmingham who seemed very friendly and efficient. With our confirmation came two visa application forms which needed to be filled out and sent to the Polish embassy along with our passports.

Apart from the temporary East German slip of paper, I had never had a proper visa before and was quite excited at the prospect of getting my first stamp in my passport. One worry was the amount of time that would be required to get the documents to the embassy in London, get them processed and back to the travel agents again in time for our departure.

I was somewhat concerned that both our passports and visas would be held for us to be collected at Dover. I didn't really fancy the prospect of setting off for an overseas trip without having my passport in my pocket but there wasn't time to handle direct.

We set off one warm and bright Sunday afternoon in early September on the train bound for London. Our eventual destination that day was Dover where the package trip actually started from - a good ruse by them to keep the brochure price down!

My travel companion had done some research into overnight accommodation and had booked us into a guest house somewhere in Dover. We had to be at the docks in the morning so that was the only way of making it and being at least half-awake to enjoy the rest of the day.

Upon arrival at Victoria Station we had a quick Casey Jones to keep us going and then headed for the platform to get our train. One of the previous trains had been delayed so there were more people than normal on ours but we still managed to get a seat. It had got dark by now and there was very little to see out of the window except blackness and the odd street light.

We arrived at Gillingham, which I found rather strange as my recollections of previous London to Dover journeys didn't include Gillingham as a stop off point.

From here everyone was herded off the train and onto a fleet of coaches which were to ferry us to some little halt in the middle of nowhere to rejoin the train, presumably due to problems further down the line.

It was too hot in the bus and I found myself sitting over the wheel and, consequently started getting travel sick rather quickly so it was a great relief when we were able to rejoin the train again.

By the time that we approached Dover the train was practically empty apart from a couple of Ferry employees discussing marker buoys and pilot boats, most of the other passengers having got off at the many little village stops en route.

We alighted at Dover Priory station which serviced the town (as opposed to the Harbour) and found a long walk with heavy bags ahead of us.

The town wasn't a very attractive place but in a frantic dash in the dark I don't suppose that anywhere looks particularly good. We eventually found our guesthouse in a row of quaint, older buildings. The rooms were actually positioned above a hardware shop and we were told that for breakfast the next morning, we had to go to the café down the road which was owned by the same people.

Having placed our bags in the room, we set off in search of food and drink. Luckily there was a pub just a little way down the road. Unluckily they had already finished serving as it was past 10.30.

With no chance of a beer we decided to settle for chips and a coke from a takeaway.

This wasn't easy either as Dover didn't seem to have much of a nightlife - especially on a Sunday night, and there wasn't much of a choice.

We decided against a heavy restaurant meal and eventually managed to find a Chinese chip shop to get some supper.

The next morning was rather hectic as we had to get breakfasted and down to the passenger terminal at the docks by 10.00 am.

The sun was shining and it was a wonderful crisp, clear day as we stepped out and walked the few yards to the café.

I looked on with anticipation as a couple of lorry driver types were being served with a plate stacked high with bacon, eggs, beans etc. Our B&B breakfasts weren't however, quite so huge, although we did get cereals before and toast afterwards.

Feeling full and ready for the journey ahead, we settled up and headed off towards the docks. We decided that, as it was a nice morning and we had time, we would walk - a nice stroll along the sea front, past the large white hotels that we had seen the night before and down the slope.

This turned out to be somewhat further than expected and we had to stop several times on the way for a rest.

Upon arrival at the passenger terminal we spied a group of people hovering around someone who looked like a trainee school teacher. This turned out to be our contact from the travel company who, luckily, had our passports, visas and boarding cards for the ferry.

We were directed towards the embarkation lounge and told that we would be met at Ostend by our coach. Another cost cutting measure - no guide for the ferry crossing!

As we all stood around in the lounge which looked out onto the harbour it was as if everybody was sizing each other up. I had arrived convinced that the whole touring party would be made up of retired school teachers and old Polish ex-patriates who wanted to return home for a short visit.

Luckily this turned out not to be the case and there was an interesting mixture of youngish and old.

The familiarisation period seemed continuous throughout the trip as each stop brought us into contact with different people.

The boat journey passed quite quickly - it was only around 3 1/2 hours - and we watched Arnold Schwarzenegger's "Total Recall" film in the ferry cinema.

We didn't really see any more of our fellow travellers (then again, we wouldn't have recognised them even if we had) until we disembarked at Ostend and assembled by the very Dutch looking man holding a card in the air, as I had often seen before but had never participated.

The Journey Starts In Earnest

There was a mad scramble for seats on the bus - obviously the others had had experience of this type of thing before. I picked a couple of seats through the window and sent Mr Hill into the melée to secure them whilst I ensured that the suitcases got loaded into the boot of the double decker luxury touring coach.

We got our chosen seats - two together facing forwards (there were others arranged in four around a table which was all right if you were travelling as a group but not if you didn't know anybody - and settled down to watch the world pass by.

Our bus was run by a Belgian operator and it was explained to us by our young female guide (long bushy hair, slightly dark skinned, slightly over-chunky) that this coach would take us across Belgium, Germany (the east/west division had ended in all but name with the monetary union that July) and part way into Poland where we would be transferred to local, Polish coaches for the last leg of the journey.

We crossed the Belgian/German border around teatime with no particular problem and continued on our journey without stopping.

Once it got dark our courier put on a video to help pass the time. Unfortunately, we were towards the back of the bus and couldn't see the small tv screen particularly well - particularly as people kept moving their heads in the way.

Equally unfortunately we were not near to one of the audio speakers that were dotted around the bus and once one of the old people who was close to one asked for the volume to be turned down, we had absolutely no chance of even hearing the film.

Just before crossing the by then defunct in all but name only East German border somewhere past Kassel, the bus came to a halt for another "refreshment and toilet break". We were jettisoned from our dozing in the snug warm coach out into an icy midnight wind at a sort of service station which had just one small kiosk and very little shelter.

Whether this stop had any particular purpose other to demonstrate how lucky we were to be crammed up in the coach was never ascertained.

Once we got back on the bus, people started preparing for the night ahead, queuing for the toilet etc. Whilst looking around at what was going on, I noticed one of the older women with some sort of collar on, like people with neck problems wear. On closer inspection it became apparent that it was an inflatable pillow that fits snugly around ones neck to cushion whilst sitting in seats, and it looked ridiculous!

I was about to point this out with some levity to Graham when I noticed that several other people around the lower deck of the coach also had these pillows. Those that didn't were taking them from their bags and inflating them. I decided in the end upon a mildly humorous comment about how daft they looked and why didn't we have any.

I hadn't been on an overnight coach journey since my holiday to Austria, five years before, which is probably why I didn't know about the inflatable pillows.

After that trip I had vowed that I would never do it again. Obviously, five years had clouded the memory somewhat......

It wasn't so much the lack of space, although a full double seat each would have been nice. I would have hated to be sitting next to someone that i didn't know. The leg room was tight so I stuck my legs out across the gangway. This was OK until somebody stumbled over them on the way to the toilet.

The biggest problem was the motion of the bus (no escaping that) and the light - both from the traffic outside and the inside "safety" lights which remained on the whole time. I finally managed to overcome this by wearing my sunglasses all night. This at least allowed me to doze a little.

We crossed what used to be the West / East German border sometime after that. The road now merely by-passed the sliproad to the customs bays and continued as if it had always done so.

The next morning arrived somewhat early for my liking. It was just getting light and we were on the East German motorway between Chemnitz (still called Karl-Marx-Stadt at the time, they had been preparing to vote on a name change) and Dresden.

We pulled into Dresden just as dawn was breaking and saw mainly grey and gloomy streets, many cobbled, and grey and gloomy tower blocks of flats. Some of the blocks had large motifs of flowers and suns painted on them to try and brighten the place up a bit but at 5 in the morning I wasn't really in the mood to be brightened up.

We arrived in the courtyard of a building which looked very much like a school or community centre. Even more so as we were ushered into a huge wooden panelled hall lined with tables and chairs.

We were given breakfast by some scruffy yet pleasant East German cook-type people and, following a quick trip to the bathroom facilities (cold, plain, no toilet paper) got back onto the bus fully refreshed and, by now, at least half awake.

As the morning went by, people were beginning to become a little more sociable and started talking a little to each other.

Polish Border

As we approached the polish border we were handed out currency importation slips to fill in to show how much money we were bringing in to the country.

It was rather cloudy and wet as we drew in to the border town of Görlitz, also known as Zgorlec on the Polish side.

After being waved through the East German controls, the coach was boarded by a very serious looking official in a green Polish army uniform. He had a ridiculously large moustache and had his cap pulled down hard on his head.

In front of him he had a sort of writing case strapped to his chest with drawers etc which opened out into his own little mobile passport control office.

He moved up the bus and, one by one, checked everybody's entry visas and stamped them. He took quite a while over each one and carefully compared the photo on the visa, the photo in the passport and the face of the holder.

This slightly over the top bureaucracy lasted a while and it was probably 1/2 an hour or so before we were on way into Poland.

Overland In Poland

We stopped off at a place called Opole for a lunch break. The morning had been, for the most part, overcast and, once we had crossed the border and got over the initial excitement of being in Poland, things began to look very similar to the German side.

There were a few roadside signs written in Polish. The whole area seemed very assimilated considering that before the second world war, this whole western stretch had actually been part of Germany.

We had actually already made an unscheduled stop at Wroclaw (formerly Breslau) when our coach's engine started making a strange noise. We pulled into a petrol station to fill up and one of the drivers went off in search of something.

It was pouring with rain and a cold wind whipping across the flat, featureless landscape blew in the open bus door. I hoped that we wouldn't have to get out as the lack of sleep the previous night had ill prepared me for too much activity.

Luckily, the problem soon seemed to resolve itself and we were on our way again.

Opole didn't, at first glance, seem particularly exciting nor attractive. We found ourselves in a hotel car park which was over looked on three sides by grim and unkempt looking "five-year plan" tower blocks. The arrival of the bus was met with great excitement by the little children playing around the area who crowded round to see what was going on. For the most part they looked fairly healthy but untidily dressed.

We were informed by our Belgian couriers that they would be leaving us here and we would be picked up by some Polish buses which would take us on to Zakopane. This was because the local buses were smaller and better suited to the twisting mountain roads that we would soon be encountering.

I didn't particularly fancy the idea of being stranded in the middle of Poland waiting for a bus that might never come but we were assured that they would wait until the other buses arrived so that we could transfer luggage etc.

In the meantime we were invited to make use of the Hotel restaurant who had a special meal prepared for us. We were ushered into the eating area. It was rather dark inside, but nicely decorated with a rustic flavour. Most people made a b-line for the toilets, having not had the chance since breakfast time, although the coach did have a toilet on board, it wasn't really the same.

The meal was served and consisted of a slice of processed meat of some description, some salad and some sauerkraut.

My previous experience in East Germany has told me that sauerkraut would be on every Eastern European menu for every meal so this was no surprise to me. Luckily, this proved not to be the case for the rest of the holiday.

We were asked what we wanted to drink and, drawing again on my previous experiences, I decided to go for cola instead of the local beers or juices, although it turned out that they did also serve imported German beers.

We were advised that the restaurant also could exchange our hard currency into Polish Zloty and everybody immediately began queuing at the little counter. As it wasn't possible to obtain Polish currency outside of the country this was the first time that most of us had seen it. An exchange rate of 15.000 to the pound made us all feel, temporarily, very rich.

When we emerged from the restaurant back into the bright light of day, we were met by the sight of the two Polish coaches that were to take us on to Zakopane. Our Polish courier for the rest of the trip, a woman in her forties, pleasant yet quick to display Eastern European firmness, called out lists of names and told us which of the two buses we should get on to.

The change of transport gave us the opportunity to meet some more of our travelling companions, none of whom seemed either interesting to talk to nor interested in talking to us, although this may well have been due to the long arduous overnight trip that we had all had to endure rather than any particular social disability.

Gliwice & Katowice

As I gazed out of the window at rolling countryside, I was also secretly counting down the kilometres on the roadsigns until we got to Gliwice. Keen scholars of twentieth century European history, like myself, will know that this town used to be on the border between Poland and Germany.

And it was here that, on 31st August 1939, the Nazis staged a bogus attack on themselves, purported to be by Polish commandos, which they used as a reason for their subsequent invasion.

Unfortunately, my fellow travelling companions (except Graham, who I had briefed in advance) didn't seem to know about this. Consequently, as we drove through the town itself, my question, out loud to anybody who was listening, "does anybody know if the radio tower is still here?" was met by silence and bewildered looks all round.

Sitting in the nearest couple of seats across the gangway from myself (having been crammed into one seat each for 24 hours on the last bus we were making the most of the extra space on this one with most of us having a whole double seat each) were two rather dull and unhappy looking women travelling together.

They were probably in their early to mid thirties and, for my money, just had to be teachers. They were both dressed in trousers and dark colours and remained so for most of the trip..

Despite going around trying to pass themselves off as teachers, even they didn't seem to know about the historical incident.

I then found myself agonising over whether to break the embarrassing ensuing silence by imposing my superior knowledge upon those around me or whether to curl back up on my nice, wide, spacious seat (it was about as comfortable as an old Routemaster) and try and doze off.

Luckily, the decision was taken for me as a young middle age gentleman with short grey hair and grey beard (looked a bit like Sigmund Freud would have done had he have been on the bus at that moment...) turned out of his seat a few further forward in the bus to ask what I was on about.

He may even have been wearing a suit for travelling in! I seized upon this opportunity and told my tale, although it really makes one wonder why people bother to go to places without knowing the background..!

Funnily enough, I don't recall seeing that man again for the whole duration of the tour.

Unfortunately, whilst all this was going on I had taken my eye off the street outside. Once I realised, all I could see was the top of a mast of some sort hidden behind a lot of trees, which may or may not have been what I was looking out for.

As we continued on our way eastwards the weather changed again from a bright and airy sky to dark clouds once again. By the time that we entered the industrial town of Katowice it was absolutely pouring with rain.

Katowice may very well have been a grim grey place already but the weather did it no cosmetic favours as we passed through.

The rain beat down on grey buildings and old battered Polish Fiats and only the most unlucky citizen who had been caught out in the rain would have observed our passing through.

We also drove past Auschwitz on our route down to Zakopane. My reading up on places of interest prior to departure had given me its correct Polish name of Oswiencim which I observed on a road sign as we passed a huge, ugly looking chemical plant.

From the reaction that I had received at Gliwice, I chose to remain silent on this occasion.

Towards teatime we stopped off for a drinks and toilet break at a "Restauracja" - a restaurant which, in effect, was a huge block building with a purple stained glass frontage that housed upstairs a smoky bar and restaurant with pinball tables etc. The downstairs didn't seem to be open and may have been used as a function room or something similar.

There were very few cars outside and the bar seemed to be full of several scruffy landworkers. Considering that this place was actually in the middle of nowhere, it was quite difficult to imagine where their custom normally came from.

This was the first opportunity that we'd had to spend our Polish currency and a few of the more daring members of the group headed off towards the bar. The majority of those remaining decided to try and find a toilet. The toilet was downstairs, near to where we came in, and turned out to be a bit of a shock initiation into Polish lifestyle.

There was a very fierce and unfriendly lady wearing an old blue housecoat standing guard. I initially thought that she was collecting money for using the toilet but closer inspection of the table in front of her proved otherwise.

On the table were spread out little bundles of individual sheets of toilet paper which she was selling for Zl 100 (0.006p) per bundle.

This caused a problem because, although we were now all flush with Zlotych, they were all large domination banknotes - Zl 10.000 or so - and the lady didn't have enough small notes to give everybody change.

Despite her not speaking a word of English, the message was quite clear: No 100 Zlotych, No Toilet!

At that particular moment I would have quite happily paid Zl 10.000 for a visit to the toilet because we didn't have such facilities on our Polish bus but it was not to be. The woman was obviously doubling her duties with something else around the complex as she lost patience with us, gathered up her prized sheets of sandpaper and stormed off.

Villa Venus – and Hotel "Hell"!

When we arrived in Zakopane, we were all allocated our accommodation for our stay. I am not sure how this was decided - whether it was down to who wanted double rooms and who wanted twins, or whatever – but it turned out that we were not all staying in the same place.

Graham and I - and a few others from our coach - were to sleep at the Villa Venus – which sounds like it ought to have been a brothel, but was, in fact, a pleasant, clean and airy "Penzion" on a pretty leafy street.

The rest were to go to a bigger hotel a bit further up the road.

The Villa Venus did not have a dining room or any catering facilities so we had to walk down to the other hotel for our breakfast and evening meal every day. It was easy enough to get to and only took 5 minutes or so – which was fine by us.

I don't actually remember the name of this other hotel and haven't been able to find all of my Poland 1990 photos yet to check it.

I can't find either the Villa Venus or this other one on an internet search either - although I notice that Zakopane has changed a huge amount since we went there in the last Eastern Bloc days of September 1990.

I am pretty sure, however, that its unpronounceable Polish name included "Hell" in the title, which we always made jokes about every time we went.

Earlier that year, there had been a TV drama on the BBC called "Oranges Are Not The Only Fruit" and the overbearing religiously fanatical mother character in it used to come out with such platitudes as "You don't need an airing cupboard if you've got Jesus" and "There'll be no breakfasts in Hell" and I always thought of that when we went there to eat.

The food there was very pleasant to be honest. I can't really remember much about what we had to eat so it can't have been horrid. It was general tourist fare – and probably not what the average Polish family would eat at home at that time – although we did have Polish herbal tea at both breakfast and dinner, so got quite used to it.

Polish visa in my passport issued by the Polish Consulate in London

You can clearly see the entry stamp made at the border crossing at Zgorzelec (or Görlitz in German) on 18th September 1990.

PB in Zakopane with (left to right): Anne & Steve from Bristol and Graham Hill

Night Club / Hotel

Once we had settled into our accommodation, we decided to go out on the town – as far as such things were possible.

There was a young student couple called Steve and Anne from our tour who we bumped into on the way out and they had the same idea so we decided to set out as a group.

We headed into the town centre clutching our photocopied street plans in our hands. They were the only things that would guide us back to the hotel again.

All the street names were totally unpronounceable. It was dark, raining and far from warm. When we reached what appeared to be the main shopping area it was totally deserted.

There were quite a few shops - all closed of course as it was late - but no bars or cafés or anything much to tempt the tourist.

On reflection, this was a good thing. Too many distractions would have meant we would lost our way back to the hotel in the dark.

It was not a good start to our stay in Zakopane. The people in the hotel had told us that it had rained everyday for the past two weeks.

We walked along the wide main street. The rain had subsided so it was more pleasant to walk. On the corner was a large building with a round tower and church/castle like front door and flagstoned hall.

This turned out to be the Orbis hotel, run by the state-owned travel bureau, which housed a night club in its cellar and cafeteria and restaurant on its upper floors, as well as high priced accommodation for rich people.

We baulked at the idea of having to pay Zl 6.000 to get into the night club and were about to walk off when we worked out that it was only about 50p in English money and, anyway, there was nowhere else open.

The night club was just like any western bar, except that it was in the cellar of such a grandiose building. There was a bar in the corner and satellite TV and a dance floor in the middle of the room with waiter-serviced tables around it.

Having studied the drinks menu on the table and noticed that the prices for the beers and juices were quite extortionately expensive – even at 15.000 to a £ - we decided to order a bottle of vodka between us.

They had several pages of different types of vodka - all with different subtle flavourings – and also in a range of sizes of bottle. I seem to think that we went for a quarter sized bottle of blackcurrant flavoured vodka between the four of us and this came served with a full litre bottle of mineral water.

The idea was that you sipped a little vodka and drank plenty of water in between so you got the benefit of the vodka but it didn't make you ill.

So this turned out to be a very pleasant introduction to our stay in Poland after all.

It had been a very long couple of days what with the journey and so on so we didn't stop too long, preferring instead to go back to our hotel and get the first good night's sleep for 3 days.

We found our way back to the hotel and I don't remember any alcohol-related repercussions the next day!

Ski Jump Excursion & Mountains

Our first excursion came the very next day. We awoke to clear blue skies and bright sunshine - a nice contrast to the weather the previous evening and the perfect start to our first full day in Zakopane.

After breakfast we were all herded onto the coach and introduced to our guide for the morning, whose name I no longer remember.

He was an oldish man who spoke good, yet heavily accented, English and dressed very much in the manner of a hill-person out of Heidi.

Our destination was the mountains - particularly the famous Gubałówka (roughly pronounced "guba-wuffka") which is a firm favourite with walkers in the summer and skiers in the winter.

The guide seemed obsessed with the desire to show us "traditional highland homes" which he mentioned more than once as he narrated our bus-assisted ascent over the bus microphone.

Our first port of call was a quaint little church up in the hills. The church was made of wood and was decorated with immaculate carvings throughout. It had been built in memory of Auschwitz survivors and contained some examples of artwork produced by the victims during their incarceration.

Making New Friends

We had observed the group of Polish people who were staying in the Villa Venus on the same floor as us and assumed that they were all one family - a mother with a loud kid, a grandfather and a few cousins / nieces who were in their twenties.

I decided that in the name of East & Western relations, I should try and bridge the gap between these two cultures. It was the middle of the evening and dark outside. Everybody has washed and showered and was going about their evening business. For the Polish people next door, this seemed to involve lots of running up and downstairs, slamming of doors and shouting at each other.

Through the strategically open gap in our door I managed to notice that two of the girls had gone back into their room, leaving the third to follow on. I went outside and hung around, very suspiciously, on the landing - trying not to make the situation look any more contrived than it already was. The furtive looks and giggles coming from our room didn't make me feel any more comfortable.

After what had seemed like an age, but had probably been around 30 seconds. The third of the girls came bounding up the stairs. It was the taller one with the dark hair and dark complexion who totally by chance had unwittingly become the subject for this initial approach and was wearing a turquoise coloured top, light blue jeans and a black waterproof coat.

She reached the top of the stairs and passed by without giving me a second glance.

Undeterred by this initial put-down, I summoned up every ounce of courage that I could muster and uttered a very shaky "Dobra Vechor..." at which she stopped, looked at me and rattled off something in Polish.

I was quite pleased to have even got a reaction as that had been the only Polish expression that I knew, having picked it up on a school trip to France years before when I overheard a Pole and a Yugoslav discussing similarities between their languages.

Not surprisingly, I returned a somewhat blank expression at this and she then said in only very lightly stilted English: "You speak Polish?" to which I had to admit that those two words were the full extent of my vocabulary.

I managed to learn that they were from Warsaw before the rest of the girls emerged from their room again and they all dashed off out somewhere.

Barbecue #1

The evening after our first meeting with the Polish girls was the farewell barbecue for another tour group who were leaving the next day. This was to be held in the open barn to the rear of the Villa Venus.

I hadn't shown any particular interest in this because the barbecue for our group would be held the week after so we could go then.

Graham and I were stood half in and half out of the room debating how we should spend the evening when the chattier of the three girls (Jola) came past and asked if we were going to the barbecue.

I explained that we hadn't bought tickets for it but she replied that it didn't matter because she and her friends hadn't either but the manager had told them they could go along anyway.

Not feeling too keen on the idea of gate-crashing a function staged by our own travel company and, noticing that she seemed to be quite well dressed, I then tried the excuse that we weren't properly dressed for the occasion.

This argument fell through when my eyes fell upon the very unelegant training boots which had seemingly been thrust rather hurriedly onto the end of her dark stockinged legs. Furthermore, it was pouring with rain and blowing a gale outside so any thoughts of elegance were quickly discounted.

I was quite keen to go along with the girls and we eventually went out of a lack of anything else to do. Everybody was sitting huddled on little benches around the edge of the dim barn looking in to the middle where a huge barrel with a roaring fire inside was being used to cook the meat which had been impaled on long sticks thrust through the flames.

Small groups were chatting amongst themselves and drinking out of plastic cups. We stood in the hotel garden just by the entrance to the barn, looking in and not really wanting to encroach further. The other two Polish girls joined us, as did someone who was probably the aforesaid "manager" who motioned for us to go in and help ourselves to the food and drink.

His view was obviously that, as everything had already been paid for by the English tourists, there was no reason why his Polish guests shouldn't go and partake for free so, being for the time being part of the "Polish Group", I took a nibble of sausage and a cup of mineral water as a token gesture

The rest of the evening was spent chatting with Jola, doing what you normally do when you meet people of other nationalities - ie: comparing passports, driving licenses etc - and talking about where we were from and what we did.

Czech Border / Mountains

I had come prepared for cool weather but not snow! That was what we encountered on our trip south into the mountains.

It was grey yet dry as we got off the bus and joined the queue to travel up to the top of the mountain by cable car.

The journey up was fairly uneventful as it was quite misty and you couldn't really see too much outside, although there did appear to be a ski run down the mountain that followed the route of the lift.

The lift station at the top was quite dark, as they normally are, and housed a newspaper stand, toilets and a rather "Eastern European" looking refectory with high ceilings and plain painted walls.

When we emerged out into the light again, it was as if we were on another planet. The view was absolutely breathtaking as the snowcapped peaks of the High Tatras spread out before us in every direction. The bright sun shone down from a clear blue sky punctuated with the odd white fluffy cloud and reflected back off the surrounding snow. It all seemed a lot brighter than at the bottom of the mountain.

This excursion was being escorted by the Managing Director of the Polish tour company who had been looking after us. He was probably late fifties and well dressed, although it's hard to tell in a thick coat. I figured that he must have been pretty rich because he wore some swish designer sunglasses with the "Adidas" marque. This particular delusion lasted only for a few days because we later saw some for sale in a souvenir shop at approx. 40p a pair.

The air was crisp and cold which all added to this remarkable high altitude experience. It was slippery underfoot as the snow had been packed down hard by the previous visitors that morning and I was having extreme difficulty making any headway in my training shoes.

To give an idea of how cold it could be up there, even in September, there was a building containing a weather centre of some sort which had ice across its windows and equipment.

Looking out across the ridges and peaks, you could see the tracks in the snow heading off into the distance which had obviously been left by hardier souls earlier that day.

We decided to be a little less adventurous and follow the main flow of ill-equipped tourists to the first long, wide ridge some 100m ahead of us. This was no mean feat in itself as the pathway was very slippery, coupled with the fact that just a few meters away on each side was a sheer drop down the mountainside.

Not the best way of getting down again! In fact, a rope had been laid along this pathway and secured at various points to give one something to grab hold of in case of slipping.

We eventually arrived at our point of destination, although not without a few heart-stopping moments on the way. Here could be seen a row of short painted poles in the ground which extended way into the distance in both directions at intervals of approximately 50 meters. They were painted white with red at the top and had the letters CS inscribed upon each one.

Closer inspection showed that these actually marked out the border between Poland and Czechoslovakia and, by standing astride the line, it was possible to disprove the old adage that you couldn't be in two places at once!

The cable car journey back down to the bottom of the mountain was chosen in preference to the reported 8 hour climb. When we had come, up the tour guy had given us all ticket stubs for our return ride in the cable car.

I had paid little attention at the time but as we were deciding what to do next, I noticed that each time the car filled up with people, a number was shown on a lit panel by the gate.

I hurriedly checked on the ticket in my pocket and came to the conclusion that this number tallied with the numbers on the tickets for the ride back down.

I noticed in horror that our number had already gone. I anticipated some East European bureaucracy in trying to get on bearing a ticket with the wrong number but, fortunately, this didn't materialise and we managed to get ourselves on a later car along with a few other fellow travellers.

Cassette Tapes

At that time there was an amazing black economy in pirate tapes of all the current artists: Madonna, Jason Donovan, Gloria Estefan etc. These were selling for Zl 11.000 which, at 15.000 to the £ was very good value for a chart album.

The philosophy behind it was simple. Normal Polish salaries couldn't afford to pay the full price for records and, indeed, "proper" tapes.

There seemed to be big organisations throughout Eastern Europe pirating these records and selling them with full colour sleeves and track listings at more affordable prices.

The only record shop in Zakopane was in a sort of log cabin and also sold badges and posters. Guns & Roses and Bon Jovi seemed to be the flavours of the month at the time.

Tapes were also sold in "Fancy Goods" shops, along with clothes and perfume and also from people with stalls out in the streets who had a tape player so that you could listen before you bought.

One of the main attractions of these tapes, cheapness apart, was that sometimes the sleeve design was different from that of the original. I got, for example, a copy of Chris Rea's 1990 album "Auberge" bearing a very 1970's picture of the artist.

Also, a copy of the soundtrack from the film "Dirty Dancing" has the song "Take My Breath Away" from "Top Gun" at the end of the second side to fill the rest of the tape up.

Tea and Cards

The next evening we were formally invited to "visit" the Polish girls next door.

We learnt that they were not, as it had seemed, one big family but two separate groups - one consisting of the woman, her son and her father and the other consisting of the three girls. The mother knew one of the girls from back home and insisted on talking with them a lot, thus creating the false impression that they were all together.

Their room was a lot bigger than ours with three beds around the walls and a dining table and chairs by the glass doors which opened out onto the balcony that encircled the top floor, as did ours.

We were offered a cup of tea which was served in typical Polish fashion in a clear glass. This tea was different however, in so much as it was a type of herbal tea and all the leaves and twigs etc remained in the bottom of the cup whilst one drank it. It was quite pleasant and soul-cleansing but little bits kept getting stuck in the teeth.

We were formally introduced to the gang:

Jola was 26 years old, liked walking in the mountains, lived in Warsaw (written Warszawa in Polish) and worked for the Polish Telephone Company as an International Operator because of her excellent English.

Maryla (also known as Marylka - Polish people put "ka" on the end of names for diminutive) was 28 years old and worked as a hospital technician in Warsaw.

Her English was good (a lot better than my Polish!) but with a slightly stilted accent and usage.

She was the poetic member of the group, was a bit tweedy, and had long dark blond hair and wore glasses.

The third member of the trio was Ella - short for Elisabeth, or at least whatever the Polish version of Elisabeth was - and may have been a little younger than the other two.

She bore an amazing resemblance to someone that I remembered from school (which stood her in bad stead straight away...!).

She purported not to speak any English but claimed to speak a little German, although communications broke down rather abruptly whenever conversation was induced. She worked at the hospital with Maryla.

The evening was spent talking, drinking cups of tea and learning a card game called "Hearts", the exact nature of which escapes me, other than the fact that you won points for hearts and must not get caught holding the queen of spades.

It became apparent from the plates and cutlery in little piles around the room that the girls were staying in the hotel on a self-catering basis and that our little jaunt down the road to the big hotel for meals was a little luxury afforded us by the holiday company.

Auschwitz

We had passed close by the town of Oswiencim on our original journey to Zakopane. I had noticed it on the roadsigns, having previously read up on the topic and knowing what to look for.

The weather was fine, although overcast - perfectly illustrating the mood for a visit to the place where thousands were murdered.

Upon arrival we were met by a local guide who was going to show us around. He had dark hair, glasses, was probably early 40's and wore a grey raincoat. His English was good, although heavily accented.

He gave a brief rundown of the history of the place before ushering us into a small cinema.

We were shown a black & white film that had been shot by the allies a few days after the liberation of the camp.

The main theme of the film was basically piles of unburied skeletal corpses and bulging eyed emaciated survivors. It was very much less watered down in content than most TV documentaries that had previously been seen of this subject but, in some respects, the impact was lessened because of the prior exposure.

Following the film show, we emerged in solemn mood and were taken to the gates of the main Auschwitz camp. There were tall electrified barbed wire fences around the perimeter and many tall green trees which belied the true nature of what had happened there.

The large double gates were open and above the opening the infamous words "Arbeit Macht Frei" greeted inmates and visitors alike.

The camp had been originally been built as a regular barracks for the Polish army and was, consequently, already in existence when the Nazis arrived. The majority of the buildings were built in blocks and rows, like any army barracks and, to be perfectly honest, didn't look particularly evil or threatening.

Large lively trees lined many of the roadways between the blocks and we were informed that they had actually been planted as seedlings by the prisoners some 50 years beforehand. Certainly, without the trees the place would have looked a lot more gloomy.

The blocks were numbered and the sequence followed a type of exhibition which told the story of the camp and the people who passed through it.

The most stirring parts of the exhibition, in my opinion, were the huge glass cases containing the personal effects of the dead prisoners: glasses, shoes, brushes, even women's hair had been cut from their heads to be recycled by their profiteering captors.

One particularly touching exhibit was the huge mountain of suitcases and baggage. Each one had the family's name and a reference number painted on.

The really sad thing was that the families had been told that they were going to be resettled elsewhere in the East and had prepared their bags with this in mind. In reality, they probably never even saw them again.

Our guide took us round all the main points of interest around the camp. We saw the building which housed the medical centre where the infamous Josef Mengele carried out his terrible experiments.

We saw the punishment blocks and the execution wall where people were tethered and shot. Interestingly enough, the prison blocks on either side of this yard had their windows covered over so that the prisoners couldn't look out upon the executions. Considering the very nature of the camp, this seemed to me a little strange.

We were walked through a gas chamber and, unlike the poor thousands who perished there, were afforded the luxury of emerging on the other side still alive. Being perfectly honest, in the cold light of day in the autumn of 1990, the gas chamber didn't look to be all that horrific - basically a concrete structure with ceiling around 2.5m high, not looking too dissimilar to a modern-day underground car park.

We saw the long metal rail, around 3m from the ground, from which 5 people (or was it 7....) were once hanged at the same time.

Once again, although unpleasant for those present at the time, in comparison to what else was going on at that time, this didn't seem to be anything major.

From here we reboarded the bus and were driven a Km or so down the road to Brzinzka, better known as Birkenau.

This was the extra camp that the Nazis had built to cope with the ever growing numbers of prisoners arriving from all over Europe.

In my own opinion, this was a much more depressing and haunting place than the Auschwitz camp.

It was a large field with barbed wire around it and had a large gatehouse overlooking the main entrance. From this tower you could see the traces of the railway tracks and the sidings where the prisoners disembarked and were selected for death, experimentation or forced labour.

A few rows of the wooden prison huts remained.

Krakow

The day trip to Poland's city of art and culture was most anticipated by all concerned. We were deposited by the banks of the Vistula river, overlooked by the daunting walls of Wawel castle.

The first port of call was the castle itself which was accessed via a curved, sloping walkway up the hill. This pathway was lined, as were most around popular attractions, by people selling souvenirs etc.

At the summit, we were met by our guide for the tour who was a short, blonde lady of pleasant demure, probably in her early thirties. Her English was very good but was ruined by awful Americanised pronunciation of some words, none the least "Crar-caww".

The fine detail of the tour of Wawel castle and cathedral is probably best handled in a specially dedicated tome. Suffice it to say, it was interesting from a historical point of view and the weather was pleasantly warm and sunny.

From there, we were led through the old Jewish quarter, given statistics of pre-and post war population figures etc and then taken to St Mary's Basilica (Bazylika Mariacka) a large church in the town centre.

This church was huge inside, all black and gold and had a huge, impressive fresco over the altar.

Back outside we were taken down an alley way to hear the ceremony of the lone piper played from the top of the tower. This is performed every day to commemorate the actions of a young piper who warned the city of an approaching invasion force thus saving them from defeat. The piper continued to play until he was hit by an attacker's arrow and was killed.

The modern day piper now plays the tune up to the point where the original piper was killed and then stops. The poignant ensuing silence bearing memory to the heroism of the fallen saviour of the city.

Our guide left us at this point. One of our number decided it would be nice to show appreciation by giving her a tip in the form of a rolled up Polish banknote concealed in a handshake which she reluctantly accepted in a state of mild embarrassment. As she attempted to escape, some of the others thought that it was a good idea and began opening purses and also proffering "loaded handshakes". Seeing the increased unease of the young lady at this, I chose to assist her by not offering her any more money.

We were then taken to the main market square (the largest in Europe, apparently) by our holiday guide and granted a few hours at leisure to walk around the city.

On our walk around Krakow, we ended up in the company of guy from Liverpool who was on his own on the trip. I don't remember his name and he was pleasant enough in small doses.

The main incumbent of the market square is the Cloth Hall - a long narrow Gothic looking building so called because it was where the cloth merchants used to gather to sell their wares. It is still used as a market hall but no longer purely for cloth, although there were some beautifully weaved carpets and cloths on sale. There were many stalls selling jewellery or other trinkets and fancy goods.

The beautiful cloudless sky had now turned to a heavy grey and rain was threatening. We decided to go and find somewhere to get something to eat.

As we stood looking around for an eatery, we were passed by the "unofficial tour" which was some of the others from the hotel who had discovered that it was possible to take the normal Polish service bus from Zakopane to Krakow for about 80p (as opposed to the £7 that we had paid, thinking it to be quite good at the time....). They obviously had to forego the guided tour but had been recompensed

Across the square from the big church was a rather large and grandiose looking restaurant. Inside was somewhat shabby and run down but quaint enough for us to want to stay. The menus were in an elegant maroon leather binder with gold lettering and contained a wonderful and extensive list of things on offer, with translations into English, French and German.

I immediately set about amusing myself looking for inaccuracies in the translations between the languages, of which there were many but nothing worthy of note.

It soon became apparent that here, as with many a grandiose looking establishment in the emerging economies of the Eastern Bloc, what was listed on the menu and what was actually available did not exactly match. In fact, only the occasional item with a price next to it on the page could be ordered - amounting to some 25% of the total menu.

The meal was nothing special, in fact, I can't even remember what we ordered now, although I do recall it was washed down with some unexciting Eastern European cola which was too warm.

We departed the restaurant and decided to have a walk around the historical town centre before the rain come down. All hopes of buying a cheap umbrella were dashed as they were all designer-expensive.

The Liverpudlian bought a Pink Floyd tape from a roadside vendor (the album with the ray of light being refracted through the prism).

Graham bought Bob Marley's greatest hits and I decided to be alternative and bought Madonna's "I'm Breathless" - more for it's unusual cover design (different from the "official" one) than anything else.

There were a lot of building works going on and it made it difficult to appreciate the true beauty of many of the obscured buildings. It was approaching time to go back to the bus so we set off at a slow march back towards the castle car park.

Milk Bar Evening

One evening we were invited out by the Polish girls to the "Bar Mleceny" (milk bar) in the town centre which served coffee, soft drinks, snacks etc. Although the days were quite warm and pleasant, the nights were getting very cold.

Walking along the dark streets of Zakopane, illuminated by the odd white street light was quite a weird, almost fairytale, sensation.

The air was crisp and icy and the mountain sky clear and still. A bright moon beamed down to light our path. The roads were free from traffic but many people seemed to be walking that evening and there was a real holiday atmosphere about the place.

We were all wrapped up in warm winter clothing (strange when you consider I was on Summer holiday - most people go to Spain, or Greece or somewhere with a hot sunny beach...) and we strung out across the width of the road - Jola, Marryla, Ella, Graham and myself chatting about the events of the day, the weather etc. As keen as ever to pick up the local language, I kept pressing them to teach me simple words in Polish, for instance hot and cold to describe the weather etc.

We arrived at the milk bar in the town centre to find that it was still open, whereas it hadn't been the night we arrived. Obviously there was some sort of system known only to the locals that we were ignorant of.

There was a bit of a queue inside which led along a sort of a self service counter à la Littlewoods cafeteria which had many empty compartments and a few un-appetising looking cakes and pieces of fruit.

It was suggested that we take an ice-cream cocktail (made up of a mixture of different ice-creams and some fruit). For drinks we were offered "juice". We enquired what sort of juice and were told "just juice....". It turned out to be some sort of longlife orange or pineapple or something, I think.

The girls all had something similar and, being the rich westerner, I thought that I should pay the bill. As we approached the till at the end of the counter, I took a Zl 50.000 from my wallet and waved it about but was totally ignored by Jola, who obviously wasn't as impressed as I thought she'd be. She paid the bill herself.

It was quite an interesting evening - we just talked about things in general. One interesting point was when Maryla suddenly announced that she didn't like Margaret Thatcher, who was a very bad person.

This seemed to go against much of what everyone else in the world (bar the British) thought about Thatcher - good, strong leader etc and further clarification was sought.

Apparently Margaret Thatcher was thought of as being a bad person because there was a poor man in prison and she let him die. The Communist Polish media of the day had obviously chosen not to mention that this poor man in prison was, in fact, Bobby Sands - a convicted IRA terrorist and that he died whilst on a self imposed hunger strike.

We spent a few moments explaining some of the actions of this victimised group of poor freedom fighters to these people who had only ever heard the censored version. It just goes to show how those in power can control what people think and believe....

Restaurant Evening

Still feeling somewhat embarrassed by having the Polish girls pay for us in the Milk Bar, we decided to reciprocate by taking them out somewhere really swish.

It was decided that we would go to the restaurant in the Orbis hotel which was, after all, the swishest place in town and we met the girls on the landing in the Villas Venus at some pre-arranged time.

I had tried to maintain some dress sense for the occasion and had put on my only proper shirt and pair of decent trousers and proper shoes that I had packed (I knew they'd come in handy sometime during the trip!).

Unfortunately, as we walked out of the hotel, we came across the Liverpudlian standing on the pavement just outside the hotel gate, obviously waiting for us. I said hello as we passed, in the vain hope that he was really waiting for someone else. This was not to be, however, as he started following and attempting to make conversation.

In an attempt to be charitable to a fellow traveller who was on his own in a strange land, I said that we were going into town and, whilst not really wanting to tell him to go away, I remained reserved in giving out an invitation to join us. He made it even more difficult by saying "if you want me to go, just say so..."

So, he insisted on following us and trying to suggest sharing out the 3 girls between the 3 of us, by running behind the group, trying to keep up and saying things like "which one do you want then, eh, eh?".

I shudder even now to think what his opinion of myself and my companions had been.

Whilst attempting to be friendly with him, I tried to avoid the topic of the girls and made a particular effort not to introduce him to any of them as we may not have rid ourselves of him ever again for the whole trip.

On reflection, perhaps I should have introduced him to Ella as it's doubtful that he spoke any German or Polish

Luckily, fortune played into our hands as, when we arrived at the restaurant, he announced that, as he had already eaten, he didn't want to go up with us. I "tried" to get him to change his mind but he insisted that he would wait in the cafe downstairs until we had finished eating.

We climbed up the wide and elegant spiralling staircase which led to the restaurant above.

It was an amazing place - wooden panelled walls with elaborate decoration, high decorated ceiling, plush deep red carpets and curtains and very impressive heavy oak tables and chairs.

We were shown to our table, a huge table set for six, in the middle of the room by a spotless, waistcoated waiter.

The menus came in large, impressive covers, as you would expect in such a place. One of the girls pointed out that they had also eaten a while earlier and that maybe they could just have an ice cream. This was agreeable to me as I was supposed to be paying for the thing so we decided to order a selection from the dessert menu.

The waiter wasn't so keen on the idea and practically said that we couldn't just have ice cream. Jola negotiated with him for a few moments in fluent Polish and he agreed to take our order on the condition that we had coffee afterwards, which we agreed.

The evening passed very quickly as we talked the night away and, before we knew it, we were the only people left in the restaurant and the waiter was hovering around waiting for us to finish.

An ice cream and coffee could obviously take a deceptively long time to consume, in the right company....!

By the time we had emerged from the restaurant, the Liverpudlian had got fed up and left – and he didn't speak to us for the rest of the trip.

PB on the balcony outside our room at the Villa Venus in Zakopane 1990.

At the top of the Ski lift on Gubałówka

PB in the High Tatra Mountains near Zakopane, September 1990

PB at Wawel Castle in Krakow, September 1990

River Trip Through The Dunajec Gorge

The raft trip down the Dunajec river (pronounced Dunayets) turned out to be a lot different than I had imagined. The brochure had mentioned it and the photo they showed made it look like something out of the "Famous Five".

The day had started off badly. I had to change some money at the Villa Venus and, knowing that the bus would call back there prior to departure, we both trotted on back there on foot after breakfast to be at the front of the exchange queue.

This backfired however as when we went to get on the bus, it became apparent that there weren't enough seats for everybody who had wanted to go. Graham ended up sitting next to an old woman and I found myself sitting on the step in a gangway towards the rear of the bus for the whole of the journey.

I passed the time craning my neck to look out of the window and listening to the mindless prattling of those around me. As we drove higher into the mountains the scenery became more and more breathtaking until you could see the high, snow covered peaks rearing up in the near distance.

We arrived at our destination and disembarked to be led down some very wide sand coloured steps down to the side of the river. We were informed that the river formed part of the Polish border and that the other bank was, in fact, Czechoslovakia.

We spent a large part of the boat trip wondering whether the ducks that we passed on the river were Polish or Czech....

The rafts weren't, as I had imagined, a flat bed of logs trapped together which we had to balance upon, but long, narrow boats made of wood with 3 rows of seats. Each raft/boat had a platform at each end for the driver to stand. He used a long oar cum pole (no pun intended...) to steer the boat through the water.

Each boat carried about 10 people, depending on how big you were, and so our group took up 5 or six boats -some more cramped than others.

Our boat was one of the last ones to leave and was therefore less cramped and a lot more comfortable than the earlier ones where people had crowded on board in their excitement.

There were no lifejackets or safety helmets issued so I assumed that rumours about rocks and rapids down river had been somewhat exaggerated.

Our boat was driven, as were most of them, by an elderly gent , his face and hands hardened and tanned from years of outdoor work, wearing a sort of uniform consisting waistcoat and hat - presumably meant to be some sort of local costume. Each driver also had an assistant on board - in our case, a young lad - in case he became incapacitated for any reason.

The sun was bright and very warm, despite that fact that it was the middle of September and we were high in the mountains. I was beginning to wish that I had left my jacket in the car until we passed through the shade cast over the water by a high rock face above us. It suddenly felt so cold that I wished I had brought another jumper!

The boat trip followed the course of the river as it flowed downhill (obviously...) and passed through some of the most beautiful scenery that I have ever seen. The sun was shining bright, as already mentioned, and the sky was clear and blue which made the hills and the fields look all the prettier.

The trees that lined the river on both sides were just beginning to enter their autumnal state and already some of the leaves were turning gorgeous reds and golds.

The river snaked through the mountains giving views of wonderful rock formations that couldn't be seen from the road. For some of the way the river was banked by a forest on the Czech side which marked the edge of a national park.

Further along was a landing stage for river rafts on the Czech side with boats moored up.

They had the colours of the Czech flag painted on the side to identify them, as did the Polish boats the Polish flag.

As we approached some flatter terrain midway through the trip, the river ran past a little village. It wasn't anything special although it had a huge church with a large yellow roof which looked rather unusual, even more so as it seemed perfectly in tune with the wild yellow flowers that were abundant throughout the fields on each side.

Our raft driver broke his monk-like silence at this point and using my skant knowledge of Russian, we managed to work out that he actually lived in that village.

Although enjoyable as a trip for the experience of river travel and the beauty of the scenery, it began to get a little cold as we approached the end and I was quite happy to be able to move again. Also, the floor of the boat had become awash with the spray from the occasional wavelet that had lapped over the side.

We said our goodbyes to the oarsmen and rushed back to the bus to dry out and warm up a little.

Gentleman in Villa Venus / Telephoning In Poland

He was the night porter at the guest house where we stayed and was tall and dark. Facially, he looked very similar to Ashraf Kharim - the second token Asian (long since forgotten) in EastEnders.

He was at the desk when I decided to phone home one evening. I used my four words of Polish and managed to indicate that I wanted to use the phone and wrote down the number.

He rang the operator and put down the phone. We waited.

And waited.

And waited.

As we waited, I tried to strike up some friendly conversation. Unfortunately, he didn't speak any English, or French, or German, or Italian, or Spanish and I soon found out that four words in Polish and a smattering or Russian (which everyone in Poland under the age of 50 learnt at school but hates to use..) weren't much use in this department so we ended up waiting in polite silence.

The call took almost an hour to come through. A similar experience a day or so later when Graham tried to make a call led me to deduce that this was a standard length of waiting time, a fact that I intended to use to my advantage in the future when planning around my activities.

This, however, backfired on me one morning when the telephone call took considerably less time to come through than I had expected.

Word was sent upstairs that my connection was ready (quicker that I had anticipated) and I ended up standing in the hotel reception area by the open main door looking out onto the street wearing only my shorts and dripping wet from a half taken shower.....

After I had finished my call (back to the original evening one, now...)

Ashraf rang back to the operator to find out the cost, which came to Zl 75.000. This was somewhat more than I expected it to come to but at approx £5 wasn't the end of the world. The only problem was that I didn't have enough Polish currency to pay for the call there and then.

I attempted to explain that I'd change some money the next day and settle up later but this didn't seem to register with him.

He just kept pointing at the piece of paper where he had written Zl 75.000 and shrugging his shoulders. English currency didn't appear to be greatly attractive either.

It looked as if we were going to be there all night as he seemed very reluctant for me to leave the reception area without paying my phone bill - despite the fact that I was going to be staying there for another week yet - until, as luck would have it, one of the Polish girls - Ella, I think it was, not the best choice from a communication point of view - came through the door and started off upstairs.

I managed to get her attention and via bits of English, German and manual gesticulations which bemused the now growing crowd of onlookers she eventually understood what I wanted her to do and she explained to the night porter that I would pay up the next morning.

He finally seemed satisfied with this, although I couldn't help thinking that he probably knew what I was trying to say all along.

Author's Note: I spent the rest of my holiday believing that Poland had a very backward communication system and that all international calls had to be patched through the operator, taking an hour or so each time. It was only during a subsequent visit to Poland that I discovered that direct dialling was also possible and, in fact, normal and that the hotel people only used the operator to be able to get the unitary charge of the call.

The Last Day: Barbecue #2, Shopping and Cards

During the previous week or so we had learnt enough about prices in Zakopane to realise that, despite the apparent cheapness of the excursions and treats by Western standards, our tour organisers were still making quite a lot of money from us. Having already been present at the previous week's barbecue and eaten for nothing, I didn't really fancy the idea of stumping up a colossal £ 3.50 for our farewell do.

The thought of missing out on the horse-drawn coach around the town and surrounding woodland wasn't sufficient to deter me from coming up with a cunning plan.

It had been raining for most of the day and our hill-walking Polish friends had had to confine themselves to the hotel.

This turned out to be quite useful as, when I mentioned my plans for the barbecue that evening, Maryla offered to come into town and assist with the shopping.

We braved the intermittent but very heavy afternoon showers and walked the short distance into town along the green tree and hedge lined streets.

At last we were equipped to communicate on level terms with the local merchants and not have to resort to sign language, mumblings from phrase books and the odd word in German or Russian to try and ask about something.

We made the most of this and did a little souvenir and present shopping - sampling after shaves and perfumes - with the assistance of our "guidka" for the afternoon.

After a while, and with the time knocking on towards closing time, we turned out attention to the main reason for the outing. We were going to buy our own meat and drinks and take them along to the barbecue, effectively having an evening out on the cheap.

We ended up in a large grocer's cum supermarket which was absolutely full of people. There was no self service and everyone queued up at various points along a long counter to be served by fierce looking assistants. The main items being purchased appeared to be vegetables and drinks.

The bizarre thing here was that you didn't just queue and buy things. You had to queue up at, say, the meat counter and then tell the shop assistant there what you wanted. She'd cut it and weigh it, put in a bag and write the price on the bag.

She then gave you a ticket with the price on and you had to go and pay at a separate cashier's window who then gave you a receipt for the amount that you had paid and you could then go back and pick up your meat.

You had to do this for each separate counter – which was incredibly time consuming.

The locals, obviously, had this off to tee and made all their selections first and then queued for the cashier's window last.

As we were learning all this as we went along, it took us bit longer to get ourselves sorted out – but it was all part of the "being on holiday" / exotic shopping experience so we didn't really mind.

Luckily, we had Maryla there to guide us through it all, otherwise we would never have got anywhere.

So, after a huge amount of patient queuing at these various counters, we managed to come away with a couple of hefty lengths of Polish sausage for the princely sum of Zl 30.000 - or £2 in English money.

We then queued at the, by now, very busy drinks counter and bought two bottles of beer for ourselves, colas and lemons for Maryla and Ella and tonic water for Jola.

As it turned out, we had made the right decision over the horse-drawn carriage ride as it absolutely poured with rain for the whole evening - particularly around the time of the ride.

It's the sort of thing that would probably have been very nice on a light summery evening – or even a clear crisp frosty moonlit night – but not in the gloom in the pouring rain

So, we waited until the convoy of little carts arrived outside the Villa Venus and the dripping tourists began congregating in the barn and then we gathered up the sausages, the drink and the girls and began to mingle.

During the evening we had a couple of conversations with the other tourists. Somebody called out to us across the barn to ask if we had missed the horse and cart ride because he hadn't seen us there.

We went over and explained our fiendish plot to get an evening out on the cheap, which he found quite ingenious. We hadn't missed much, anyway, as it had been pitch dark and pouring with rain.

One of our Polish friends asked about the difference between the United Kingdom, Great Britain and the British Isles. Although I could probably have explained the difference with a lot of huffing and puffing, I decided to put the question to our "map expert", ie. the well spoken man with the cockney wife.

He took up the matter with great resolve. Unfortunately, I had to go and tend to our sausages which were in danger of being incinerated on the barbecue and so never did hear the final answer.

As the evening wore on, our interest in socialising with our fellow coach travellers began to wane, particularly in the knowledge that we would soon be spending some 36 hours crammed inside a bus with them all.

We were invited back to the Polish girls' room to play cards for a while and to get some more of that herbal tea stuck between our teeth.

Autumn 1990: Nordic No-Go

You can probably guess from the title here that my next little story doesn't really have a "happy ever after" sort of ending - but it is still worth an airing.

After I had got back from my holiday in Poland with Mr Hill in September 1990, I still had that vague "back to school" feeling.

There was a light autumn feel in the air and in the quality of the light. I had the urge to go out and buy a new uniform and shoes for school and get a new bag for the new term and fill it with a load of pens and pencils.

I always feel that way every September even though I haven't been at school or university for years now – but there's still that vague "new beginnings" feel that you can't just shake off.

Anyway, full of new beginnings feelings, I was walking home from work at Baker Perkins on Westfield Road, down Priory Road, to my bachelor pad on Williamson Avenue – which, according to "Google Maps" is 0.5 miles away, and used to take me between 5 and 10 minutes, depending on how much of a rush I was in.

As was my wont, I often used to drop into one of the shops on Mayors Walk on the way home to get something for tea. Back in those days – being a young free and single lad in his early 20s - I wasn't very well organised with catering and didn't do big weekly shops and have things lined up for planned meals as I might do now.

So I went into the shop and was looking for something like a packet of Vesta Chow Mein or the similar packet curries they used to do.

Yes, I know that sounds quite revolting now but, back when I was little, it felt like real exotic cuisine – and it was easy to cook for somebody like me who had enough trouble boiling an egg.

Pot Noodles also fell into that category – as did the really lazy option of just pigging out on large packets of crisps and biscuits...

Well, I couldn't find the thing I wanted on the shelves but there was a nice girl stacking tins just a bit further along so I asked her and she went and got me one from round the back.

She was very pleasant, very polite – a bit timid - and quite nice looking in a "I'm at work, wearing a dowdy overall – what do you expect...?" sort of way and she gave me a nice smile.

I didn't remember seeing her there before – although I had been away for two weeks, of course, and couldn't tell whether she had just started working there, or was just doing different hours or what.

I saw her in the shop a few more times and I managed to work out that she worked all day on Saturdays and a couple of evenings - and that screamed out to me: "College Girl"!

That would explain why she was a bit shy – because she'd only been doing it since the new term started at the Tech College in September and working in a shop and dealing with customers wasn't really her thing – she was more academic and was just doing it to help support her studies.

Now, Ironside – that's the American TV detective, not the British WW2 general - once said in an episode of, well, "Ironside", actually: "if there's something you feel you GOTTA do, then you better go and do it" (or, at least, words to that effect, anyway...).

And, interestingly enough, Lucy expressed the self same sentiment to me very recently as well – albeit on a completely different subject matter. So, having tenuously been given retrospective approbation by my wife to pursue this historical bird some 30 years earlier, this is what I did:

I went into the shop one day, bought something and asked the girl on the checkout counter what the other girl's name, was. With an odd smirk, she told me that her name was "C---".

Her name wasn't actually "Sea Dash Dash Dash", by the way -not like the guy in NCIS Los Angeles whose first name really is "G".

I'm just being gentlemanly and discrete here so as not to embarrass the poor girl in case this book becomes a worldwide best seller.

(I learnt later, by the way – much to my huge embarrassment - that this other girl was actually C---'s older sister...)

Armed with this information, I went to a florists in town a few days later and order a small bunch of flowers – nothing too expensive or ostentatious as I couldn't be sure that they would

a) get delivered at all and
b) what the reception might be,

so it was just a token posy of some sort - to be dropped off at the shop on a day that I knew C--- would be working, and then left things alone to develop.

I avoided the shop for a few days, just to leave time for the dust to settle, and had to rely on the chip shop and the Chinese take away for sustenance in the meantime.

Then in true "Katy" literary style, this is what I did next:

I took one of my swish works business cards that we had been given for going to the Drupa exhibition in Germany earlier in the year, wrote my home phone number on the back and took the plunge.

I marched into the shop to where C--- was filling some shelves – and asked if she had got her flowers. She said she had – but I didn't think she seemed QUITE as surprised to find out they had been from ME as I might have expected, although I was too nervous to worry about that at that particular moment.

I handed her my card saying if she'd like to meet up and "do something some time" to give me a ring - and then marched straight out again in a huge fluster.

If anybody had seen my exit, they might have reasonably thought that I was a fleeing shoplifter – and I rushed home in a mad panic of nerves.

I seem to think that this might have been on a Tuesday and nothing happened until the Thursday as I avoided the shop like the plague.

I remember this next bit quite distinctly. It's funny how some relatively trivial things stick in your mind and other more important things can get forgotten about over time.

Anyway, I was at home in my Bachelor Pad watching Top of the Pops and the phone rang - it was C---.

She said something along the lines of thank you for the kind invitation, she would like to meet up and do something - and we arranged to go to the cinema on the Saturday evening.

Interestingly enough, Maria McKee was live on TOTP performing her theme song from the new Tom Cruise film "Days Of Thunder" just at the time that I was talking to C--- on the phone and, as a result, if ever I hear that piece of music, it always takes me right back to that moment.

They recently arrived at covering that particular era on the re-runs of TOTP that they show now on BBC4 and, when I saw that live clip being played again, for a very brief moment I was right back there as a nervous 23 year old lad in my Bachelor Pad. It's very unnerving – but I AM a very sensitive chap.

So the evening arrived and I drove round to C---'s house and knocked nervously on the door. Luckily it was she herself personally in person who answered and not some enraged parent, so that was a good start but I was given a very close once over by her mum after I had been invited in.

We went and had a pizza before the film.

I can't remember where we actually went now but it must have been on the same leisure / retail park as the cinema complex as we parked just outside and didn't have to walk every far.

We had a nice chat over the meal and she told me that her name was actually spelt K--- – not C---, and that the flowers had arrived at the shop on a day when she wasn't working.

She then told me it had been her sister who I had originally asked about her (which explained the comical smirk...) and that she had rushed home from the shop in great excitement to tell her that some flowers had been delivered for her.

We went along to the cinema next and, while I had a couple of films in mind that it might be nice to see, K--- didn't want to see either of those, which was fine by me. I figured that she had probably already seen them with some of her college chums and was too polite to say, so we saw something else instead.

(Did you notice what I just did there? Staying true to the events of the timeline as it actually happened, I altered the spelling of C--- to K--- in the exact order of my finding out about it...! Clever, eh..?)

In the end we settled on the film "Presumed Innocent" starring Harrison Ford and Greta Scacchi, which was a murder mystery with lots of twists and turns in the plot.

It is actually a very good film but tends to get overshadowed by Harrison Ford's other blockbusters like Indiana Jones, Star Wars and The Fugitive etc.

There was time for a quick drink after the film but K--- didn't want to go to the pub so I dropped her off back home.

I went round to hers one evening the following week (by prior arrangement) and she answered the door and said that she needed to talk to me, so should we take walk...?

My heart sank at this point as I thought I was about to be given the old "heave-ho", which was a shame as I thought the cinema evening had gone rather well.

But no – she said she had really enjoyed the evening out as well and that it would be nice to do other things together. But there was SOMETHING that I ought to be aware of.

My mind raced. Was she a Jehova's Witness...? Oh gawd, not again - surely not! How come I could only ever manage to hit on Jehova's Witnesses...? NO – it wasn't that.

Was she, in fact, gay – and didn't really like boys - and had only gone out with me out of pity...? NO – it wasn't that either.

Did she, then, have a terrible disease of some sort? Perhaps even one that was easily transmittable while sharing pizza and going to the cinema? PHEW – Nor that.

However, it did turn out that the rather convenient back-story that I had single-handedly concocted in my mind to explain K---'s domestic and academic circumstances was not entirely accurate.

Instead of being an 18 year old business / professional / technical student at Tech College, she was actually a 16 year old A Level student at Sixth Form College!

OOOOPS!

Oddly enough, I found this revelation more reassuring than annoying. It immediately explained why she hadn't been keen to see the two 18 Certificate films that I had suggested at the pictures and also why she didn't want to go for a drink afterwards.

Most 16 or 17 years olds of my acquaintance in the past – me included – had always been desperate to go and see films that they were not old enough to be able to watch (that's in the pre-internet days, of course, when things weren't so easy to access as they are now) and also to go out boozing at every opportunity.

So I respected her very much for sticking to the rules and not taking advantage of being out with me to get up to things she shouldn't have done.

I said that her age didn't especially phase me as we seemed to get on well together but, bearing it in mind, I'd make sure we didn't go out late anywhere and only at weekends when it wouldn't affect her studies too much.

We both seemed satisfied with the outcome of this tête à tête and I took her back home again.

Over the following weeks, we did quite a few nice things together.

- We went and saw the Patrick Swayze / Demi Moore film "Ghost" at the pictures
- We went to a sophisticated party at Anne Castellano – my colleague from work's - house
- We went to see the big bonfire night firework display at Ferry Meadows
- And we went to my mum and dad's to have tea once as well.

However, in the background to all this jollity, something was definitely going on.

I was aware that her mother wasn't over keen on me due to the age difference. There didn't appear to be a father on the scene and I never asked why. If anything, I was just privately happy that it meant there were fewer parents in situ to disapprove of me.

But since the first meeting with the mother - when she had reportedly said afterwards: "Phew - he's nice. I could go for him myself..." – I hardly ever saw her, which a shame as it meant that she didn't have the opportunity get to know me and see how nice I really was.

So I got the impression that K--- was probably getting hassle at home about me and one Sunday afternoon when I went round, she told me that she didn't want to see me anymore.

I knew that it was nothing that I had done as I had always been ultra-correct and hadn't done anything that could in the least be construed as negative.

Thus, I feared it must be due to pressure on the home front and, bearing in mind her age and situation, there wasn't much that could be done, so she had to go along with it.

Once again, although I was obviously disappointed, I respected her greatly for at least telling me to my face. She could just as easily have told me over the phone or sent me a note.

So, time for another change.

Thus, having just been unceremoniously dumped by a 16 year old, I decided to give up the Bachelor Pad – in spite of its handiness for getting to work – and move back in with my parents for a while in order to save some pennies and regroup.

*****

I saw K--- once more - over a year later on the town bridge in Peterborough. I seem to think that the twice yearly fun fair was on (once in spring and once in autumn) and I was walking into town on the Friday night with some of the lads to go for a few post-amusement drinks, and she was coming in the other direction towards the Fair Meadow with some of her mates.

We said slightly embarrassed "hello"s - as you do in that sort of situation - and stepped to one side to exchange a quiet word. I had previously noticed in the local paper that she had passed whatever exams it was that she had been studying for, so congratulated her on that and – aside, from establishing that she was OK in general - that was about it really, and we all wended off on our respective ways.

The walk into central Warsaw from Jola's flat. You can see in the distance the silhouette of the much maligned "Palace of Culture and Science" which everybody hated because the Russians built it. (Author's Photo)

April / May 1991: Polish Pursuits - Visit To Warsaw

I have to admit that I did fancy Jola but I imagine that everybody else who ever met her did as well so she was probably immune to it.

Certainly the whole time we were together - meeting up in Poland in 1990 and 91 and then in England in 92 & 93 - she never once gave the slightest hint of being interested in me as anything other than a friend but I was perfectly happy with that.

Jola worked for the Polish Telecom company in Warsaw and, as she spoke good English, she was an operator on the international exchange. She particularly liked working the nightshift because that meant there were no managers about and she could do what she wanted.

So, when it was a quiet night with few international calls to worry about, she used to ring me at home and we'd have long chats at the Polish Telecom's expense.

We'd just natter about everyday things, she'd teach me a few Polish words and phrases and I'd also help her with her English.

If she had come across something during the course of the week that she didn't understand, I'd explain it to her and, once we had run out of things to talk about, I'd give her little pronunciation exercises to practice.

What I would do is pick out pairs of words that sound similar and which foreigners often have trouble getting right in English and I'd get her to repeat them over and over again.

So we'd have "teeth and thief", "poppy and puppy", "sheep and ship" and other things like that and she'd say them over and over until I was happy that she'd got them right.

I'd never had any teaching or linguistics / phonetics training as such but I could at least hear and explain how words were meant to sound in English and I like to think that she gained some benefit from these little chats.

Leaping ahead somewhat - I was driving up to a roundabout in Preston one day with my later, German girlfriend Hanja, when I had to suddenly slam on the brakes as a car coming round hadn't performed the manoeuvre that I had expected it to.

I probably sighed and muttered something like "jeeez" under my breath and then suddenly from the usually peaceful and passive passenger seat came the words:

"F*cking indicate! For f*ck's sake....!" bellowed towards the windscreen.

Somewhat taken aback, I wondered where she might have come by such unlady-like vocabulary.

I knew that the German education system was supposed to be very good but did they really teach articulate swearing in their English classes....?

I did, however, notice that, over a period of time, her conversation did also gradually become littered with such other useful words as "p*ssheads" and "w*nkers" – and the ubiquitous catch-all German term of "scheisse" was regularly replaced with much more relevant apposite English terms, all with their correct intonation and usage.

So, I can only conclude that - somehow or other - I must have been a very good teacher – if not an especially good role model!

But luckily, I never taught Jola any English swear words and she never asked me about any either – which was good.

Well, after several months of exchanging letters and chatting on the phone, I was invited to go and visit Jola in Warsaw and this visit took place at the end of April 1991.

The flight over to Warsaw was quite memorable – albeit not for the best of reasons.

It left quite early in the morning from Heathrow and I had to get the first train of the day from Peterborough to make sure I was there in time.

I don't remember how I got to the station but I know I was still half asleep. It was pitch dark – being about 5.30am - and there were only about 3 other people on the entire train, all half asleep as well – but at least I avoided the commuter rush!

The rest of the journey down to the airport is a bit of a blur. I seem to think that I saw Mark Eastwood's dad on the platform at St Neots, waving somebody off but can't really be sure if that was the same trip or not.

The actual flight, I still remember very clearly indeed - as I was petrified the whole time.

It was a Lot Polish Airways flight and the aircraft was a Russian built Tupolev - a similar sort of size to a Boeing 737, I imagine.

Well, having actually flown on some modern British Airways Boeing 737s in previous years – and a very nice Air France flight to Paris on one occasion as well, I found this Tupolev very medieval looking in comparison. They had big mechanical levers on the main doors instead of nifty little buttons and keypads and, having heard horror stories about Russian airliners regularly crashing in Siberia, I was not fully at my ease.

Having been up since some ridiculous time in the morning and having refused to pay £10.00 or whatever it was they wanted for a cooked breakfast in the cafe at the airport, I was quite peckish by now and looking forward to the passengers' meal.

However, this being a Polish plane full of Polish people - plus me – the catering was geared to a Polish clientele and the breakfast dish was some sort of Polish sausages in gravy.

Had it been later in the day, ie lunch time or tea time, and had we not been up in the air - with its associated turbulence, I might very well have liked to try some traditional Polish fare but

a) not for BREAKFAST, and
b) not when I was feeling like sh*t and worried that we were about to crash at any moment.

As it was, the smell of these sausages in gravy just wafted all around the plane and made me feel even sicker than I already did.

I think, in the end, a kind stewardess brought me some coffee and some bread and butter and I made do with that.

We finally arrived in Warsaw – without crashing – and I went through the passport and customs controls, which was a bit daunting.

Don't forget this was outside the EU / EC / Common Market so they were a bit more in your face and stricter than I had been used to in recent years.

But I didn't have any contraband or anything in the least bit suspicious looking so was able to pass through without let or hindrance (like it says in the UK passport) and Jola was waiting for me on the other side of the barrier.

*****

Jola was living in a flat in the Ochota district of central Warsaw. I am led to believe that it was somebody else's flat as I was given strict instructions never to open the door if anybody knocked.

Because she would have to work for some of the time of my visit, she gave me a set of keys and an A to Z of Warsaw - and told me how to get to the main shopping areas.

So I spent a few days out on my own exploring. I stuck to the main streets as I didn't want to wander and get lost, especially as my Polish knowledge was practically non-existent.

On the first day that I was at Jola's, it snowed. The rest of the time it was hot and sunny so it was difficult to know what to wear because I had brought mainly cold weather clothes.

Wilanow with Anna

On my first full day in Warsaw, Jola had to work so she got one of her friends to take me round some of the sights. She was called Anna and, while she didn't speak very good English, her French was pretty good so we spent our time nattering in French as we looked around.

Above: PB outside at Wilanow Place in Warsaw with Anna, April 1991

Below: The Tomb of the Unknown Soldier in Warsaw

She took me to look around the elegant Wilanow Palace – a former home of the Polish kings and often described as the "Polish Versailles".

We also saw the Tomb Of The Unknown Soldier, which had inscriptions of the many campaigns where Polish troops had been involved and was permanently guarded by polish soldiers.

I believe that there is now a separate monument to the Monte Cassino campaign, but that wasn't installed until 1993.

Of the things that I did with Jola during my visit, these were the most memorable:

English Classes

On one of my days there, Jola took me along to the two English classes that she taught – presumably she did this once a week at each location. I don't know much about the Polish school system but these appeared to be private kindergarten establishments in nice leafy neighbourhoods – rather than state schools - and the kiddies were probably aged about 7 or 8.

The classes were only about half an hour each so as not to over-tax the little darlings and she did a mixture of basic conversation, playing games and singing little songs ("I have a car. Broom broom my car").

We had to rush from one straight to the other so I didn't get much of a chance to really see what the places were like.

But it was an interesting morning.

PB next to the Chopin monument in Lazienki Park

Lazienki Park & Chopin Statue

Lazienki Palace – a former royal palace situated in huge decorative grounds which form the basis of the Royal Baths Park - the biggest park in Warsaw.

On the way back from the Lazienki Palace we saw the famous Chopin statue, which is in the park grounds. The original one had been destroyed by the invading Germans in 1939 and this current one was put up in 1946.

Sunday Church Service

On the middle Sunday of my visit to Warsaw, Jola and I went to a church service.

Religion had been frowned upon during the communist period but now that democracy had returned to the country, the churches were full and they actually had to run extra services back to back on a Sunday morning to cater for the number of people who wanted to go.

We went to an upbeat version of the service with singers and guitars which was especially aimed at a younger audience. Even though it was the 3rd or 4th service of the day at that same church, we had to queue to get in and then had to stand at the back as it was so busy.

Needless to say, I didn't understand anything that the priest said but could follow the basic drift of what was going on as I gather that most Christian masses are more or less the same whatever language they are held in.

1st May – Lech Walesa

One day we saw Lech Walesa –the former Solidarity trade union leader who was at the time President Of Poland. I think it might have been 1st May as he was going to some sort of function in an official building. He drew up in a chauffeur driven car and waved to the gathered crowds on his way in. And that was that. Interesting experience though...

The 1st May 1991 was a Wednesday and in Poland it was - and still is - a national bank holiday. Back in the communist times, they used to have grandiose military parades but now people just have the day off and spend time with their families.

That Wednesday afternoon we went to visit Jola's mum in her flat in Warsaw and Jola's brother Piotr was also there.

We sat around and had tea and cake and, as Piotr also spoke very good English, we had a nice chat about all sorts of things.

There was a documentary on the TV about the history of the 1st May military parades and how it had all changed since the fall of the wall.

Piotr and Jola explained to me that, while the parades seemed to be very popular, with crowds of people cheering and waving flags, that was only because everybody was actually forced to go along and watch.

If you didn't have a valid reason for not being at the parade, ie a doctor's certificate or working in a vital job, the police would come round to your house and make you go. And anybody that didn't comply got fined or - in extreme cases - put in prison!

Piotr told me that, in later years, there had been lots of unrest and counter demonstrations on 1st May and that the police used to use tear gas to disperse the protesters.

He showed me where a piece of masonry on the window ledge in their living room had been damaged by a bullet fired from a passing police car one time when he and his mates had been hanging out of the window making rude gestures.

Top: 1ˢᵗ May 1991: You can't see him clearly – but I can assure you that the chap directly under the red stripe on the long hanging Polish flag (that's the dark one if you are viewing in black & white) is Lech Walesa. And he waved at me! And everybody else, obviously...   Above: PB outside Lazienki Palace

PB outside Warszawa Centralna railway station, along with a load of Polish cars.

Above left: Jola in Warsaw Old Town. Above right: PB at the Soviet War Cemetery in Warsaw

Karta jednorazowego wstępu bezpłatna

ZAMEK KRÓLEWSKI W WARSZAWIE
SALE SEJMOWE I KOMNATY DWORSKIE

TRASA I

data

godzina

№ 0097052

*Entry ticket for the Royal Palace in Warsaw - dated 25th April 1991, time 11.50am.
It looks as if the price was Zl 30.000, ie about £2.00*

Royal Palace

The thing I have to say about all of these historic buildings was that they were all very well looked after and fascinating to walk round.

Bearing in mind that the Germans razed most of Warsaw to the ground when they retreated in 1944, everywhere has been remarkably well restored.

They had a system in place where you had to book a specific time in advance to go round the buildings so that they didn't get too many people inside in one go. I suppose if you took pot luck and turned up at a time when there was nobody much else there, you might get in straight away, but we bought our tickets the day before and made sure that we were there for our allotted time the next day.

Also, when you were inside the buildings, you had to wear throw away protective covers over your shoes – like they use on crime scenes in "CSI" – to protect the surface of the floors.

I'm afraid I can't tell you very much detail about the various palaces and houses that we visited now – other than that they were very beautiful and ornate. I had so much information thrown at me about the various kings and Polish history that it was quite a lot to take in.

But I can assure you that, on a nice day, Warsaw can be as beautiful and interesting to visit as any other major city in the world.

Chinese Meal.

One evening, we went and had a meal in a Chinese restaurant as a bit of a special treat. I'm not sure whether it was the first one to open in Warsaw but it was certainly still a rarity at the time that I was there. By now I had become quite accustomed to Chinese food both in England and in France and I had particular dishes that were my favourites.

Unfortunately, none of these appeared to be on the menu at this place and, as far as I could tell, everything was heavily padded out with either cabbage or beetroot.

I fully appreciate that exotic restaurant dishes around the world are designed especially to appeal to the local community where they are being served and that the Chinese food we eat in Peterborough will probably not closely resemble what normal people eat in China on an everyday basis.

So it was completely reasonable that the Chinese food that was being offered at the pioneering exotic restaurants in Poland at this time would give more than just a passing nod to the traditional Eastern European ingredients that people were familiar with.

I have never liked beetroot and didn't used to be overly keen on cabbage either (it depends how it is cooked and what else you have it with). Luckily there was enough sauce and other bits and pieces that I was able to cope with the cabbage element and overall it was a very pleasant meal - if not, in my opinion, overly Chinese-y.

What was slightly odd in this Chinese restaurant was that there did not seem to be any actual Chinese looking people there at all. All the waiting staff were obviously Polish – although the women did try and look the part by wearing Chinese style dresses.

I never saw who was doing the cooking behind the scenes so there could have been some Chinese food experts round the back – but who knows...?

This phenomena isn't restricted to Chinese restaurants in emerging economies in Eastern Europe, by the way. I have been to one in Huntingdon that appeared to be completely staffed by white people as well...

Soviet WW2 Cemetery

One day we went to see the vast Soviet WW2 cemetery in Warsaw. As you might expect, this had huge imposing monuments and statues of Russian soldiers and thousands upon thousands of individual graves.

The interesting thing here was, in place of the Christian cross that you would see on the majority of war graves in the west, these individual plots all had the Soviet star marker instead as religion was not allowed under the communist regime.

Warsaw Zoo

It's a zoo – they had animals. What more can I say? It was a nice warm sunny day and we had a good look round.

On the days when Jola was out at work, I quite happily amused myself walking around the main shopping areas of Warsaw, armed with my trusty A to Z.

After a day or two when I had built up enough confidence to know where I was and how to get back to her flat again without getting lost, I decided to try further afield and track some of the more interesting historical monuments.

Among the things that I saw out on my own were the following:

Warsaw Uprising Memorial

On one of my walks armed with my trusty Warsaw A to Z, I went and found the Memorial to the Warsaw Uprising of 1944. This is a modern memorial and was only built in 1988 as, during the post-war communist period, the incident was not acknowledged by the ruling Soviet – influenced regime, for reasons that will become obvious.

Basically, what happened was that during August and September 1944, with the Russians already having liberated Polish territory to the east of the capital, the Polish resistance forces were encouraged to rise up against the German occupation troops to help speed up the liberation of Warsaw.

However, instead of joining in the assault, Stalin ordered the Soviet forces to wait until the Poles and Germans had fought it out among themselves so that the Russians would have an easier job of taking over the city.

The Germans crushed the uprising in 63 days and, while the Russians sat by and watched, expelled the entire population from the city and spent the whole of October, November and December 1944 looting Warsaw and destroying whatever was still standing.

The Russians finally entered Warsaw in January 1945 after the Germans had abandoned the ruined city.

Warsaw Ghetto

(Please note that I wrote this account in the mid 1990s so it is more clearly remembered - with better detail – than some of my later reminiscences.)

I had not spent years studying Nazi history to come all the way to Warsaw and then not see the infamous Warsaw Ghetto.

Everybody that I had mentioned it to had dismissed the idea saying that there was "nothing there anymore", and that it had all been built upon.

Undeterred by this, I set off one morning with my Warsaw atlas in my hand. I had already researched where the "Pomnik" (monument) was and decided that I would head for it. It was a fresh early May morning as I strode out. The busy shopping and business streets gave way to residential areas the further out I went. The odd statue in a tree-lined square caught my eye as I passed but none of these was the one I wanted.

After what seemed like an age, I finally arrived in the middle of a bland, relatively new residential area full of identical box-like blocks of flats. In the middle was a wide square which had pavements leading to a concrete central area, which had a square lump of stone as its centre-piece.

There were a couple of lean-to information boards standing at one corner of the concrete and a man was walking around taking photos.

Having once again checked on my map that I was in the right place, I marched forward towards the structure. Despite being late morning, there was no-one else around and I felt very exposed walking out across the quiet, open square on my own. The other sightseer had gone, leaving the way clear for me to photograph away.

The monument itself was fairly plain, dark and rectangular. Its various sides were etched with views commemorating the horrors of the ghetto.

As I stood back, taking photos, I noticed in the corner of my eye an untidy little old man approaching the monument from one of the blocks of flats.

Feeling a little unsure of myself, knowing very little Polish and being in a district quite a way from where I was staying, I decided it might be better to keep out of his way.

I wandered over to look at the info boards. These were clearly a very recent addition and were black wooden boards, about 1.5m high which had been hand painted with information about the ghetto and the victims of the holocaust.

The little man appeared to be sauntering towards me in such a manner as if he didn't want me to notice. I decided to go back around the other side of the monument to avoid him but was unlucky enough to find myself cut off.

He came up to me and said something in Polish. I managed to explain that I didn't speak Polish and asked if he spoke English. He didn't but we did eventually compromise and spoke in German. His was a lot better than mine but I was quite surprised at how much I could understand.

He was a short, rather untidy man with white hair and a lot of stubble. He wasn't particularly well dressed and I was rather concerned that he wanted to scrounge something off me.

Instead, he started telling me a little about the Ghetto and how the area had looked at the time. He said that he had been there and that he and his family had been sent to the concentration camp at Treblinka – and showed me his camp tattoo on his arm.

He gestured across to where another line of flats stood a few hundred meters away behind a fence and some waste ground. That was where the Ghetto wall had been built , he said. It was constantly patrolled by Nazis with dogs and Ukrainian guards. Also in that direction was the area where they used to force the people onto the trains and ship them off to the concentration camp.

He invited me to follow him. I still felt wary at this point but felt that if I didn't, I'd probably never get another chance of seeing what he wanted to show me.

We walked away from the square and through some small, bland streets through to another square lined on all sides by flats.

On the way he pointed out a house where some famous Esperanto professor lived or had lived.

The next square was smaller and I was led to a small grassy hump to one side. Upon this hump was a crudely engraved stone which had recently been decorated with flowers and red and white ribbons.

He told me that this marked the spot where some 200 Jewish resistance fighters had been murdered in a cellar by the Gestapo in the famous "Mila 18" incident, which I had in fact heard of. The rebuilt street is still called Mila but I was unable to see whether there was still a number 18.

From here he took me on a little further out of the housing estate and across the main road. Two large dour buildings stood on either side of the road.

These were the SS and Gestapo building respectively and were the only buildings left standing in the area after Jurgen Stroop and his men had razed the area to the ground during the last days of the Ghetto.

Close by was a bright white walled structure which marked the point where the rail sidings had been. There were inscriptions both in Polish and in Hebrew to commemorate the atrocities that had been carried out there.

The "tour" ended here. I thanked the little man and was about to walk off when he asked whether I could "help" him as he was old and didn't have much money etc.

He had been such a great guide to me that I was more than happy to give him Zl 100.000 - about £5 to me - which he gratefully received.

I suppose I'll never really know if he was a survivor of the Ghetto or not, but he certainly told a great story!

PB in the former Warsaw Ghetto, May 1991.

Photo above: The Gestapo building behind was the only structure left standing.

Left: The Mila 18 Jewish resistance monument.

Below (left): The Warsaw Uprising memorial and (right) the Warsaw Ghetto memorial

Tea With Maryla

One afternoon I went to have tea with Maryla – who I had also met on the holiday in Zakopane the year before – and her parents.

They had a very smart grandiose apartment in Warsaw and the living room was dominated by a huge oil painting of her father in uniform.

He was some senior official in the Polish Forestry Ministry (hence the uniform) and I imagine that he had been similarly important under the previous socialist regime for them to have had such a nice place to live in.

The afternoon was very pleasant and the food was nice although I don't remember what we ate.

Despite being very prim and proper - and almost 30, Maryla showed an almost school-girlish delight in showing me her room and all of her vast collection of English literature classics – Dickens, Brontës etc.

I would probably be able to have a much better conversation about books with her now than I could back then as my reading tastes have widened greatly since I was 24 - and I seriously doubt that she had personally read many Sven Hassel "SS punishment battalion on the Russian Front" books or Len Deighton cold war spy novels in the past.

Anyway, she insisted on reading me her favourite poem (I suppose that having captive English people to talk to was still quite a rare thing in Warsaw in 1991...).

I can't remember what the poem was or who it was by but I do clearly remember that she absolutely refused to believe me when I told her that "bird" was pronounced like "bird" and not like "beard" - which was quite sweet, really.

I have also had trouble with Germans in the past who refuse to pronounce Leicester as "Lester" and we also had a German salesman at work once who always referred to Chelmsford as "Kelm-es-fort" but we just left him alone with that one as it just sounded so typically German and endearing.

Despite being a lofty government official, Maryla's father was very pleasant and welcoming, although he spoke very little English. He kept plying me with wine during the meal and then brandished cognacs afterwards.

Poles In Wimbledon

Maryla told me that she had a friend who was living in London – in Wimbledon - and she asked whether I might take some things over for her when I went back home.

My flight back from Warsaw to LHR was fairly early in the morning (that's why it had been so cheap, I suppose...) so, as I was going to have to cross London anyway on the Underground – and I had nothing particular that I needed to do for the rest of the day other than getting home, I readily agreed.

I asked Jola about the girl I was supposed to be going to meet and she said that she knew her – but couldn't say that she liked her as such... But nothing ventured, nothing gained!

Don't forget - this was all way before the 11th September 2001 hijackings and all the subsequent airline security checks that came in after that.

But, in the wake of the Lockerbie Pan Am bombing in 1988, they did ask you things at the check in like "did you pack the bag yourself?", so you still had to be careful about carrying things for other people.

Having said that, of all the people that I have ever met in the whole of my life, Maryla is definitely the least likely person who you could ever possibly suspect of being involved in contraband smuggling, drugs or people trafficking - so I had no reason to doubt the contents of the bag that she gave me to take to Wimbledon.

In fact, she insisted on taking everything out and showing me in the minutest of detail what it all was – basically packets of Polish brand sweets and biscuits that they presumably couldn't get in England at that time, unlike now - before allowing me to go off with it.

So I got my flight back to England without incident and took the Underground in the direction of Wimbledon. Unfortunately, part of the line was closed for repairs so I had to take a replacement bus for part of the route – which wasn't very handy with me lugging my suitcase as well as my hand luggage bag – but I eventually arrived at my destination around lunchtime.

Don't ask me now how I found the address - but I obviously did. It was a pleasant semi in a nice leafy suburb – exactly what you'd expect to see in Wimbledon, to be honest – and I rang the doorbell, albeit a little nervous as to what might await me.

A pretty blond girl answered the door and it turned out that it was she I was supposed to meet. So far, so good.

She invited me in (I'm afraid I can't remember her name...) and sitting around a large table in the kitchen were 4 or 5 more young Poles, who I was introduced to - and whose names I can't remember either.

We sat and had a coffee and I handed over the goods I had brought with me. Everybody seemed really pleased when they saw one or other of their favourite nibbles from home.

They asked me if I was in a rush to go and I said I wasn't so, as the weather was nice and sunny, they suggested going to the park for a bit.

I always imagined that this was Wimbledon Common (of "Wombles" fame) but looking on the map now, there are several different parks in that area and it really could have been any of those.

They had brought some bottles of water and coke with them so we sat on a rug and took sips of the drinks, sunbathed for a bit – and generally enjoyed the atmosphere in the park.

They all seemed keen to chat to me and make me welcome and I got the impression they didn't have much social contact with normal English people and quite probably only ever mixed with other foreign workers. Anyway, it was a nice way of finishing off my Polish adventure.

After a while we headed back to the house and they asked if I would like to stay for something to eat. I said that I would and we all ended up sitting round the table grating potatoes to make Placki – which are Polish potato pancakes.

I'd had these already with Jola one day so I knew how labour intensive the preparation was - and it was all hands to the pump with 6 or more people to feed.

We ate the Placki with some goulash stew of some sort and it was really a good way of making a basic meal go a long way. As I was getting ready to leave I asked to use the toilet and was shown upstairs. Here I saw an incredible sight that has stayed with me to this day.

All around the upstairs landing were airbeds with sleeping bags and pillows laid out on them. There were more airbeds like this in the bedrooms (that I could see) so it looked as if there were considerably more than the 5 or 6 people that I had already met who were living in the house.

There may have been more beds in rooms that I didn't see – quite possibly in the loft space as well - so I couldn't even guess how many people were using that place. And it made sense that most of them would be out at work at that time of day.

At that time people from Poland needed entry visas and work permits to be able to come to England so I figured that there was probably some illegal activity going on here.

But everybody had been so nice and welcoming to me that I decided not to put them in a difficult position by asking about it - and went on my way to get the train back to Peterborough.

Passport visa stamp issued by the Polish Consulate in London.

Stamped 21st April 1991 upon my arrival at Warsaw airport and 3rd May upon my departure.

Home sweet home for the first 35 years of my life – on and off. And a regular stopping off point in between Bachelor Pads.

1991: A Little Bit Of Lynda

If you have ever lived away from the family home for an extended period and then had to move back there for some reason or other, you will know that it isn't necessarily easy.

While everybody may be very pleased to have you back and move things round to accommodate you, you still have to fit in with them and what they do - so it can lead to little niggly frustrations.

Luckily we had plenty of room at our house so nearly all of my furniture from the Bachelor Pad went in the garage – to join all the other stuff that had languished in there since I had moved it out of the rented house in Dogsthorpe at the end of 1989.

I was stuck in the small bedroom at the front of the house as my brother had commandeered the big back bedroom after I had left in the first place – but that didn't bother me as it was cosy and comfortable.

I didn't have too many clothes at the time, having led a bit of a laddish nomadic existence for a while and there was plenty of room for them in the built-in cupboard in the corner. This was because my mum had thoughtfully had cleared it out and, in the process, disposed of all my cherished toys a while previously without telling me.

That's all my Action Men ie: the Tank Commander, the bearded adventurer one, the original one with the useless hands, my 6 Million Dollar Man action figure, my Kirk and Spock Star Trek figures – even though there were a different size, my Action Man tank, all the Lego, the Matchbox cars, all the toy soldiers (both sizes), Airfix models, my toy fort, (probably) Gary's car garage with the lift, cuddly toys of various vintages....the LOT!

Bitter...? Grudges – me? Surely not.

To quote Richard Gere in the "Pretty Woman" film: "I was very engry" about it at the time - but have since some to realise what a blessing it has been not to have even more stuff to have to cart around with me every time I have shifted abode since then. She did me huge favour. Hurrah for the minimalist approach!

Anyway, I still had my TV, video and music player from the Bachelor Pad and, after a couple of initial nights uncomfortably shoehorned into a single bed pushed up against the radiator, I managed to convince my dad to get my big bed out of the garage and swap them over.

It took up most of the room but it wasn't as if I was going to want to play Scalextric or Subbuteo in there.

As part of a special offer that was going when they were trying to install cable television in our street, we had cable receiver boxes in the living room, my bedroom and Gary's bedroom so I could watch whatever I wanted from the wide assortment of channels without having to battle over the telly downstairs.

I also had a telephone extension put in next to my bed so that I could ring people in private.

So I was able to be comfortable, independent and do my own thing but, by this time , I actually had a very full and varied social calendar and consequently wasn't really at home very much.

One issue that we had to contend with on a regular basis was car parking. We were not too badly off with our house as it was the last plot of the private houses before the council houses started and, as such, it had a longer driveway than many of the others on our road.

But by the time I moved back, I had a car as well as a motorbike and, while the motorbike could easily go in the garage (we never did once have a car in that garage all the time we had it – it had been built where the shed and coal bunker had originally been but was always too full of other stuff!), my car was more of a problem.

We had 4 cars in our household by then: my dad's 1965 Ford Zodiac which parked under the car port nearest the house and only he ever drove, my mum's Morris Marina estate which everybody used from time to time as a convenience car, my brother's Austin Allegro and now my sporty yellow Datsun that I had acquired after passing my test in August 1990.

You could fit three cars on the driveway fairly easily – although in later years when I had a Vauxhall Cavalier Commander estate, that used to hang out over the footpath a bit – but we also had the problem of who needed to go out first the next morning so we regularly had an evening session of moving all the cars round so that we were parked in the right order.

Because I had a slightly more active nocturnal life than all the other family members, I would often be the last one home at night so would usually park on the grass verge directly outside the house.

That saved me having to worry about letting other people off the driveway again and meant I could always zip off easily when I needed to.

You couldn't really park on the side of the road outside our house like you could further up because we had a side road directly opposite and it would have caused a dangerous obstruction, so this was a good solution for me.

The downside was that it did get a bit muddy when the weather was bad and the grass surface of the verge got rather churned up.

What the local council started doing – and I thought this was a very good idea – was laying those big paving slabs that you sometimes see in car parks that have gaps for the grass to grow up. That meant that you could still have a grassy verge but that the surface was protected underneath by concrete. Apparently they are called "permeable" – because they also allow the rainwater to drain away.

They started putting these in at the top of the road - up by the Carpenters Arms - and I watched the progress carefully, looking forward to when they did ours. Unfortunately, they never got that far down the road and, I think, didn't even get any further along than Chapel Street before they stopped doing this. What they then did instead, which I can fully appreciate was probably a much cheaper option – was to put up "No Parking On Grass Verges" signs the rest of the way along!

Anyway, having already established a common-law right to park my car there, I always ignored this and never once had any comeback from it.

*****

As I mentioned earlier, I had a pretty good social life by this time.

On Friday evenings I used to go out for a few drinks with the lads – depending on who was about, that would be one or more from Steven Garratt, John Ludman, Graham Hill and my brother Gary.

On a Saturday afternoon several of us would go to football to watch the mighty Posh in action. If Alan Platt was up from London for the game, I would meet him in town and have a few drinks beforehand.

Saturday evenings were often taken up with travelling back home if some of us had been to an away game.

On Sunday lunchtime I would play squash with Simon at the Cresset and then we would have a drink at one of the two pubs nearby afterwards.

Sunday evening was taken up watching the Peterborough Pirates ice hockey team.

Monday evening I did Karate at Eastholm School

And quite often I'd do something else with Simes during the week like play squash or badminton at any number of different venues.

Add to that regular outings with people from work for meals out, birthdays or leaving dos and whatever, and I had quite a happy existence.

I also had a couple of pleasant female friends– this sounds seedy but is really isn't - who would happily make up the numbers (on a "no strings attached" basis – ie no canoodling...) if I needed somebody to go with me so as not to look like a spare tool at a proverbial wedding from time to time.

One was Jane Barnet from work - who actually, for example, really did go with me to Alan & Louise's wedding party as I had already asked her in advance before I had met Karen (she of shirt ironing fame) - and the other was Lynda who was a barmaid at one of the pubs where Simes and I often ended up going for the quiz night and a drink after midweek squash.

In fact, I seem to think that we just went in once quite by chance after squash and found that the pub quiz was about to start. We decided to enter it just for a bit of fun and the pair of us actually won the quiz!

The prize was 10 free pints – or something like that – which luckily, you didn't have to drink all at once, so we had to keep going back there so that we could use them up before the deadline. And that's how I came to know Lynda.

She was very pleasant and chatty and she told me that she was learning to be a personal fitness instructor and spent a lot of her time at the local sports centre in the gym.

She said that she was hoping to learn Spanish, go and live in Spain and work there as a fitness coach out there but had to wait until the next academic year started (this was in the middle of winter – my guess would be January 1991...) so that she could do a conversation class at the college.

Being a bit of a linguist myself, having been doing some Spanish at work and – let's face it: as I am THAT KIND OF GUY – I offered to help her learn a few words and phrases to whet her appetite until she could start a proper class, and she readily accepted.

So I used to pick her up from her house on one of her evenings off and we'd go to a pub somewhere and sit in a quiet corner with a drink and look at the pages from my Spanish learning book that I had photocopied at work for her.

It was only very basic stuff like "My name is Lynda", "I am English" and so on as I didn't want to dampen her enthusiasm too much without worrying about genders of nouns, tenses of verbs and other bits of grammar that she could always graduate on to later.

And I have to say that it was probably just as well, as she had enough trouble trying to remember the basic stuff that I had shown her in the first place.

Don't get me wrong here - I'm not being at all nasty – but everybody is different. There are those of us who have a particular interest in - and natural aptitude for easily picking up - languages.

And then there are those of us who have a natural aptitude for going to the gym and being a fitness instructor – and Lynda definitely fitted into the latter category.

The following week when we were going to recap on what we had done last time – and that she had supposed to be practicing at home in the meantime … - it tended to be a whole load of "oooh, hang on… No – don't tell me… I remember it's… erm … ".

So it was quite clear from very early on that our Spanish lessons were not really going to have much of a long lasting impact.

One particularly humorous incident that did occur while we were having our Spanish evenings together was one time when we went to the Hero of Aliwal pub in Whittlesey. My friend Wiggy from school had moved to Whittlesey by then and he happened to be in this pub on that particular evening and came over to say hello.

I introduced Lynda said we were "having a Spanish lesson", to which in all seriousness, he turned to her and asked which part of Spain she was from.

There followed a bit of an embarrassed silence and I then had to explain that it was ME teaching HER Spanish - not the other way round – and he said "Oh" and went off to carry on doing whatever it was he had originally been doing.

In all fairness, we did have a "quid pro quo" with these Spanish sessions and I asked Lynda in exchange to take me to the gym and show me some basic exercises that I could do to keep in shape.

So we had a few sessions at the sports centre where she taught me how to properly use the various bits of equipment and also showed me some simple floor exercises that I could do easily in the gym or at home.

Over time, the Spanish lessons fizzled out but we went on to do other things instead on an occasional basis.

It's probably quite hard to imagine for anybody reading this but this was always a purely platonic friendship throughout.

Lynda was nice looking and fun to be with – but I never once fancied her in the slightest. In all the time we were together, we never once flirted, exchanged glances, kissed, hugged or even touched – except for maybe in the gym when she was correcting an exercise posture.

I'd met both her mum and her dad on different occasions when I had been round to pick her up and I also unwittingly knew her brother.

He was a designer at Baker Perkins where I worked and I didn't actually KNOW him but we were in the same meeting once and he must have known who I was because he spontaneously introduced himself as Lynda's brother – so I had obviously been talked about among the family!

Now, if I was reading all this now for the first time, as an outsider, I would also find it hard to believe that this wasn't a full-on relationship as well - but it really wasn't.

I did later have another friend like that - Jill from University, who you may read about another time in "Germany Calling".

While Jill and I did spend a lot of time together - and may have exchanged the odd hug, because we helped each other through some difficult moments – we never actually fancied each other either. So I have first-hand experience – twice over - that such a relationship is possible.

Anyway, among the other things we did together, Lynda went with me to see "Terminator 2" at the cinema when I couldn't get anybody else to go with me and one Sunday we had a drive down to Cambridge for the day.

Don't ask me why because there was nowhere open and nothing to do but we stopped and had lunch at that Megatron hamburger restaurant at the side of the A1.

It was shaped like a flying saucer and had a space themed menu with things like "Black Hole Burgers" and "Cosmic Chips" or whatever...

I believe it is still there to this day and is now a McDonalds.

I seem to think that we went down to the Notting Hill Carnival once as well – parking at East Finchley and then taking the Underground the rest of the way – but my memory is a bit vague about that one.

My brother Gary actually "borrowed" Lynda once as well to go to a work Christmas do with him.

They were going on a boat trip up the River Nene and having a meal at the Dog & Doublet at the far end - and it was an event for wives and husbands and partners to go as well.

Gary didn't want to miss it and didn't want to go on his own so we asked Lynda if she would go. She agreed and, as far as I remember, they both had an enjoyable time.

One Lynda story that I had completely forgotten about until writing up these others has flashed into my memory and I simply must tell you about it, before we move on.

It actually concerns one of my old friends from school - who we have mentioned already - but I am not going to name him in this instance as he is now happily married and I don't want to cause any ructions or embarrassment. So, in the best interests of all involved, we'll call him "Reggie".

Anyway Reggie was "between girlfriends" - as we like to call it – and he told me that he had met somebody he quite liked and she'd - somewhat hesitantly - agreed to go out for a drink with him.

He didn't want the evening to come across too much like a formal date between him and her and asked if I might go along and take somebody suitable with me to make up a four so it wasn't quite so awkward.

I told Lynda what the plan was and she readily agreed to come along.

I can't for the life of me remember where we went now. It must have been a high end bar of some sort with a dance floor as I remember we sat up on a balcony looking down, but it can't have been a night club as the music wasn't too loud and it was during the week.

Anyway, it was a very refined and "polite" occasion and I think we were all nervous. Both Reggie and I had jackets and ties on and the other girl (can't remember her name – sorry) looked very nice and pleasant but came across as very shy.

Lynda – I have to say this – was wearing a dazzling slinky red dress and she looked absolutely stunning. I had only ever seen her in jeans and t-shirts before – or sportswear when we had been in the gym – but, for this evening, she had done something with her hair and put some make up on (another first in my company) and she looked really gorgeous.

She had really taken on board what I told her about our "mission" for the evening (should we choose to accept it – to try and make it look as if "Reggie" had nice, respectable, sophisticated friends...) and she even toned down her usual raucous East End London accent for the occasion.

So WE had an enjoyable evening at wherever it was, anyway. I hope Reggie did. I don't know about the other girl, whether she twigged that it was some sort of artificial set up for her benefit or not, as I never saw her or ever heard about her again!

I lost touch with Lynda after I started working in Preston in April 1992. Although I came home every weekend, Lynda and I normally did things together during the week so it wasn't really relevant any more as I was in Preston all week long.

Like I said already, it's not as if we were an inseparable item and we just both moved on and did other things.

I had actually not thought about Lynda for years until now, so it has been quite nice to re-live a few pleasant memories that didn't finish up with a nasty falling out saga!

A Few Words About Whittlesey

There used to be a lot of rivalry between Whittlesey and Stanground and, despite them being only about 5 miles apart, huge cultural differences between the two places.

Whittlesey retains its old fashioned farming town character whereas Stanground was a lot more "towny" and metropolitan even in the time when I was still living there and, with a lot of expansion having gone on since then, I would imagine that it is even more so now.

Most Whittlesey natives tended to have the "Fen" way of speaking – so they would pronounce computer as "com-poo-ter" whereas as I would say "com-pew-ter", for example.

In fact, when I was little there used to be stories about big gang fights between the Whittlesey Mob and the Stanground Mob. I never saw any of this but a few of my friends from school claimed to have done.

Happily, however, at the time I am talking about now - in the early 1990s, it was perfectly safe for people from Stanground to walk the streets of Whittlesey and, indeed, enjoy a pleasurable evening out and there was no worrying about being pounced upon by fabled hordes of ritualistic hooded yokels.

In fact, with Wiggy by then living over there and knowing his way round, we went quite often for a bit of a change – particularly after I had passed my test and had my own car.

Our favourite pub in Whittlesey – well, mine anyway - was always the "Hero Of Aliwal" which was named after Sir Harry Smith.

He was a Whittlesey-born soldier who led the British to victory in the Battle of Aliwal, in the Punjab in the 1840s. There is also a school in Whittlesey that bears his name.

A girl who worked with me at Baker Perkins called Lorraine came from Whittlesey and she used to help out behind the bar there some evenings so it was always nice to drop in and see her for a chat.

The Hero was a bit away from the main street – so you could park easily in its car park. It also had a restaurant attached so it generally attracted a more genteel crowd.

The other pubs that I remember going to in Whittlesey were the Letter B (apparently, at one time, there were so many pubs that they ran out of names and started calling them by letters...) and the Morton Fork.

I occasionally went and played badminton in the evenings at the Manor Leisure Centre – usually with Simes or my brother Gary - and I do remember on at least one occasion playing a four with Simes & Rosie and one side and Jane Barnet from work and me on the other.

These highly energetic sports sessions almost always finished up with a stop off at the Hero of Aliwal for a period of recuperation afterwards!

*****

There used to be a good Sunday market on some old waste ground on an industrial estate in Whittlesey that had different stalls and wares to what you might usually find elsewhere so I often used to go there on a Sunday afternoon if I had nothing else to do.

There was a similar, but much bigger one at Wisbech as well, although that was a bit further away and needed a bit more planning. You couldn't just pop to it like you could the one in Whittlesey.

This isn't my actual Whitney Houston ticket but you can see as an example where it has been overstamped with the rearranged date.

31st August 1991: Whitney Houston at the NEC Arena

I saw a couple more world famous artists perform concerts during 1991. Whitney Houston had been due to tour the country early in the year but had to postpone due to illness and the shows eventually took place in August / September of 1991.

I'd got tickets for the original show at the National Exhibition Centre near Birmingham and the rearranged date was on Saturday 31st August – which was a sod as it meant having to rush off straight after football to catch the coach. (Peterborough drew 1-1 at home to Stoke City, by the way...).

I'd booked the tickets via the Steve Jason agency in Peterborough and the package included coach travel to the venue. Unfortunately, the coach actually broke down somewhere on the A47 and they had to get a replacement to come out and take us the rest of the way.

This meant that we were a bit late arriving and had to be shepherded in through some back entrance and then there was a panic to try and find the correct seats in the huge auditorium.

It took the shine off the evening a bit as I was too flustered to be able to relax and really enjoy the show properly.

Although it was good to see Whitney Houston in person, I didn't think that the show was especially memorable. We were quite a long way back from the stage, even though they were relatively expensive tickets. Plus a lot of people further forward stood up all the way through making it difficult to see past them as our group wasn't on the tiered seating.

Overall I rated seeing Belinda Carlisle in Peterborough for a tenner much more enjoyable – even though that had been standing only.

According to our friends at setlist.fm, the running order for this show was, apparently:

I Wanna Dance With Somebody (Who Loves Me), So Emotional, Saving All My Love for You, How Will I Know, Love Medley (All at Once / A House Is Not a Home/Didn't We Almost Have It All / Where Do Broken Hearts Go), All the Man That I Need, Sack Full of Dreams, My Name Is Not Susan, In Return, Revelation, Who Do You Love, I'm Your Baby Tonight. Encore: I Belong to You

20th October 1991: Roxette at Wembley Arena

The Roxette concert – at Wembley Arena on Saturday 20th October 1991 - was a completely different kettle of fish and was really superb.

We had really good seats for this – up on the posh tiered balcony–not miles away from the stage - and had a really great view.

This was the first time that they had toured outside of Scandinavia and the London shows on 19th and 20th October were the first that they had ever played in England, so it was a very special occasion.

The show was as good as you'd expect from a world class act on a 100-date international tour and they sang all their famous songs.

The set list was: Hotblooded, Dangerous, Fading Like a Flower (Every Time You Leave), Church of Your Heart, Sleeping Single, Spending My Time, Watercolours in the Rain, Paint, Knockin' on Every Door, Dance Away, The Big L., It Must Have Been Love, Dressed for Success, The Look, Encore: (Do You Get) Excited?, Joyride, Listen to Your Heart, Perfect Day.

The whole concert was recorded by BBC Radio and broadcast one time on Radio 2 over the festive period. I have a copy of it somewhere which is nice souvenir – and you can also find it now on YouTube as well.

The only downsides that I recall from the evening were having to pay £7 to park the car in the Wembley Arena official car park and then taking the wrong turn on the M25 to come home and having to drive miles to get to the next exit to be able to turn round.

But that wasn't enough to put a damper on anything and overall I really enjoyed the whole experience.

Route of the Orient Express – 1935. from Railway Wonders of the World by Amalgamated Press, London   (source: www.railwaywondersoftheworld.com)

September 1991: Inter Rail

The above map is quite interesting as it shows the route that was followed by the famous Orient Express train back in 1935 – around the time of Agatha Christie's famous Hercule Poirot mystery story.

We didn't actually set out to emulate the Orient Express when we were planning our rail trip across Europe. We just looked for the furthest point that we could travel to on our ticket – ie Turkey – through the most number of countries, and decided on the most interesting route to get there.

I actually got the inspiration for this trip from watching Michael Palin's BBC series "Around The World In 80 Days". I had seen it when it was originally broadcast in Autumn 1989 and found it fascinating - and then, in the Spring of 1991, it was repeated during the afternoons at a time when I was off work for some reason or other, with one episode on per day.

By this time, I was the veteran of numerous travels across Europe – had been to Poland twice, East Germany, Amsterdam, France on several occasions and I felt that I was ready for a really big adventure.

I worked out that, if I saved up £200 a month – instead of going mad and spending everything that I got like I normally did, I would be able to afford to get an Inter Rail ticket and have enough left in hand to pay for food, accommodation and fun on a 3 week trip across Europe.

I went with my friend Simon who I had known since 1986 when we had met on a course at the Technical College in Peterborough and we played squash together every weekend.

I somehow managed to convince him that it would be fun to go haring across Europe on a train for a few weeks so we both spent the summer months saving up and, in September 1991, that is exactly what we did.

The timing of this was quite important because, back then, you could only get an Inter Rail ticket if you were under 25 - and I suppose it was originally aimed at students who wanted to go travelling during their summer holidays.

Basically, it was valid for a month, cost £125 and covered all second class rail travel in 26 countries right across Europe.

You had to pay local supplements on top of that if you wanted a sleeper berth or couchette or any special reservations but, in theory, if you didn't mind taking pot luck, planned your itinerary carefully and didn't mind and sleeping every night in a regular seated train, you could have a very cheap pan-Europe holiday and only need to pay for food and entertainment.

We planned our route so that we had a mixture of overnight train travel and more comfortable stays in youth hostels and pensions.

As a rule we only planned to have one night on the train at a time and then 2 or 3 nights in proper accommodation to be able to freshen up and recuperate in between.

They have different versions of the Inter Rail ticket these days and there are various tickets of differing durations if you want to concentrate on one particular country or go for a shorter time period.

There are also different age groups now as well so that adults and retired people can make the journey if they so wish.

But, back then there was a strict age limit of 25 so autumn 1991 was the last chance that I would have to be able to do this before my 25th birthday in April 1992.

I didn't keep a note of any of our travel dates for this trip, unfortunately. The "modern day me" would have kept a detailed diary or internet blog all the way through ready to publish it – but I wasn't a writer back then.

I can, however, narrow it down fairly well due to a happy chance memory that has stuck with me over the years.

We were sitting at an outside cafe somewhere around the station in Amsterdam, late summer sun shining down, and a cool draught coming in off of the harbour, enjoying a post-breakfast coffee before taking the train into Germany.

I distinctly remember seeing that the back pages of the newspapers were full of news of the British relay team – Roger Black, Derek Redmond, John Regis and Kris Akabusi – pipping the Americans in dramatic fashion to win the 4x400m gold medal at the World Athletics Championships in Tokyo.

That was on 1st September 1991 and it was reported in the newspapers on Monday 2nd so it must have been Sunday 1st when we travelled over to Holland on the ferry.

Now, that was the day immediately after I went to see the re-arranged Whitney Houston concert at the NEC in Birmingham and I don't really remember having zipped off on holiday the day after that – but I suppose I must have done.

I had a lot more energy and oomph back in those days of my early 20s so it wouldn't have fazed me as much rushing from one exciting venture to another.

These days, following a serious illness and the various Covid pandemic lockdowns, if I can manage to do one - not especially exciting – thing a week, I count myself lucky!

Anyway, accepting Sunday 1st September 1991 as Day 1 of our trip, I will try and estimate the rest of the timeline based on that, with help of visa stamps in my old passport. It might not be 100% accurate as I might not recall how many nights we stayed in which place but, looking back 30 years on, I don't suppose it really matters too much – and you will certainly get the general idea.

Day 1 (Sunday 1st September 1991):
Drove Peterborough To Harwich (200km)

Simon's mum and dad drove us down to Harwich to catch the ferry to Holland. As it's cross country and not main roads all the way, it usually takes the best part of three hours to get there.

Day boat Harwich to Hoek van Holland (200km)

Train Hoek van Holland to Amsterdam (80 km)

Overnight stay in the Youth Hostel at Vondelpark. We got to the Youth Hostel just as it was beginning to get dark, stashed our stuff there and went off in search of food and a good evening out.

Based on my previous Amsterdam experiences, I knew that we should head straight to the Leidseplein and Red Light District – and I was able to show Simes round the best bits.

Above: Non Stop Erotic Cabaret – PB in Amsterdam's Red Light District
Below: Simon outside Amsterdam Centraal Station. Both September 1991.

PB with Dutch penpal Nadah Dekker in Enschede

Day 2: Train to Enschede (160km)

Afternoon spent with Nadah Dekker – her dad used to be a professional basketball player and was very tall like she was.

Nadah was a Dutch penpal of mine who I had acquired through appearing on a Satellite TV programme.

Having been enjoying my recently re-found single status and the extra travelling opportunities that this had allowed – and meeting up with Jola and her friends in Poland – I had embraced the idea of having penfriends all over the place and going off to visit them.

There used to be an afternoon programme on Superchannel called "On The Air" which broadcast right across Europe and beyond and they had a weekly penpal slot where people could write or phone in.

I went on one day in June /July and ended up with a stack of letters from people.

Nadah was one of these and, as she was living right on the Dutch border with Germany – and on the direct route of our train journey from Amsterdam to Berlin, we arranged to meet up with her.

I actually met my eventual German girlfriend of 6 years, Hanja, through this batch of penfriends as well, although she lived a lot further north - and not on our proposed Inter Rail route - so I didn't meet her until later.

As it was a nice day, we sat in the Dekkers' garden and ate crisps and drank coke all afternoon.

After a sandwich tea, she took us to the railway station and we got the overnight train for Berlin.

Overnight Train Enschede to Berlin (500km).

We had a sleeper car so we got a decent night's sleep.

PB outside the Youth Hostel in Tegel, Berlin

Days 3 & 4: Berlin

We arrived in Berlin early on the Tuesday morning and headed for the Youth Hostel at Tegel. This required a bus or S-Bahn trip (I don't remember which) but it meant that we had 24 hour tickets for going exploring with.

Having already been to Berlin the year before, I knew how to get to the main attractions so we made the most of the nice sunny day to get round as many things as we could.

It was interesting to see how the areas where the Berlin Wall had been had already changed in the short time since my last visit and there were lots of building works going on all over the place.

We visited the area where Checkpoint Charlie had previously been and that was now just a big open area that had been cleared for construction.

257

There were some bits of left-over wall that had been put on display and a sort of open air makeshift museum, which was interesting to see.

We also visited Alexander Platz, the Brandenburg Gate, saw the memorial to the victims of the Wall - which had been moved since my previous visit and now had more names added to it – and then went to the Olympic Stadium where the infamous 1936 Olympic Games had taken place.

It was a very impressive building and the sun was just going down as we got there so the long shadows made it very eerie.

It was good that we had done our main sightseeing on the Tuesday as the next day was a bit gloomy and mizzly.

We set off for the Eastern part of the city to go and see the Russian war memorial in Treptower Park. We found the park OK but couldn't find the memorial – despite it being rather huge and impressive, so we left disappointed.

We bought another 24 hour metro ticket – timing it so that it would last until we were ready to go to the station the next day – and spent the rest of the time on the U-Bahn and S-Bahn, zipping between places of interest.

Without spending a lot of time - or going inside anywhere - I seem to think that we had brief glimpses of the Citadel at Spandau and the palaces at Charlottenburg and San Soucci in Potsdam.

Berlin, September 1991:

Top left: PB in the area where the former East German border control post had been at Checkpoint Charlie. Top right: Berlin Wall Museum at Checkpoint Charlie Middle left: PB at Brandenburg Gate, Middle Right: PB with the Berlin TV Tower in the background. Bottom left: PB in Alexanderplatz.

PB at Leipzig railway station

Day 5 – Thursday 5th September 1991:
Day Train to Leipzig. (190km)

We got the mid morning train from Berlin to Leipzig and it took about 2 hours to get there.

I didn't really know much about Leipzig back then so hadn't earmarked anything particular to see there.

I suppose – looking back now - it would have been a good idea to go and see the Lokomotiv Leipzig football stadium - or the iconic Opera House and Old Town Hall which featured in the opening sequence to the 1960s DDR musical film "Heisser Sommer" (check it out on YouTube...!).

But, if I'm completely honest – back in those heady days of the early 1990s with Europe opening up, me being young, free and single and having just re-discovered the excitement of travelling and meeting new people after a few years in the doldrums (that's a state of mind, by the way - not a place...) – it didn't even occur to me that this might be the only time that I would ever go there.

I did travel to Germany many more times during the 1990s and visit lots of different places – especially along the northern coast – but I have never (so far...) gone back to Leipzig again.

However, at the time of this particular trip, Simon and I were more interested in the fact that Leipzig was close to Colditz - and we were keen to go and see the famous WW2 prison.

We wasted a bit of time by rushing unnecessarily to the Youth Hostel on Kathe Kollwitz Strasse because I had misunderstood "ab" on the telephone.

I thought that we needed to check in before 2pm whereas it was, in fact, after 2pm so we got there early and had to hang around when we might otherwise have been having lunch.

Apart from not letting us check in before 2pm – quite why, I don't know as it's not as if there was anybody else there and nothing else happened – in fact we all just sat there looking at each other for an hour (just the typical Germanic fascination with sticking to the rules, I guess...) - anyway APART from that, the guy on reception at the Youth Hostel was very pleasant and helpful.

Although he didn't really appreciate why we wanted to go there – he obviously had never seen the 1970s BBC wartime drama starring Anthony Valentine and David McCallum - he took the trouble to look up the train times for us to see about getting to Colditz.

Now, I don't know what it is like now - but back then, it was still - apparently - just an old castle in the middle of nowhere that had been shut up and left to ruination for years.

There was no Colditz museum, or visitor centre or any tourist infrastructure at all set up around it to encourage visitors and the trains ran at very inconvenient times.

We could have got there on the train which took an hour and bit - but the train to come back on was very late in the evening and would have meant us hanging around there for hours.

As we didn't know how easy it was to get to the Castle from the station in the first place and whether we'd be able to do anything once we got there, we decided not to waste a whole day of our trip on a wild goose chase and didn't go. (Apparently the castle itself is now a Youth Hostel..!)

I had read somewhere that Weimar (of 1920's "republic" fame...) was close to Leipzig (130km by train) and that, from there, you could get a bus to the former Buchenwald concentration camp. So we found out the train times to Weimar and headed there instead.

The train to Weimar passed through very pretty countryside and took about an hour and half as it stopped at every little place you could imagine.

Weimar is close to Jena (of Carl Zeiss repute) and Erfurt (about whose football team I wrote a book a while back), which are both interesting historical towns in their own right and might, under other circumstances, been worthy of further study and attention, but on this occasion, we stuck to our guns and sought out the Weimar bus station.

The bus "station" in Weimar was easy enough to find from the railway station as the whole town wasn't very big. In fact, it wasn't a station at all as such but a series of bus stops set around a green leafy square.

We walked all round the square twice looking at all the signs and timetables trying to find out how to get to Buchenwald with no success.

I ended up going and asking at the information /ticket office but nobody there appeared to speak English and the guy on the desk spoke German with such a bizarre local accent that I didn't understand a single thing that he said.

Now, there's another thing to flag up here about the German mentality. I'm not being racist or nasty here – it's a cultural thing based on their particular history and it's just how they were brought up.

I have always had a keen interest in history. General history, sports history, family history, military history - WW1, WW2 - you name it.

However, after spending more time with native Germans in later years, it was explained to me that if you demonstrate an interest for the Holocaust and in the WW2 concentration camps, people seem to think that you are some sort of ghoulish Nazi sympathiser, rather than a respectful knowledgeable connoisseur of the past.

That being the case, and bearing in mind that we were in a small provincial town in the former East Germany, less than a year into re-unification - which was sufficiently off the beaten track to not have had its fair share of western tourists, I can fully appreciate how the sight of two strapping young nordic males going around asking about Buchenwald may have rung some alarm bells.

So we didn't go to Buchenwald either.

But I did know that there was a famous statue in the town square of the famous German writers Goethe and Schiller who had both lived in Weimar, so – determined to at least salvage something out the day's labours, we went off to find it.

Find it we did and we took our photos in front of the two famous literary figures and then headed back to the station.

The train journey back to Leipzig was pleasant enough. There were very few people on the train and we had a compartment to ourselves pretty much the whole way.

This one also stopped at every tiny village and halt along the route and it won't be like this nowadays so it is definitely worth mentioning here.

Each stop had its own little station building and most of them were very old and falling to bits. They were propped up by girders or scaffolding and looked very unsafe.

All of these buildings looked very sooty and dirty – like factory houses used to in industrial towns in England – and the station signs were all written in Gothic lettering!

Now, if you know your German history you'll possibly know that Gothic (or, if we are being pedantic, actually "Fraktur") was the official script for a while under the Nazis during the 1930s until it was abolished in 1941 for having "Jewish influences".

So that meant that those station buildings had probably not had any maintenance, or even a lick of paint, since the 1930s - all though the war years, the Russian occupation and the DDR period. The walls would have blackened with soot from the passing trains in the intervening years and the buildings left to crumble.

I forever regret not having taken at least one photo of these station buildings now as they really were a fascinating relic of a bygone age. I can only assume that I didn't have any shots left on my camera at the time.

This was back when you had to load a film in your camera and had 24 or 36 shots before having to take it out and get it developed.

You never knew if your photos had actually come out until much later and photography was much more haphazard than it is these days with digital devices.

When we got back to Leipzig we had a shower and freshened up before heading for an evening out.

I have to say that this Youth Hostel had superb facilities and was the best I have ever encountered anywhere.

It was an ornate old fashioned 4 or 5 storey building and had comfortable twin rooms for the guests. The showers were in the basement and the whole place was very well laid out.

It was quite dark by the time we went out so we didn't want to go very far and run the risk of getting lost.

A few minutes' walk along a straight road we came to the Johannapark and there was a pleasant bar / cafe / restaurant there with candlelit tables outside.

We sat there, had a drink and a snack and listened to the piano music coming from inside the restaurant - bar and it was a very nice way to unwind after a long day spent mainly on trains.

Left: PB at the Goethe & Schiller Statue in Weimar, September 1991.

Day 6 – Friday 6th September 1991: Leipzig / Dresden / Prague

The next day we got the morning train to Dresden (115km), which took just over an hour, and then caught a train for Prague (150km).

Here again, the time that we spent on the platform at Dresden Hauptbahnhof is the only time that I have ever set foot in this remarkable historic city.

With the benefit of hindsight, I would have probably taken half a day at least to check out the Frauenkirche - which is a huge elaborate church that had stood in ruins since the Allied bombing in WW2, but has since been restored – the Dynamo Dresden football stadium and the baroque Zwinger Palace. But it's easy to be clever after the fact.

I did travel through Dresden twice more - by coach on the way to summer camps in the Czech Republic in 1996 and 97 - so was able to see a few of the historic buildings on the way past, including the impressive Zwinger Palace illuminated in the dark. But, once again, Dresden as a travel destination remains very firmly on my "to do" list...

PB and Simon on the Charles Bridge in Prague, September 1991.

Train to Prague (150km)

Off the top of my head, I couldn't remember if we stayed for 2 or 3 nights in Prague.

My passport doesn't actually help on this occasion either as the entry stamp states that we arrived in Czechoslovakia crossing the border at Děčín on 5th September - although that can't possibly be correct as, if you have read any of the foregoing, you'll know that we were definitely in Leipzig and Weimar that day.

I'd argue that we travelled into Czechoslovakia on the 6th and that their date stamp hadn't been properly adjusted for the next day.

The exit stamp says that we left the country on the 8th September at Štúrovo – which is now in Slovakia – and that tallies with a two night stay.

The train journey only took about two hours but it was a truly fascinating experience. The border area between Germany and Czechoslovakia is very mountainous with thick forests and steep narrow passes.

The railway line passes through some wonderful scenery and in places the views are quite breathtaking.

However, one very interesting point arises from having made this journey - and somebody referred to it later in our trip.

You could certainly see why Hitler exploited dubious political means to annexe the Sudetenland – the area of Czech territory to the north and west bordering with Germany in 1938 in the run up to World War 2 . A full on military assault across the mountains and through the narrow passes and forest terrain would not have been possible.

I actually travelled that way twice more – by road in the summers of 1996 and 1997 on a coach on the way to summer camps in the Czech Republic (as it was known by then) - and can tell you that, even then, the main road from Dresden to Prague was very narrow and precarious with hairpin bends and steep inclines.

I had arranged for us to stay with a penpal of mine – Aleš who lived with his family in a flat in Prague 8, which was one of the big sprawling residential suburbs of the Czech capital.

He was waiting for us when our train pulled into the station and was holding up a handwritten sign with his name on so that we would find him easily. I haven't a clue now how we arranged what time to meet up as we didn't have mobile phones or internet in those days – but that is what happened.

I have lost touch with Aleš over the years - which is a bit of a shame as he was a great guy. His English was very good as, before I had come to know him, he had spent a summer in England / Scotland working casual agricultural jobs like strawberry picking - and sleeping under hedges in a sleeping bag!

The first thing that we did was go and have something to eat in the station restaurant. We would have been quite happy with a sandwich or a burger from a stand outside the station but Aleš insisted that we had something "proper" to eat, in his own words – and I think that his mother had probably given him some money especially to make this happen.

So we went and sat down and enjoyed some tasty local meat and dumplings dish and then took the bus out to where he lived.

Aleš lived with his mother and father and younger brother in a two bedroom flat and it soon became obvious that he and his brother were vacating their bedroom for the duration of our stay and were going to sleep in the living room.

I felt bad about this and immediately said that we would go and stay in a youth hostel and just meet up with him during the day – but they were adamant – all of them, that they wanted us to stay with them in their flat.

I couldn't really work out whether it was just for the kudos of having some western foreigners stay with them – the sort of thing that just two years earlier could seen them all hauled off to prison – or whether it was the lure of the western currency that we were going to exchange (presumably illegally) with Aleš for Czech Koruna.

I had already come across this in Poland when I had gone there the year before – in most places that you went to in Eastern Europe during the early 1990s, you often got local people coming up asking to buy western currency off you.

Western currencies like US dollars, Deutsch Marks and GB Pounds, had kept their value while the local communist era currencies had all collapsed and local people could – apparently - buy certain things using these notes that were otherwise difficult to obtain in those depressed domestic markets.

We had been told before departure that US dollars were highly prized across the poorer areas of Europe so had brought a stash with us, along with GB traveller's cheques, so that we were prepared for any eventuality.

So when I told Aleš that we wanted to change some money when we got to the station, he told me in a low conspiratorial voice that he would change it for us at home - and he could even give us a better rate than the official bureaux, who took a large commission.

Now, the relative cost of living in Czechoslovakia at that time was very low compared to ours. Everything seemed embarrassingly cheap compared to what we were used to paying in England, so we weren't overly bothered about getting a competitive rate and were just happy to give him what he wanted in terms of USD.

Karlštejn Castle

The next morning we took the train to Karlštejn – which was 30km away from Prague and had an interesting castle.

According to Wikipedia, "Karlštejn Castle is a large Gothic castle founded in 1348 by Charles IV, Holy Roman Emperor-elect and King of Bohemia. The castle served as a place for safekeeping the Imperial Regalia as well as the Bohemian Crown Jewels, holy relics, and other royal treasures."

We didn't actually go in but had a good walk around the walls and enjoyed the views of the surroundings.

We spent rest of the day back in Prague catching up on the rest of the sights and saw among other things:

Wenceslas Square - The scene of the 1989 demonstrations that led to the overthrow of the communist government

Karlov Most (Charles' Bridge) - A medieval stone arch bridge that crosses the Vltava river. It has the most beautiful ornate statues along its length that depict various saints and patron saints who were venerated at the time of its construction.

Prague Castle / New Royal Palace - There is a bit of confusion here – on my part, at least - as there is the Old Royal Palace and the New Royal Palace, both of which are centred around the impressive Prague Castle complex.

From comparing photos, it was definitely the New Royal Palace that we saw, although that would, obviously, have also been quite old as well at the time.

St Vitus Cathedral - How about that! A cathedral named after Sonny Crockett's boat on "Miami Vice". You can't get much more "Bachelor Pad" than that!

Old Jewish Cemetery - The name speaks for itself. Interesting stonework and monuments - very moving to see.

Alchemists Street (Zlatá Ulička) - Where Goldsmiths used to live in the 17th century. Apparently writer Franz Kafka stayed here for a while when his sister was living here in the 1920s.

Prague Orloj (Astronomical clock)

Here again, Wikipedia can explain this much more concisely than I can: "a medieval astronomical clock attached to the Old Town Hall in Prague, the capital of the Czech Republic.

The clock was first installed in 1410, making it the third-oldest astronomical clock in the world and the oldest clock still in operation."

"The clock mechanism has three main components — the astronomical dial, representing the position of the Sun and Moon in the sky and displaying various astronomical details; statues of various Catholic saints stand on either side of the clock; "The Walk of the Apostles", an hourly show of moving Apostle figures and other sculptures, notably a figure of a skeleton that represents Death, striking the time; and a calendar dial with medallions representing the months."

This clock was really beautiful - and fascinating to watch in operation. We were lucky enough to be there on the hour when it did its full set of movements.

Unfortunately, it was dark by then so I didn't manage to take any photos - but you can find out all about it on the internet easily enough. I also saw a similar one in the Czech town of Olomouc in 1996.

Czech Beer Evening

On our last evening in Prague, Aleš gave us a real treat and took us to an authentic Czech bar. What I mean here is a bar for normal working people that hadn't been updated and modernised into a trendy cafe or wine bar aimed at tourists, and was presumably still the same as it had been before the fall of the wall.

It was accessed via a courtyard off a side street very much off the beaten track in the centre of Prague and if you didn't know where it was, you'd never have known it was there.

Even from standing outside you wouldn't necessarily have known what it was and it was clearly a hidden gem that the locals were keeping quiet about for themselves.

It was rather like an old working's men's club in England from the 1970s, full of people (nearly all men, in fact) drinking and smoking at long heavy tables – bare wooden floor, no frills and no piped music.

If you think of the old comrades meeting scenes in the films "The Odessa File" and "Night of The Generals", I'd say that the room layout and atmosphere was rather like that – although I doubt there were any former Nazis in this place.

We took a seat at the vacant end of one of these long tables and Aleš ordered some beers. He told us that the Czechs drink their beer cold and fast – which suited me down to the ground.

As it happened, I really liked Czech beer anyway – not the watery Americanised Budweiser – but the proper traditional lagers, like Staropramen and whatever others are available now.

I couldn't tell you what actual brew the beer was that we drank but it was wonderful. There didn't appear to be a bar counter with fancy taps with different brand names on and the glasses didn't have any markings on them either.

They did have beer mats scattered around – but I'm afraid I never kept any – which is a bit of shame, in hindsight.

My guess is that this beer would have been some local brew – which, like most things, tastes best when it is served in its own region of origin. If you bought a load and took it home, it would not taste the same when you got there - and neither would buying an imported version.

People say that Guinness always tastes better in Ireland and so I imagine that the same was the case for this local Czech beer.

The serving girl brought the beers out and marked down what we'd had on a beer-mat – like they do in Germany. She also put down a pot of salted pretzel sticks.

These went down well as an accompaniment to the beer which – as Aleš had promised - was cold, refreshing and very tasty.

I don't know whether the salty pretzels sticks were a chargeable extra - or just put out to tempt the guests to drink more – but the total bill for our evening there consisting of 3 or 4 beers each and several servings of these snacks came to considerably less than what we had paid for one round of drinks at a touristy city centre bar the night before.

The odd thing was that, despite having guzzled a large amount of Czech beer, whilst I felt happy and very slightly intoxicated, I wasn't at all drunk nor did I have get the slightest hangover afterwards – so it must have been really good pure stuff!

My guess is that we were only allowed in the place because we had been with Aleš and I feel very lucky to have had that experience as I doubt that such places exist anymore now.

Prague tram ticket. This has been stamped at 16.12 hours on 6th September 1991.

Simon and Aleš on the walk up to Karlštejn Castle.

Zmrzlina is Czech for "ice cream"...

PB at Karlštejn Castle

PB in Wenceslas Square, Prague

PB in Heroes Square (Hősök tere), Budapest – September 1991

Day 8: Day Train to Budapest (525km rain)

According to "Google Maps", the distance between Prague and Budapest is some 525 km and takes about 7 or 8 hours on the train.

Now, I don't remember it taking anywhere near that amount of time – I'd have said about 3 hours tops - so either we went on a super duper express train that doesn't exist anymore, or I slept most of the way – or the adage that "time flies when you're having fun" must have come into effect.

Anyway, I suppose that we must have left Aleš's after breakfast, got the train and arrived in the Hungarian capital around tea time.

I remember that we went through Brno and Bratislava and that's about it.

We met a couple of Americans on the train – one was girl called Jenny who was travelling on her own – and who we will mention ago later - and the other was a guy called Tim Wilkins.

When we got off the train, we had no particular plans on where we were going to sleep, however, with Budapest being a big city, we were sure we'd find somewhere easily enough.

As it turned out, there were a lot of local people meeting the train holding up cards in the hope of renting out private rooms and hotel places to well off foreign tourists (a bit like the evacuees scene out of "Carrie's War"...) so Simes, Tim and I we went along with one of the less dubious looking ones of these.

We ended up at a nice clean new looking hostel run by an Indian guy who appeared to employ young Romanians to tout for business at the station on a room and board basis. The place seemed nice enough so we booked in for two nights

The following day we went out with Tim and saw all the main tourist sites - Buda Castle, Fisherman's Bastion, St Stephens Basilica, Parliament building , Liberty Statue, Elisabeth Bridge and so on.

They mostly followed the banks of the beautiful River Danube so it was quite easy to get from one to the other.

Sime's girlfriend at the time Rosie had Hungarian parents and she told us that we HAD to go and see Heroes Square as it was so impressive. So we did that one evening and I saw a load of people doing Tai Chi in the park next door – something that wasn't as widely know about then as it is now.

While looking at the impressive statues of former Magyar chieftains and Hungarian leaders in the square, we came across the American girl - Jenny - who we had seen on the train on the way down from Prague.

She said that she had discovered a great local restaurant where they served proper Hungarian Goulash – and would we all like to go? So there we went and we dined on proper traditional Hungarian Goulash – in Hungary!

Top photo: PB overlooking the confluence of the rivers Sava and Danube from Kalamegdan Castle in Belgrade, Yugoslavia. Above left: PB with an anti aircraft gun at Kalamegdan Castle. Above right: Belgrade tram ticket

278

Day 10 – 10th September 1991
Morning Train: Budapest to Belgrade (380km)

We left the hostel and took the train southwards towards Yugoslavia. Oddly enough, I don't really remember very much about this journey – apart from going past Budapest's Nep Stadium as we left the city.

But it is interesting if for no other reason than the fact that "Yugoslavia" no longer exists as a country. So, while you can still go to all its former constituent parts – Slovenia, Croatia, Serbia, Bosnia, Montenegro etc - rather like "Czechoslovakia", a trip to "Yugoslavia" per se is no longer possible.

We crossed the border at Subotica and, despite there being a vicious civil war going on in Yugoslavia at the time of our visit and our train line running relatively close to the besieged Croatian city of Vukovar at one point, we never saw any signs of fighting or destruction.

The journey took about 6 hours in all and we spent an interesting afternoon / evening in the Serb capital. It was fascinating to see all the signs written in Cyrillic lettering.

In Serbia and neighbouring Croatia, they actually speak the same language - Serbo-Croat - but, in Croatia, it is written in normal Latin script and in Serbia in Cyrillic.

For a country that was supposedly at war with its neighbours, the main shopping area was very bright and colourful – and the shops were all open late.

We changed a bit of money in the Exchange Bureau at the station so as to be able to go and have something to eat. We were warned that because of hyperinflation brought on by the collapse of the previously controlled economy, they were in the middle of revaluing the currency.

As they were introducing the new versions over a period of time, there was a mixture of old and new notes in circulation and we, as tourists needed to be careful that we didn't get ripped off.

Apparently you had to knock a number of zeros off the end of the values of the old notes - an old 10.000 Dinar note was probably now worth 10, or whatever it might have been.

Despite this pep talk, the old and new notes all looked very similar to me - all pretty yellows and oranges with pictures of hard working peasants on them - but as we had only changed enough money to buy sandwiches with anyway, we weren't overly concerned.

We had some street food – cheesy pastries that were really nice - and then went up to Kalamegdan Park. This had a castle on a hill top with great views and also an interesting collection of WW2 military vehicle.

It was a warm sunny evening and there was a stunning sunset – probably caused by the pollution in the air, Simes suggested. From the castle walls, we also had a great view of the confluence of the rivers Danube and Sava.

*A Yugoslav 1,000,000 Dinar note that was official currency
from 1st November 1989 to 15th July 1991*

*The new 100 Dinar note that was officially used
from 1st March 1990 to 31st December 1991.*

*Because of the continual revaluation of the Yugoslav currency - and the regular
issuing of new updated banknotes, and all the associated confusion, both of these
versions were still in common circulation at the time of our visit to Yugoslavia in
September 1991.*

Above: Approximate route from Belgrade in Yugoslavia to Istanbul in Turkey - via Sofia, Bulgaria. This map shows the journey by car route so the train route will have been slightly different (Source Google Maps).

Below: Entry and exit stamps in my passport for Bulgaria - dated 11th and 13th September 1991 respectively.

PB in "Saturday 9th September Square", Sofia - on Wednesday 11th September 1991. The impressive Largo building – former home of the Bulgarian Communist Party is in the background, as is the TZUM Department Store.

Night train to Sofia (400km)

Our welcome into Bulgaria was rather a rude one as we were awoken in our sleeper compartment at the border by a rather gruff and dodgy looking customs official. He didn't look like any of the other customs officials that we would see over the whole of our trip – or, dare I say it – anywhere else, ever. He didn't have a uniform or an official ID badge or anything like that – he just rapped on our door and came in.

He wore a very scruffy suit and overcoat and looked just like the rather comic KGB men you'd see in 1960s black and white spy films.

He smoked all the time he was with us, dropping his ash all over our bedding and our passports –and would you believe - he wanted £50 to give us a visa each to enter Bulgaria.

We hadn't had to pay out at all for crossing into any of the other countries thus far so this was a huge shock and, luckily, we had enough English cash between us to be able to scrimp it together.

After he had gone, Simes raised the question that we had both been thinking about – was he really a customs official or just some crafty conman pulling a fast one and preying on half-asleep tourists?

Anyway, nobody else came to check our passports afterwards so he must have been the real McCoy after all. But it was not a very promising introduction to Bulgaria and Bulgarians.

It may well have been a bit more tourist-orientated in the coastal resorts but I didn't like Sofia very much at all. It was still relatively backward compared to the other emerging economies that we had visited in Eastern Europe – but that was, after all, one of the reasons that we wanted to visit these places.

On arrival, we headed for the main tourist office as they had a very clever system in place where you could book tourist room accommodation in people's private houses.

You paid the fee up front for however many nights you wanted to stay and they gave you a key and a map and instructions of how to get there. We decided to go and dump our luggage at our accommodation first and then come back into the centre and check out the sights of the Bulgarian capital.

Our room was in a flat in a residential area on the outskirts of the city and we needed to take a tram to get there and then walk another 10 minutes or so.

It was in a big block set among other similar blocks and I was glad that we were trying to find it in daylight. The flat we were to stay in was pleasant and clean enough, although the decor reminded me of England in the mid 70s with lots of browns and faded yellows.

There was nobody there when we arrived but the door to the guest room had been left open so they had obviously been told we were coming – and we could see where to put our things.

These Bulgarian tourist rooms were "bed and breakfast" in the true sense of the word. They gave you a bed for the night and breakfast in the morning and that was that – although it only cost something like £8 a night for both of us so you couldn't really complain about value for money.

However, when we went back to the flat after an evening out, we had a bit of a shock. Everywhere was in darkness. And I mean everywhere. Once you got away from the tram stop on the main road, there was no street lighting along the path to the blocks of flats or in the courtyards between them – or if there was, it certainly wasn't working. It was pitch black.

Luckily, Simes had a tiny pocket torch with him or we would have been totally scuppered.

You could see lights on in the rooms of individual flats and most of the entrance foyers to the blocks had lighting of some sort but it was still very disconcerting for two western tourists to be walking through this dark labyrinth of a housing estate. It might have been my imagination but there were sounds coming from all the shadowing depths as if people were watching us - and we felt quite lucky to get back to our accommodation without being accosted.

I drove through a run-down area of Burnley on 24th June 2001 when a riot was actually going on - but this was far more scary than that!

Another very eerie thing about Sofia was that the walls around the city were plastered with what looked like missing persons posters.

These weren't official police posters but clearly home-made a4 photocopies, each bearing somebody's photo and some text in Bulgarian Cyrillic script. And there were hundreds and hundreds of them - on every spare bit of wall that you saw.

Quite who all these people were and what had happened to them I'd hate to think but it was all very un-nerving.

Anyway, back to fun things. Or, at least, as close as you could get to fun in Sofia in 1991...

On the main wall in the Tourist Office they had a big plan of the city centre that showed where everything was. It showed the position of the Tourist Office with a "YOU ARE HERE" marker and from that you could work out which way to go to find things of interest.

This was handy as they didn't seem to have anything by way of tourist maps to hand out – or even to sell.

One place that we were keen to go was the "Saturday 9th September Square".

It had originally been known as the Tsar's Square because it was also the site of the former royal palace but during the post war period it was renamed 9th September to commemorate the date in 1944 when a coup established the first communist government.

The square is now – by the way - called Prince Alexander I Square, after Alexander I, the first prince of modern Bulgaria – who reigned from 1879 to 1886.

But back then we had an absolute pig of a job trying to find this famous 9th September Square because the Tourist Office map had clearly been hung the wrong way round. We even went back to it several times to check that we were heading in the right direction but always ended up going the wrong way.

The Tourist Office was quite a smartly decorated building – certainly compared to the rest of Sofia – and it later occurred to me that it might have been quite recently moved from its original location and that the big wall map had been transplanted without being re-hung in the right place for the schematic directions to fit properly with the streets outside.

The really helpful young guy who we had seen earlier in the Tourist Office when we had organised our guest room had disappeared and that was a shame as he spoke reasonably good English.

He had been replaced by a grim Stalinist looking woman who purported to speak no English, German, French or Russian and this did make me wonder what sort of tourists they were expecting to cater for in the main Tourist Office of the Bulgarian capital.

Of course, in all fairness to her, she might easily have been the cleaning lady who had just been asked to watch over the counter for 5 minutes while everybody else went off for a smoke break – and been trying to explain this fact in polite and eloquent Bulgar – but it certainly didn't come across that way.

Anyway, we eventually found the square and wanted to see the Georgi Dmitrov Mausoleum. In its Communist heyday, this was the centrepiece for all the elaborate military marches and parades on significant occasions and, on normal days, it was open to the public where they could see the embalmed body of Bulgaria's original communist leader who died in 1949.

The tomb was ceremonially guarded day and night by armed soldiers and was an impressive place of pilgrimage for dyed in the wool socialists - rather like Lenin's tomb in Moscow.

Unfortunately, by the time we got to see it, the ceremonial guards had gone, the mausoleum was sealed up and the structure had been daubed with anti-communist graffiti. So that was a disappointment. But at least we did get to see it – which nobody else will ever do now as it was demolished in 1999.

Bulgarian Nightlife

On our first evening in Sofia, we decided that it would be a good idea to phone home and let everybody know how we were getting on.

I had sent postcards to my mum and dad from the various places that we had stopped in but you can never be too sure how long they might take to arrive.

It turned out that, for members of the public to telephone abroad or long distance in Bulgaria in 1991, you had to go to the main post office building where they had row upon row of telephone booths.

You had to queue up at a desk, write down the number of where you wanted to call and were given a numbered ticket – rather like at the deli counter in a lot of British supermarkets or the local council offices.

When your ticket number came up, you were told which telephone booth to go and use and your - somewhat crackly - call was put through. When you finished, you went to another counter and paid however much the call had cost.

Needless to say, we were not the only people who wanted to phone abroad on that balmy September evening and the place was absolutely heaving. There were a lot of people who were obviously tourists like us, lots of others who could have been immigrant families or migrant workers - plus an inordinate number of local people who, presumably, didn't have their own telephones.

And the endless queuing was excruciating. You had to queue to get into the building, then queue at the enquiry desk, then hope to get a seat, then wait for ages for a booth to become free and for your call to be connected and then queue to pay and get out again!

So all this took absolutely ages – with hundreds of sweaty smelly individuals all impolitely milling around and pushing.

Luckily, Bulgaria was two hours ahead of English time so whatever time we finally got our calls through, it wasn't especially late in the evening back in Peterborough.

The following morning, I decided that I wanted to ring my friend and colleague Anne back in the office in Peterborough to touch base and see what was going on in my absence.

I couldn't bear the thought of spending a large part of the day queuing at the post office again in the hope of getting a call put through and was also concerned about avoiding her lunch hour with the 2 hour time difference.

So, this is a bit "revolting English person abroad" but I came up with a strategy.

There was a large ornate hotel on one of the main thoroughfares near where we were – all wood panelling and chandeliers - and I marched straight up to the reception desk and dramatically slammed my Rockwell International business card on the counter.

I announced in a very loud important sounding voice that I needed to get in touch with my company by telephone immediately and could they please arrange it. To my pleasant surprise, the very polite man behind the counter answered in perfect English and pointed me to a discreet dark oak panelled booth over in the corner.

The call was connected almost immediately and I had a nice chat with Anne over a perfectly clear line for a good 10 or 15 minutes.

I appreciated that the call would probably cost a lot more than going via the Post Office but, as nothing in Bulgaria was very expensive in western terms at least, it was certainly worth the extra expense to have a speedy and more comfortable telephone experience.

Back to the night before - after our harrowing Post Office telephone experience, we decided to unwind and check out the Sofia nightlife. And, would you believe – there wasn't any. Or if there was, we certainly never found it.

We eventually found a bar/cafe that had a pleasantly lit outside terrace so we sat there in the cool evening air and had a local beer there.

I ordered a "pivo" as I knew that was what beer was called in Russian, Polish and Czech so it was reasonable to assume that it might be the same in Bulgarian.

Oddly enough I can't remember having anything to eat all the time that we were in Sofia, which is very odd as my near photographic memory is usually very good with trivia details like that.

We must have had breakfast at the tourist room /flat as that was included in the price. Coffee and rolls at guess, but I certainly don't remember. And we must have had something for lunch and dinner all the time were there as well. How odd to have forgotten all that.

All I can say is, that it can't have been memorable, whatever it was!

Shopping In Sofia

Shopping in Sofia was difficult because there wasn't anything to buy. Nothing by way of souvenirs for tourists - and nothing at all, in fact.

They had a huge elaborate department store as part of the imposing Soviet - built Largo complex, called the TZUM or central department store.

It would have been wonderful in its heyday – on a par with the GUM in Moscow and KDW in Berlin – and full of all sorts of exotic things from all corners of the eastern bloc, the Russkies and their allies around the world.

Unfortunately, by September 1991, the free market economy was kicking in, the former Soviet based central economy had collapsed and there was hardly anything in there.

Certainly nothing you'd want to buy, however cheap it might have appeared to western pockets.

I later looked round the grandiose Lewis's department store in Blackpool just before it closed down in 1992/93 and this place had a similar depressing abandoned feel to it.

The only thing that I clearly remember looking at – for interest value rather than as a potential purchase – was an incredibly old fashioned looking transistor radio with Cyrillic text for the tuning settings.

It was heavy and cumbersome and hardly portable and looked like the sort of thing that somebody might have thrown out in the early 70s in England - so it was quite a surprise to see that sort of thing on sale in the top shop in Bulgaria in the 1990s.

From looking on the internet, I believe that the TZUM eventually picked up and got taken over by proper business people who returned it to some modern semblance of its former glory. It is once again the place to go in Sofia for all the top name brands – and I am very happy for them.

In most places that you went to in Eastern Europe during the early 1990s, you often got local people coming up asking to buy western currency off you.

After the fall of communism and the introduction of free market economies in those countries, their own currencies nosedived in value and there was hyper-inflation and constant revaluations.

Western currencies like US dollars, Deutsch Marks and GB Pounds, par contre, kept their value and could – apparently - be used to buy certain things that were otherwise difficult for locals to obtain in those depressed domestic markets.

I had previously heard that you could sometimes get a better deal when buying something off street traders if you offered to pay in western currency rather than local dosh, so Simes and I had come prepared and brought a stack of US dollars with us for that eventuality.

Now, apart from giving some to Aleš - who had been keen to do some home currency dealing – and out of gratitude for letting us stay with him and showing us around Prague - I hadn't had cause to use any of my "dead presidents".

That's until we came across a guy in the centre of Sofia who was selling those pirated audio cassettes that were rife at the time.

As I have already explained earlier in my write up about Poland in 1990, you could purchase dubious copies of current chart albums for less than £1 from these street sellers – and they were perfectly adequate for listening to on your walkman while you were travelling.

Some of them had different / extra tracks on them to the official albums, some had different sleeve designs and I actually still have most of the ones that I bought on those travels even now.

So, we looked at the guy's tapes and figured that there might be two or three worth getting for a quid and asked about a deal for paying in US Dollars.

He gave us a price in dollars for what we had selected and, to my surprise, it seemed to work about exactly the same as if we had been paying in Bulgarian Lev.

I began bartering here – which I never normally do, anywhere, ever – but I had read somewhere that these street traders LOVE to barter and will usually give you a good deal. Except this gloomy sod who didn't.

The price per tape was the same whether you bought one or two or three - and irrespective of whatever current you wanted to pay in.

It took some doing but we had managed to come up against the only person in the whole of Eastern Europe who wasn't interested in acquiring any western currency.

So we walked off without buying anything – and left Bulgaria never to return again.

We had originally planned to go to Romania after Bulgaria but hadn't managed to go to the official Romanian Tourist Office in Berlin when we were there to get the necessary advanced entry visa.

Apparently the economic and social conditions were considerably worse in Romania at the time than they were in Bulgaria so, on reflection, it's probably a good thing that we didn't go...

NB: As a conciliatory note, it did occur to me - in later years, ie: just now, really... - that the lad selling the tapes might not have been a young entrepreneur as I had imagined at the time – and might have not been his own boss.

He might have been employed to sell the tapes by some underworld crimelord, with the finances closely scrutinised, and that might have explained why he was reluctant to do any deals.

Top: PB outside the St. Alexander Nevsky Cathedral in Sofia (built between 1882 and 1912). Saint Alexander Nevsky was a Russian prince.

The cathedral was created in honour of the Russian soldiers who died during the Russo-Turkish War of 1877-1878, as a result of which Bulgaria was liberated from Ottoman rule.

Left: PB outside the National Palace of Culture, Sofia. The largest, multifunctional conference and exhibition centre in south-eastern Europe - opened in 1981 in celebration of Bulgaria's 1300th anniversary.

Bottom: The Dmitrov Mausoleum in 9ᵗʰ September Square, Sofia.

294

Final Destination: PB at Istanbul station, September 1991
The platform was actually being guarded by a policeman armed with a machine
gun but he discretely moved out of the way so that we could take this photo!

Day 13: Friday 13th September 1991
Night Train To Istanbul (550km)

Our welcome to Turkey was a lot more cheery than when we had
arrived in Bulgaria as we were greeted by a pleasant, chatty,
smiling, smartly uniformed border guard who came along the
platform and politely tapped on each compartment window.

He was selling passport entry stamps for £5 a go, which was a
perfectly reasonable amount to pay, in my opinion, and certainly
much better value than the £25 each we'd had to pay to enter
Bulgaria.

The journey time for the night train was around 11 hours so I was
glad that we had a sleeper compartment.

We crossed the border at some god awful time in the morning like 4am and it was only just getting light and freezing cold - but it certainly made our arrival in that particular country more memorable.

By the time we arrived at Istanbul station it had got noticeably hotter and we were pleased that we didn't have to traipse round carrying our luggage trying to find somewhere to stay.

That issue had been easily resolved on the station platform by a well-dressed middle aged man with car who was touting for customers for an hotel in the main tourist area of the city centre.

So we had an interesting - if slightly hair-raising drive along the waterfront and teeming back streets of Istanbul as he took us to this hotel, which turned out to be very clean and pleasant.

Entry visa in my passport for Turkey and an exit stamp dated 16th September 1991

PB at Istanbul Waterfront – with the Asian side in the distance

Needless to say, the weather was very warm and sunny all the time we were in Turkey and the streets and sights in Istanbul were vibrant and colourful. They were full of people all day long – locals traders, visitors and there was a fascinating melange of nationalities and cultures.

Obviously, it was a moslem country so you would hear the call to prayer wafting out across the roof tops from the numerous mosques that were dotted around the city but there was certainly nothing repressive about it and the whole atmosphere there was very bright and cheerful.

Despite the national religion, they weren't over-strict about foreigners back in those days and tourists were allowed – indeed encouraged - to frequent the bars and cafes and pretty much spend as much on booze as they wanted.

Over the two days that we spent sightseeing in Istanbul we visited the following:

Topkapi Palace.

This is a highly impressive 15th century palace that was originally built as the main residence and administrative headquarters of the Ottoman sultans.

It is now a museum and was made famous in the 1964 film "Topkapi" starring Peter Ustinov and Maximilian Schell.

We didn't actually go into the museum but explored the extensive grounds and messed about on the stage in the amphitheatre.

Blue Mosque

This is a very beautiful building and is best appreciated from a distance where you get the clearest overall view of the fascinating architecture. It is unusual in so much as it has 6 minarets instead of the usual 4.

According to Wikipedia: "The Blue Mosque has five main domes, six minarets, and eight secondary domes. The design is the culmination of two centuries of Ottoman mosque development.

It incorporates many Byzantine elements of the neighbouring Hagia Sophia with traditional Islamic architecture and is considered to be the last great mosque of the classical period."

Sophia Mosque (Hagia Sophia)

This is another very elaborate and eye catching building. It is especially interesting because it pre-dates the Moslem Sultanate period in Istanbul and was originally built by the eastern Roman emperor Justinian I as the Christian cathedral of Constantinople for the state church of the Roman Empire between 532 and 537.

At the time, it was the world's largest interior space and among the first to employ a fully pendentive dome. It is considered the epitome of Byzantine architecture.

Minarets were added as it was converted to a mosque in the 15th–16th centuries under the Ottoman Empire.

In 1935, Ataturk – founder of modern Turkey – transformed the building into a museum and it attracted millions of visitors from across the world over the years.

It was controversially re-converted back to use as a mosque in 2020.

Waterfront / Fish Stalls

The water front was a fascinating place to simply hang out and just watch all the people going about their business. There was whole network of ferry boats that zipped across the Bosphorous from the European side of Istanbul to the Asian side with different ports of call along the coastline and they ran very regularly with very little waiting time for the next one.

There were also stalls where local fishermen of were selling freshly landed fish – which smelt awful after a short time in the hot sun – and other traders as well.

Although it was hot, there was nice cooling wind coming in off the clear blue water which made it a very pleasant place to drink in the atmosphere.

Galata Bridge

This is the famous bridge that crosses the Golden Horn in Istanbul and has shops and cafes underneath the roadway across its entire length – it really is the most unusual thing to look at, but a very practical use of space.

The actual bridge that we saw in 1991 has gone now – the so called 4th "floating bridge" (built in 1912). It was apparently severely damaged by fire in 1992 and replaced by a new one on the same site.

We staunchly resisted the various street traders who randomly offered to shine our shoes, sell us little glasses of tea or tell us how much we weighed – but Simes did buy a pair of knock off black Levi 501 jeans for a couple of US dollars. They didn't have any jeans in my size but I was tempted to buy a "Cartier" wristwatch but never had the opportunity to go back to the same market.

We were also tempted briefly into one of the many carpet warehouses but were luckily not conned into buying an overpriced Turkish carpet – magic flying variety or other...

Evening Out

We had a very pleasant evening out around the old town in Istanbul dining on street kebabs and then sitting at an outdoor cafe, soaking up the atmosphere drinking Efes beer and sampling the Turkish version of the aniseed aperatif Ouzo, which is called "Raki".

Setting foot in Asia. PB on the far side of the Bosphorous in the Asian part of Istanbul, September 1991.

An Hour in Asia

On our second day, we took one of the many ferries that criss-crossed the Bosphorous Strait and headed for the Asian side of Istanbul.

We had toyed with the idea of travelling further into Turkey as our Inter Rail tickets covered the whole of the country and not just the bit in Europe. So we could, in fact, have gone as far as Kapikoy on the border with Iran, had we so chosen – or the inland capital Ankara - or Izmir and Iskenderun on the Mediterranean coast bordering with Syria.

However, we decided to have a quick look at the other side of Istanbul first before making any decisions about further travel.

Not knowing where to go on this initial foray into Asian Istanbul – having not researched what was actually there on the other side, we just stayed in the area around the ferry terminals.

Oddly enough, the small part of the Asian side that we saw looked a lot more modern and westernised than the actual western part of the city that we had just left – so that was a bit of a disappointment.

So we didn't stay in Asia very long and crossed back to the higgledy-piggledy vibrant streets of European Istanbul to continue exploring.

A Sudden Curtailment

On our second night in Istanbul, I ate something that didn't agree with me.

Having eaten mainly snacks and street kebabs for the whole of our stay so far, we decided to go to a restaurant and have a proper meal for a change - and I spent all night evacuating at both ends and feeling really ill.

I stayed in bed all the next day and told Simes to go off out sightseeing as I didn't want him to waste his holiday sitting in the room looking after me.

He dropped back in from time to time to check that I was OK and brought bottles of water and plain things for me to nibble on.

The day after that, I felt a bit better and managed to go down for a bit of breakfast but I certainly didn't think I'd be up to spending another week charging around Turkey and Greece on various trains.

This caused a problem as we had flights home booked from somewhere in Greece (I don't remember where – Simon had organised them...) for the following weekend and, as they were tourist charter flights, the reservations couldn't be changed.

The hotel owner was very helpful and rang round the airlines in Turkey - but any flights from Istanbul back to England were either very expensive or didn't leave for another 3 or 4 days, so in the end, we decided to go back the way we had come and take the train.

Approximate route from Istanbul to Thessaloniki (Source: Google Maps)

Day 16: Monday 16th September 1991
Day Train: Istanbul to Thessaloniki (600km)

As I have already mentioned, we had planned on spending the last week of our trip travelling around Greece, seeing the sights and doing a few beaches. We even had flights booked home for the following weekend. But I didn't feel up to much and wanted to go home so we opted for the cheapest option – which was to use the train tickets that we had already paid for to cover the route back.

The train followed a picturesque route along the Turkish and then Greek coast – until we got to Salonika (as Thessaloniki used to be known to the Brits during WW1). Unfortunately, we only had a couple of hours until our next train connection so we didn't really have enough time to go and look at anything - nor did we, in fact, know what there was to go and look at.

So we just stayed in the station, soaked up the Greek sun for the short while we were there - and bought some sandwiches for the overnight trip up through war-torn Yugoslavia.

Passport entry stamp to Yugoslavia, 16ᵗʰ September 1991. Gevgelija is now in the independent country of Northern Macedonia but back in 1991 it was the main border crossing point between Greece and Yugoslavia.

Night Train: Thessaloniki to Budapest (1000km).

We took the overnight train up through what is now known as North Macedonia, along the edge of Kosovo and the length of Serbia, with stops at Nis, Belgrade and elsewhere

This was a really horrible journey and, had it been the first time I had ever been on a train, or at least the first day of our Inter Rail experience, it would certainly have put me off forever!

There were no sleeping berths available and we had to use a normal 6 seater compartment and sit up all night. Luckily, we ended up sharing with another English guy who we had met on the platform who was travelling on his own. He was decent enough and was heading back to England the same as we were. We'll call him "Sam" as I don't remember his name.

As far as I could tell, the whole train seemed to full of bizarre and unsavoury characters – probably smugglers, gangsters, war criminals, mercenaries, you name it – and all they all spent the whole night wandering up and down the train opening doors and trying to steal things.

Now, I do occasionally have a tendency when I am writing to get carried away and "over-dramatize" certain things to make them more interesting to read about. But there is no bullsh*tting here at all - this was REALLY scary. I even saw some dubious looking character threaten somebody with a big knife at one point.

It would appear that a large part of the train had been closed off – we knew not why – and was all in darkness, which was no fun for getting to the toilet... But this also had the knock—on effect that there were not enough seats available therefore a lot of people, particularly those who had joined the train in the areas adjacent to the war zone, were having to camp in the corridors.

It was such a threatening situation that we ended up barricading ourselves in the compartment and taking it in turns to stay awake and keep guard over our stuff.

We somehow managed to survive the night without getting robbed or killed and arrived in Budapest a little the worse for wear. Add to that the fact that I was still feeling queasy after my bout of food poisoning and you can appreciate that this was not really the best bit of our trip.

Days 17 & 18: 17th & 18th September 1991
Day / Night train Budapest to Paris (1490km).

From Budapest, we picked up the Orient Express route to Paris travelling via Vienna, Munich, Stuttgart and Strasbourg.

Any other time, I would have loved to have stopped off along the way to explore - but I still wasn't feeling right and we had already decided that we would head straight for home.

Now, I am bit vague about this whole journey due to still getting over my dicky tummy but I seem to think that we travelled the whole route from Budapest to Paris in one go without having to change trains.

I also "remember" that we did all that and then zipped home from Paris all on the same day. But, as the Trainline.com says that the trip from Budapest to Paris takes 15 to 18 hours, that can't possibly have been the case.

But, if we left Budapest around midday on the Tuesday, travelling through the west of Germany and east of France in the dark, which would be why I don't remember it, we would then have arrived in Paris first thing on Wednesday morning.

Add to that a cafe breakfast in Paris, 3 hours train to Calais, the ferry to Dover, the train from Dover to London and another train from London to Peterborough and that would account for an early evening arrival back home. So that must be what we did!

The Inter Rail Expedition In Figures:

There	Back Again
Peterborough To Harwich (200km)	Istanbul to Thessaloniki (600km)
Harwich to Hoek van Holland (200km)	Thessaloniki to Budapest (1000km)
Hoek van Holland to Amsterdam (80 km)	Budapest to Paris (1490km)
Amsterdam to Berlin (660km).	Paris to Calais (300km)
Berlin to Leipzig (190km)	Calais to Dover (85km)
Leipzig to Prague (265km)	Dover to London (125km)
Prague to Budapest (525km)	London to Peterborough (160km)
Budapest to Belgrade (380km)	
Belgrade to Sofia (400km)	
Sofia to Istanbul (550km)	
Total There: 3450km	**Total Back: 3760km**

Presents

CHRIS REA

NO SUPPORT

MALLARD PARK, PETERBOROUGH
Saturday 7th December
8.00 p.m.
Tickets £15.00 (inc. VAT)
This is an unreserved ticket
which entitles the bearer to sit
or stand subject to availability

002238

Chris Rea / Spain – 7th December 1991

Chris Rea was due to play at the Mallard Park on Saturday 7th December 1991 as part of his Auberge Tour and I had tickets!

However, a rather odd work-related incident prevented me from going – as I had to go to Spain instead.

In my memory, this trip to Spain was arranged all in a rush on the Friday morning but, thinking about it now, I suspect that it may well have been planned the day before. Our company Baker Perkins was installing some printing presses at a company in Madrid called Rotedic. It was a multi-million pound contract and it was very important that everything went according to the agreed timescale.

It turned out that one of the gearboxes that had been delivered for the machine was faulty and another had to be sent over quickly, so as not to hold things up on the installation.

Normally everything would be sent via a freight company but the weekend was quickly approaching and there were a number of festival days coming up in Spain over that period.

That meant that the amount of time that it was likely to take for the shipment to arrive, be unloaded and be processed by customs was unacceptable as it would delay things too much.

It was decided – by somebody who knew about these things – that the only way to get the gearbox to Madrid quickly and avoid all the holiday delays was for somebody to take it on a regular passenger flight as "luggage".

So the next thing I knew I was being driven to Heathrow Airport in a van with an air ticket in my pocket and this gearbox stashed safely in the back.

I don't really know why it was me that had to go. I used to get quite a few of these unusual little jobs to do and I suppose it was because I was the youngest - and most single - person in the office and suddenly having to zip off somewhere or other would cause fewer ructions to my domestic situation. It could also be that I was just the most expendable - but who knows...?

Anyway, upon arrival at the airport I had to dash to get to the check-in because I needed to be there early because I had this extra baggage to worry about.

The company had rung ahead and booked an extra luggage allowance of however many kilos it was for the plane to be able to carry this gearbox and, when I looked at the ticket I was surprised to see that the extra baggage had cost considerably more than the air fare itself.

The charming check in lady was processing my ticket and, the next thing I knew, the van courier chap arrived with three porters who were struggling to carry this ABSOLUTELY HUGE piece of mechanical equipment, strapped to a wooden pallet about 4 feet x 4 feet for safety – round the back of the check in area. So that was my extra baggage!

I don't really remember much about the flight – so that must have been incident free. The big problem came when I got off and went on to the baggage hall to reclaim my gearbox.

I noticed that there was a doorway over in the far corner and the baggage handlers were bringing items out through there that wouldn't fit on the conveyor properly.

This was one of those conveyors where the suitcases come out at the top, slide down a little ramp and then go slowly round and round on the carousel so that the passengers can pick their bags up.

So, as I only otherwise had hand luggage for overnight, I left everybody else doing that and I went and waited over by the unusual items door.

They brought a bicycle out – and then a bag of golf clubs. A framed picture of some sort that was in secure packaging. Some skis – that sort of thing. But my gearbox didn't arrive. So I waited.

And waited.

And waited.

By this time, the baggage hall was almost clear and the airport staff were preparing to close up and go home, so I figured I ought to ask somebody.

All of a sudden I heard the most enormous crash emanating from the direction of the baggage carousel followed by a terrible clunking and whining sound.

You guessed it – somebody had sent this huge heavy gear box through the baggage system and the conveyor was now straining under its weight.

A porter arrived with a trolley and somehow managed to tip the gearbox on to it, levering the palette over the lip of the carousel.

As I went through passport control and customs, with the porter following behind, I was immediately pounced on as expected.

Luckily, Rotedic's local customs clearing agent had been warned in advance of my impending arrival and was standing there with all the paperwork.

Having achieved my mission for the day – and physically got the gearbox into Spain – with great relief I handed over responsibility for this important piece of kit to the customs agent and he disappeared off with the customs officers - all babbling away in Spanish.

I went through to the arrivals hall and was pleased to see that the PMC engineers were waiting to meet me, as I didn't have a clue where the hotel was that I had been booked into – nor even what it was called.

I feel really bad about this - but I can't for the life of me remember who the engineers were that evening. I know Simon Moulds was there (Electrical Engineer – formerly with AL Electrics) as I remember talking to him about ice hockey the next morning when we were sitting around in the factory, but I don't remember who the others were.

That may sound strange if you have seen the minute detail that I can often go into regarding some things but all I can say is that this was quite late in the evening, after a really odd day, and I was really tired.

I remember that we drove through the moonlit streets of Madrid and the guys pointed out certain attractions along the way. We went to a restaurant for a meal and, probably, a few Spanish "cervezas". I couldn't tell you what I ate because I was really tired by then but I am sure it was very nice.

One thing that I do remember was that the restaurant was quite empty when we got there at around 10pm but by the time we left an hour or so later it had started to get really busy.

It was explained to me that, as it is so hot during the day time, the Spanish spend all afternoon resting, go back to work in the early evening and their "evenings out" didn't usually start until about 11 o'clock at night.

That certainly explained why whenever we tried to telephone anybody at Rotedic during the afternoon, we'd always be told that he was "at lunch" even if we were about to go home for the day at 5pm.

With Spaniards also getting up early to make a start before it gets too hot, that also explains why the typical Spanish breakfast consisted of strong coffee and sweet pastries to give them a sugar rush to jump start the day.

So, on the basis of "when in Rome..." I had a sticky sweet sickly typical Spanish breakfast at the Novotel that we were stopping in and then travelled with the guys in to the Rotedic factory.

Despite it being a Saturday morning, they had something that they needed to get on with so weren't able to take me and show round anywhere, which didn't really bother me as I was still exhausted from the night before.

Also the Rotedic factory was a new build development on a new industrial zone in the middle of nowhere so there wasn't anything near there to see either. It was a very overcast gloomy day, so not a good day for sightseeing and seeing Spain at its best anyway.

I therefore spent the only morning that I have ever had in Spain sitting in a factory in the middle of nowhere, not doing anything.

I chatted to whoever wasn't busy at any given time and drank plenty of fluids as, even though it was gloomy and December, it was still very humid indoors.

Then it was time for me to get my flight back so somebody dropped me at the airport and off I went.

I had secretly hoped that I still might get back to Peterborough in time for the Chris Rea concert but it was about 10pm by the time I came out of the station so decided to go straight home instead.

*****

Another occasion when I had an usual task to perform for the Rotedic contract was when I had to go down to London to present a Letter Of Credit to release a large contract payment.

According to the "Oxford Languages" website, a Letter Of Credit is *"a letter issued by a bank to another bank (especially one in a different country) to serve as a guarantee for payments made to a specified person under specified conditions."*

Now, I don't know what they normally did with other letters of credit for this and the many other contracts that our company dealt with but, on this particular occasion, there was a huge fuss about meeting the presentation date and it was decided that "somebody" needed to go down to London on the train and hand it in personally to wherever it needed to go.

And I bet you can guess who that "somebody" was that was sent off to carry out this task..!

I was given a train ticket from our travel department. As far as I could tell – they had blank books of rail and plane tickets, and also traveller's cheques, kept under lock and key, so that they could quickly fill one out if people needed to travel in a hurry – which was very well organised.

I rang my friend Alan – who worked in the purchasing department at London Underground to see if he wanted to meet up for lunch once I got there. Unfortunately, he said that he had something arranged already and suggested I try Louise instead. He gave me her office number – she was free - and we arranged to meet up on the steps outside St Paul's Cathedral, as that was easy to find and handy for where her office was.

I got to St Paul's, found Louise, and we went off for a drink and sandwich somewhere or other - nothing too elaborate as I was, after all, down in London to deposit an important financial document, not to wine and dine other people's wives...

After a pleasant lunch I managed to find the place I was supposed to be going, which turned out to be an upper floor office in the Hays Galleria near London Bridge. I don't remember now what the company was but they were in a lovely air conditioned building, which was very nice as it was a warm sticky day in London.

They had a wonderful panorama from their window looking out across the River Thames and had a great view of HMS Belfast, which was just as well as I had to hang around for a while until they could authenticate the document.

It was all in Spanish and they couldn't take my word for what it said so we all had to wait around until they could find somebody to translate it. That eventually got done and I was given a receipt of some sort and my task for the day was completed.

I rang through to my office to report back and then took the train back to Peterborough. I arrived back later than my usual finishing time but that didn't really bother me as I'd had an interesting day out of the office and not had to do very much.

The first time I did that sort of thing for work was a couple of years earlier – quite possibly 1988 or 1989 - and I had to go on my motorbike to Odhams Sun printers in Watford to pick up a cheque.

I had never driven to London before – usually going on the train – and this was a lot further than I was used to going on my bike in one go, so it was quite an adventure.

I rode down the A1, then the A1m and took the M25 round until I got to Watford. Luckily, it was a nice day and there wasn't too much traffic at the time I was travelling.

I picked up the cheque – for £250.000, would you believe, but the next bit wasn't quite so easy as I had to take it to the main branch office of the Nat West bank in central London to pay it in.

It was a "Town Cheque" which - so far I understood it , meant that it could only be paid into a bank account that was domiciled within the City Of London. Going back to the old days of cheque clearing before we had all electronic banking access, this was an extra safeguard and guarantee mechanism to enable cheques for large sums to be cashed easily.

The cheque itself had the letter "T" at the end of the account number – as did the account number on the Nat West paying in book that I had been given – to highlight that this was a Town cheque and a Town bank account.

I asked the guy in the accounts office at Odhams what the best way was to get to the Nat West that I needed to go to and he told me that, if I didn't know my way around London very well, I'd be better off going on the train.

So I rode back to Watford Junction station which I had passed on the way there, parked up my bike and jumped on the next train to central London.

I managed to find the Nat West building. I don't recall now where it was but it was a huge impressive old fashioned place with lots of wood panelling - and I imagine they'll have closed it by now and moved to somewhere more streamlined.

It was just before 4pm by the time that I got there and the place was about to close. There was a uniformed commissionaire standing the door trying to stop people going in and I somewhat rudely rushed past, waving my crash helmet at him, and went over to one of the cashiers' windows that was still open.

Back in those days, interest rates were still quite high so it would have made a great difference whether a cheque for £250.000 was paid in one day or the next.

The fact that they had sent me down to physically carry this cheque to the bank showed how important it was to get it done that day.

So, like Phileas Fogg in "Around The World In 80 Days", I slapped the cheque and the paying in book down on the counter just before the clock began to chime 4 o'clock and looked beseechingly at the cashier.

He gave me a rather superior look and, seeing my leather jacket and crash helmet, must have thought that I was a despatch rider.

"What time did you pick this up?" he asked me in a rather disdainful manner, quite possibly trying to make out that I had been slacking on the job in some way.

I launched into a long spiel about how the company I work for had told me to go to Watford to pick up this cheque and then I had to take the train and find my way here, etc, etc

He eventually sighed, stamped the cheque, stamped my book and promptly slammed the window shut.

On the way out, I found a phone box and rang the office to report that the cheque had been successfully deposited and I then had to go back to Watford to retrieve my bike.

The traffic was heavier on the way back as it was approaching rush hour but it was quite a nice day so I enjoyed the ride home.

Once I was back on the A1, on territory that I was more familiar with, I stopped for a toilet break at a Little Chef. As it was tea time and I hadn't actually had any lunch, I decided to let the company treat me to a burger and chips, bearing in mind how many £000s I must have made for them in interest through my heroic endeavours.

The only other time I went anywhere on my bike for work was to Allan Denvers, who were one of our customers based in Milton Keynes. I can't remember what I went for but it chucked it down with rain all the way home and I got soaked.

BTEC HNC class on a day trip to London, 1988. Left to right: Richard Mason, Vivian Turner, Steve Virgo, John Semple, Rudi Cavalieri, PB, Glyn Mayley (tutor) & Simon Blanchard.

Squash 1985-1995

One leisure activity that was quite prominent during my Bachelor Pad years – and also a bit before and after – was playing squash. I was never really any good at it but I enjoyed playing and it was good for keeping in shape and for socialising.

I first learnt to play in December 1985 off my friend from school Alan Platt. He was away studying at Reading University and had learnt to play while he was there and, when he came home for the Christmas holidays, he taught me.

We both went on my motorbike to the Cresset Centre at Bretton where they had a big sports hall, squash courts and other leisure facilities. As well as booking a squash court for 40 minutes at a time, you could also hire racquets and balls – which was handy if you were just starting to learn.

Alan showed me the basics of the game and I quite enjoyed it so, over the course of the holidays, we went and played several more times and I slowly got the hang of it.

After Mr Platt had gone back to University, I got my brother Gary to go and play with me. I taught him what I had learnt and we had some good games together. At this point I also splashed out and bought my own racquet and balls to save on the hire fees and to be able to get used to the regular feel of using my own equipment.

So this pattern continued - playing with Alan during the holidays and Gary during the term time and, over that time, we graduated from the easier to play with (ie: bouncier) "blue spot" squash ball through to the harder (less bouncy) "yellow spot" ball.

I believe that there are different types of ball now – and that they can also vary between brands - but we had blue / red/ white / yellow, if I remember correctly, going from beginners to competition level.

After Alan finished at University in 1988 he got a job in London and moved into a flat there. He was not at home in Peterborough anywhere near as often after that, which meant that we very seldom got to play squash anymore - but we still met up for football, music events and drinking sessions when it fitted in.

But all was not lost!

In September 1986 I had started doing a day release course at the local technical college. It had been organised by my employers and was a BTEC Higher National Certificate in Business and Finance. It ran over two academic years and we had to attend the college all day on a Wednesday – which was a nice break in the working week.

This was a general business qualification and the class attracted a fascinating mixture of ages and backgrounds.

There were several people from Thomas Cooks and Pearl Assurance, there was a guy from Metal Box, one from British Gas, me and somebody else from Baker Perkins (although he was in a completely different section and I didn't actually know him beforehand...), a chap from Beezer Homes Construction, a couple of people from the RAF who wanted to pick up new skills before being demobbed and several others who ran their own businesses and wanted a bit of extra know how.

I won't tell you about all of them for now because they are not relevant as far as squash is concerned – but we may come back to them at a later date.

Suffice it to say that, over the duration of the course, some of them dropped out and those of us who remained formed a tight knit group and ended up doing lots of socialising together as well as studying.

One of the guys from Thomas Cooks was called Simon and it turned out that he lived just up the road from me in Stanground.

I never really enquired about this - but I imagine that his family must have moved there comparatively recently because he never went to any of our schools and I never came across him when I was little.

He had separate friends of his own who he socialised with – who were not Stanground based - and they never went to any of the local pubs, usually meeting up in town instead.

Anyway, over the course of the HNC course, Simon and I somehow gravitated towards each other.

I managed to interest him in learning to playing squash and we ended up having a regular squash game on a Sunday lunchtime.

Despite that fact that it was ME that taught HIM how to play, he ended up doing better than me and usually won.

That didn't really bother me as I still won sometimes and it was a nice regular social occasion.

With him living on the same road as me - and him having a car and me not - he used to pick me up and we'd go and play at the Cresset in Bretton.

Afterwards we'd go and have a drink (non alcoholic) - usually orange and lemonade, or something similarly refreshing - at The Beacon which was the pub inside the Cresset complex. We later discovered another pub within walking distance at Bretton Centre called The Roundhead and sometimes went there for a change.

The Roundhead used to have a karaoke on a Sunday lunchtime. It was never very busy when we went in there and it seemed to be the same few people there ever week.

That being the case, the same handful of people seemed to sing their favourite couple of songs all the time - and there were two that I quite fondly remember.

One was a girl who every week without fail sang "Mad About You" – the song by Belinda Carlisle.

I hadn't heard the song before. It had been her first single release as a solo artist in 1986 before she became worldly famous and never made an impact on the UK charts.

The other memorable song was "Endless Summer Nights" by Richard Marx, which some guy made a good job of singing every week.

Here again, Marx went on to have international chart success with later releases such as "Right Here Waiting for You" in 1989 and "Hazard" in 1992 but this earlier song from 1988 didn't really get anywhere and I had never of it before either.

Anyway, this Sunday squash became a regular thing and Simes was kind enough to keep picking me up - even when I moved away from Stanground for a bit.

We sometimes had an extra game one evening during the week if neither of us had anything else happening and we would play at different venues depending on where was available at the time that we wanted to play.

Peterborough was pretty good for sports facilities in those days as all of the new expansion satellite "townships" had sports centres included when they were built. As well as the Cresset at Bretton, there was the Bushfield Sports Centre at Orton and a sports centre at Werrington Centre, which was also used by Ken Stimson School during the day.

These all had big sports halls as well as squash courts so we would sometimes play badminton for change or if the squash courts weren't free. There was also the Manor Leisure Centre at Whittlesey where we occasionally played badminton as well.

Oh – and if the weather wasn't too bad we would sometimes play tennis - which I was also completely useless at – on the hard courts outside, or on the grass courts in Peterborough Central Park during the summer.

As we liked the same sort of music, we often did other things as well. Simes started singing in a band so I went along to watch them play whenever it was convenient. We also did a video shoot for a special live performance by the band in Peterborough's Cathedral Square one day – but that story will also have to wait for another time.

As he had a few music friends that were taking part, I remember that we went to watch a karaoke competition at the Arena Nightclub in Peterborough. This was very odd place as it was out in the middle of an industrial estate and was done out like a Roman courtyard with columns and whatnot.

The advantage of this place over the other clubs in the town was that there was big car park outside, so there was no problem with parking and getting in.

They had an elimination round one week and then a couple of weeks later they had the grand final, where the judges were Ross Kemp and Steve McFadden – who played the Mitchell brothers in EastEnders.

After I moved to Preston for work in 1992 (I'm jumping ahead here - but it is relevant to just round off the story ...), I wasn't in Peterborough quite so often so the squash games became less and less regular.

I did, however, find some squash players among my new northern colleagues so we often played at one of the several sports centre around the town. That continued until I gave up working there in 1995 to go to University after which I lost touch with everybody – and moved on to do other things instead.

As a post script to Squash and to Simon in general.

Following on from our Inter Rail trip in 1991, Simon really got the travel bug and he did actually travel around the world for a year, taking in India, the Far East and Australia.

He cut his navigation across the USA short, however – which was a bit of a shame as I had planned to fly out and join him in San Francisco and we were going to take the train across America together to New York, stopping in interesting places along the way.

So that never happened.

Peterborough United on the pitch at Wembley Stadium for the Play Off final against Stockport County on 24th May 1992.

Football In The Bachelor Pad Years

I wouldn't go so far as to suggest there is a direct link here between my domestic arrangements and success on the football pitch but it just so happens that Peterborough United enjoyed their best period of success – arguably ever - during my Bachelor Pad years.

The first time I ever went to watch a football match was 19th November 1977 when Peterborough played Plymouth Argyle. No – even I haven't got that good a memory - I just looked that up. All of these things are really well archived on websites like www.11v11.com.

I went with my friend from school John Ludman (we sat next to each other in Mr Walker's class at the time, I seem to think) and his dad, who was a season ticket holder.

The Posh won that game 1-0 but just missed out on promotion at the end of the season. The following year, they adopted an Argentina- style playing kit with light blue vertical stripes in the hopes that they might be able to emulate the success of the new recent World Cup winners. Unfortunately the new garb did them no favours at all as they got relegated down to the 4th Division.

The next time I actually went to a game was 14th February 1981 when Peterborough played Manchester City in the 5th round of the FA Cup. I went with Richard Ellis and his dad and I remember that we had to go and queue up outside the ground on freezing cold Sunday morning a couple of weeks earlier to get tickets.

There was a huge 27000 crowd there for the game – you couldn't have that many people these days because of safety regulations.

Man City won the game 0-1 and went on to reach the final where they lost out to Tottenham Hotspur – and that famous Ricky Villa goal - after a replay. That is the only time in history that Peterborough had ever played Manchester City so it was very a special occasion, even though we lost.

(Note: As I am writing, this situation has now changed as the mighty Posh were drawn to play City again in the 5th round of the FA Cup – with the game due to be played at the end of February 2022.)

Having got the bug, Richard and I went to the next home game as well – a 1-3 defeat at the hands of Torquay United in the league – but we never went to a game together again after that.

In run up to the 1981/82 season, Chris Lamb – a friend from school - suggested that we all get season tickets as there was a special offer at the time where juniors could attend all home games for just £10 for the whole season.

So there was a group of us and we all used to meet up and stand together on the Glebe Road terrace (which was considered a bit more genteel and less yobbish than going in the London Road end behind the goal).

There was me, Alan Platt, Chris Lamb, Paul Winskill and few others who didn't go all the time. Wiggy used to go with his dad and I think Steve Garratt went with his dad - Paul Jinks used to be a ball boy, so we often used to see him as well.

Over time, as we grew up a bit and got more used to going, we eventually gravitated to the London Road end and have stood there for games ever since.

I also got a junior season ticket for the 1982/83 season and went to matches with the others but, in the summer of 1983, I got a job in Colton's bike shop in the town centre that meant I had to work all day on Saturdays. I still went to home games that were played on a midweek evening or on bank holidays but it wasn't really worth me getting a season just for that.

So I missed the major part of seasons 83/84, 84/85 and 85/86 due to working on Saturdays and I went off football a bit as I had got into ice hockey which was faster and more exciting to watch – and it was played on a Sunday night, which I could get to more easily.

However, a couple of things happened during 1987 that changed that (we are getting to the important bit – really... Just bear with me!)

The first thing was that Mark Eastwood was working for Barclays Bank at the time and they were main sponsors of the Football League. Part of their sponsorship deal meant that they were allocated a fixed number of hospitality seats at every single Football League game over the whole season and these were distributed out between the Barclays employees at local branches.

In October 1987, Mark was offered two seats for the home game against Cardiff City and he asked if I'd like to go with him.

At that time I was living on Oundle Road and it was a very easy walk to the ground. We had to dress smartly to go in the Executive Suite and we had posh seats and tea and biscuits at half time.

It was an exciting game and Peterborough won 4-3, with the Cardiff fans providing some light relief by invading the pitch at the end.

Anyway, although I never went to a game with Mark again, and didn't go in the Executive Suite again for quite a few years, this experience had a catalytic effect and I decided that, as I was no longer working at Colton's on a Saturday afternoon, I would start going to all the home games again on a regular basis.

This arrangement had the added advantage that I could get out of the house and avoid any brewing arguments that might otherwise have occurred.

This period that I am talking about now – ie the whole of the 1980s – was ironically referred to by the Posh fanzine "The Peterborough Effect" (or TPE for short) as the "Glory Years" because, despite starting every new season with lots of promise, the team never actually achieved anything of note.

And now we finally arrive at the Bachelor Pad years!

For the 1989/90 season, former Liverpool player Mark Lawrenson joined as manager and things began to look up. The Posh finished 9th in Division 4 but hopes were high for the following season.

Midway through the 1990/91 season, something weird happened behind the scenes and Lawrenson left for reasons that were never properly explained. After a few weeks of uncertainty, former Posh player and ex-Cambridge manager Chris Turner was announced as the new manager.

Then things suddenly started to happen. The team pulled together, the fans really got behind the new boss, and over the 22 games that Turner was in charge until the end of the season, Peterborough only lost 2 of them.

A spectacular run of results catapulted them into the top places in the league table and they sealed promotion with a 2-2 draw away at Chesterfield on the last day of the season – 11th May 1991, which I went to see with Paul Hornsby from work.

The following year, the roller coaster continued. Turner's team had a very good run in the League Cup – beating Wimbledon (who were a First Division team at the time), Newcastle and Liverpool before meeting Middlesbrough in the quarter final. The home game was a 0-0 draw so it went to a replay which Paul Hornsby and I drove up to the North East to see, with the Posh losing 1—0 in extra time.

Another excellent run of results in the latter half of the season put Peterborough in the promotion play off places and they beat Huddersfield over 2 legs to reach the Wembley final (you can read more about that later...).

On a boiling hot sunny day over the May Bank Holiday weekend, they beat Stockport County 2-1 to reach the second tier of English football for the first time ever.

For the 1992/93 season I was working in Preston during the week and coming back to Peterborough at weekends so I was able to see most of the home games and, through careful planning of my travel arrangements, quite a few games as well.

The Posh finished in their highest ever league position – 10th in Division 1 - that season. The next year they struggled and were relegated and have been up and down like a yo-yo between various divisions ever since then.

So – what do you think? The three best ever consecutive Posh seasons coincided exactly with my Bachelor Pad years. Spooky or what?

*Before and After: Outside Wembley stadium for the
Play Off final on 24th May 1992.
The open top bus victory parade for the mighty Posh's play off triumph arrives at
the bottom of Fletton High Street on Bank Holiday Monday.*

Ice Hockey In The Bachelor Pad Years

So having already demonstrated with almost scientific certainty that the Peterborough United football team enjoyed their greatest ever period during my Bachelor Pad years, would you Adam and Eve it...? - the Peterborough Pirates ice hockey team did pretty much the same thing!

OK, the years don't coincide quite as nicely as for the football, but you'd have to admit that me and my Bachelor Pad must have sending out some pretty positive vibes for any of this to have happened at all.

I have written numerous books about ice hockey already and could ramble on all day about nothing else but, just to précis:

In season 1987/88, the Pirates finished 10th out of 10 teams in the Heineken League Premier Division – which was the top tier of ice hockey in this country at the time – and had to beat Telford Tigers in a relegation play-off game to stay in the top division. Which they did.

In season 1988/89, they finished 7th out of 10 teams in the HBL, which was a great improvement, and they also won through to the English Final of the prestigious Autumn Cup.

The played the mighty Durham Wasps on 18th October 1988 in the first leg of the final at the East Of England Ice Rink. There was huge crowd for the game (you can see highlights on YouTube) and, according to official figures, it was the biggest ever attendance for a match at that venue. Apparently they were so many people there that the police were called at one point but they couldn't even manage to squeeze in and they went away again.

The Pirates went 1-6 down after a disastrous first period but they were roused by the fans and fought back to draw 7-7 by the end of the game.

Unfortunately, traffic problems caused half of the team to arrive late for the away leg a week later in the north east and they lost 17-3 on the night and 24-10 on aggregate.

But it was still a great achievement to get that far – and it was the only time they ever had any major success in that competition.

In season 1989/90 the Pirates finished 8th of 9 teams - but wait for it – in season 1990/91(which was my main BP period...), under the stewardship of former NHL player Rocky Saganiuk as newly arrived head coach, they had their BEST EVER SEASON, finishing 3rd in the HBLP league table and reaching the British Championship play-off final at Wembley Arena, for the first time and only time ever.

This season saw first time wins over teams who had usually hammered them in previous years, including a highly memorable and entertaining 7-4 win over last season's winners Cardiff Devils in the Wembley semi final.

In the Play Off final against Durham Wasps, the Pirates were within 10 minutes of causing a major shock before eventually succumbing to a 7-4 defeat.

I didn't go to the Play Offs at Wembley Arena that year. In fact, I never went to the play offs at Wembley ever – and there were several reasons for this.

Firstly, at the start of the 1990/91 season, nobody really expected the Pirates to go on and have the success that they did and therefore the Wembley dates were not necessarily blocked off in peoples' diaries.

Also, tickets for the Wembley play offs used to go on sale ages before anybody knew which 4 teams would actually be playing in them.

This meant that, while supporters of the perrenial top teams like Durham, Cardiff and Murrayfield could reasonably assume that their teams would figure and splash out on tickets, the fans of the other less likely teams would have to wait and see how the season panned out and then try their luck with any leftover sales nearer the time.

Because of these factors, I had already organised to go and visit Jola in Poland over the time of the Wembley Play Offs at the end of April 1991 so had no chance of altering my arrangements once it became clear that the Pirates would be appearing there for the first time ever.

Luckily the matches were shown live on BBC's Grandstand sports programme at the time and my mum recorded them both for me on video so that I could watch them when I got back.

I copied the recordings off the original VHS tape onto DVD a while ago and still have them – and highlights of both games can now be seen on YouTube as well courtesy of Pyro Media so that everybody can relive those thrilling moments again and again.

Now, I have to say all this success that this wasn't necessarily all down to me being in my Bachelor Pad at the time. Some of the credit has to go to main team sponsors British Sugar - who used to have a big factory in Peterborough and who, through their Silver Spoon brand, put a lot of money into the team over several seasons

The proof of that particularly pudding came when, in the 1991/92 season, that successful sponsorship deal came to an end and British Sugar were replaced by the Norwich & Peterborough Building Society in a less lucrative deal.

That season the Pirates only managed 7th place out of 10 teams in the league but still got to the Wembley play off semi final where they lost 7-3 to Nottingham Panthers after drawing 3-3 early in the third period.

Sadly, after that it was all downhill for the Pirates and they never quite managed to achieve that level again – but what a few great years to look back on!

I'm the one in white with the puck! This was a training session for the Peterborough Spartans C (rec) team and I imagine I probably got clobbered by that huge defenceman very soon after this photo was taken! That's John Tweedie, by the way, who was a great rec player and very nice fellow.

Recreational Ice Hockey 1987-1990

Although I had been watching ice hockey since 1983, and skating (after a fashion...) since 1981, I didn't start playing until 1987 by which time I was 20 and probably too old to be much good. We certainly didn't have all the "learn to play" and "learn to skate" courses that are around now and the lessons that were available were more aimed at figure skating rather than ice hockey.

The Spartans - as far as I can remember - were started by Robin Colton who he had been involved with getting ice hockey first started in Peterborough along with people like Phil Tilley, the Hunter clan and Granville Raper who moved down from Bradford.

I never actually learned how Robin was able to skate or play ice hockey before anybody else in Peterborough but he had quite an interesting life generally so nothing ever surprised me about him.

When the Spartans were still an embryonic idea and before they were given the name "Spartans", they were initially known as "Robin's C team" and I had heard this being discussed among the crowd at Pirates matches.

The "C team" aspect basically referred to the fact that they would be furthest down the pecking order in terms of adult teams – after the Peterborough Pirates Heineken League team and the Peterborough Titans Division 2 team (who had actually started off as the Pumas).

The idea of the Spartans was that they would be a recreational team open to anybody who wanted to play and, while occasionally some of the players were able to progress and be picked up by the Titans team   - Cassie Dawkins went on to play for the Pirates for good many seasons as well – there was never any initial intention that it should be a competition based team.

As it turned out, there ended up quite a lot of players at varying ages levels and abilities and over time the main Spartan team – composed of the better players - did become a more competitive unit, going in for competitions etc and sort of Spartans B team evolved for the rest. I seem to think that they eventually came to be run as a completely separate team called the Falcons, although I wasn't involved by that time.

I actually knew Robin already because I had worked in his dad's bike and motorbike shop in the town centre called Colton's Cycles. I started there part time when I was 16 in the sixth form doing A levels and remained on and off for three years, doing extra hours in the holidays. Alongside helping run the bike shop, Robin also had a business on the side selling ice hockey gear and getting skates sharpened etc so there was always a fascinating procession of people coming in wanting to see him.

After his dad died and the bike shop had to close, Robin opened up his own ice hockey supplies shop in Millfield (Windmill Street...) and that became a busy hub of activity for ice hockey enthusiasts.

It had never actually occurred to me that I might ever play ice hockey myself. A bit like football and whatever, I enjoyed watching it but was never any good at it.

Anyway, push came to shove and I got into playing – albeit not very well.

This photo at the top was a Sunday morning session and the kit I am wearing there has quite an interesting story attached to it. I first started playing at the grand old age of 20 and needed to get some kit quickly so that I could join in the training sessions properly.

There was a guy where I worked called Steve Brattan who, at that time, ran the Peterborough Ravens ladies team (first ever English ladies champions in 1984/85...!) and had also played for the Pirates when they first started and, presumably, other places before that.

He agreed to sell me some old stuff so I went to his house and picked out some bits and pieces, the more interesting of which were:

A Tilburg Trappers shirt (with some advert in Dutch printed on the front) which he had picked up on a tour match once.

A pair of the original Pirates orange socks (-- lots of darning)

There is another claim to fame here- albeit somewhat spurious regarding the ice hockey shorts I am wearing in this photo - in fact, in all these photos as they are the only ones I ever had.

They actually used to belong to Kim Strongman - daughter of the great Les Strongman of Nottingham Panthers fame, a GB women's international in her own right and one of the top woman players in England during the 1980s and 90s.

When I met her, she was playing for the Peterborough Ravens, who were one of the leading women's teams at the time – and Nottingham didn't even have a women's team back then. And I have her shorts..! No dirty jokes please....

MY ASSIST!

I played my first proper game away at Medway – against the Medway Rangers, who were rather good.

Things started off badly as another Spartans player turned up wearing the same number as me – 26. This was in the days before compulsory registrations when rec hockey was still more or less in its infancy... so this sort of thing did happen – there were even two players with names or numbers at all. Luckily, the other guy was on a different line to me so we coped.

For this match I was centre ice on the 3rd line. The third line was basically a mixed bag of people who had never played in a proper game before and this was just to give everybody a go.

It was very fairly done actually, because each line played for two whistles and then went off, irrespective of how the game stood or who had what penalties or whatever. This meant that everybody on the team got more or less the same time on the ice – not just the "star players" on the first line.

I was never going to be fast enough to play as a forward so my time at centre ice only ever lasted that one game. I seem to think we got hammered by Medway and then had a similar experience in the home game (to which they brought a huge amount of fans...).

My best position was right defence. This was helped by my size/height and the fact that everybody else always wanted to play up front.

I played on what we called the "Mamone Line". Come to think of it, we didn't, actually, call it that at all. I have just made that up – but it sounds good...

It was generally known by everybody else as the third line – or "I suppose we'd better let them have a go then..." or something else equally as uplifting.

There were three Mamones on the team. Mark was a bit older than me, I think, and a much better player so he played on the first or second line, depending on who else was available.

Dave was the middle brother and a bit younger than me and the youngest was Steve - who hadn't had at that time had his growth spurt so was still quite little. Despite this, he played left defence to my right and Dave played up front.

My problem as a defenceman was that I couldn't skate backwards properly and was, therefore, at a disadvantage when faced by attacking players coming forward.

One thing, however, that I was quite good at was defensive clearances off the boards to get the puck out of my blue zone.

Having previously been criticised for incurring icing calls with my enthusiastic clearances, I developed the tactic of slamming the puck into the boards so that it ricocheted off at an angle and pinballed through whoever was between me and the opposite end - and this seemed to work better.

In fact, one evening in the ice rink bar Dave Mamone (probably at the highly popular Friday or Saturday night Laser Blades disco session) staggered over to me in a mildly drunken state and told me in no uncertain terms how much he LOVED picking up my long clearances off the boards - so we then started to use that as a positive tactic.

Now, I'm leading up to something interesting here, so do bear with me. I'm going to tell you about my assist.

Yes, goal scorers tell tales about the various goals that they score, I'm going to tell you about my assist. Just one – once ever – away at Oxford.

I can tell you the date – Sunday 12th June 1988 - it was the day that England lost 1-0 to the Republic of Ireland in the 1988 European Championships as that was on the TV at the rink when we were getting ready to go home. We had 2 games against a rec team at Oxford that former GB player and coach Darryl Morvan was running and, indeed, playing in.

We played the B game swapping lines after two whistles and around midway through the second period it happened. The puck came in my direction on the right side of defence. It crept over the blue line with me in pursuit.

Knowing that I was about to get clattered by one or more charging attackers, (yes, this does sound like that scene in Porky's where he scores the winning shot in basketball by mistake...) I flicked at the puck with the back of my stick, glancing over my left shoulder (not...!), smashed it against boards, out of the bluezone and off up the ice.

The charging attacker still clattered me (this was rec hockey after all...) we both fell over and, while I was still getting up, a goal went in. We had scored. The announcer announced "Goal Mamone" (probably, anyway , I think he was 20) "Assist 26 Breeze"!

So there you are – my and only solitary competitive point – ever. But what fun, eh?

We won that B game and I think we also won the A game which was more competitive. I was a reserve for the A game and actually got onto the ice for 10 seconds in the last minute in preparation for a face off. AC Stan Asplin told me to go on for a bit of ice time and Captain Mick Trollope promptly told me to get back off again....

But there you go – that's the story of my assist – and one I'll never tire of telling, however boring it may be for everybody else.

MEDWAY RANGERS

v

PETERBOROUGH

FACE OFF

5.15

SUNDAY 22 MAY 1988

Left: Front cover of the match programme from the first ever game I played in. No - they didn't have our names inside – communications weren't that good back in those days!

Above: This is my Peterborough Spartans shirt from 1988 – it's a bit snug these days. I think it must have shrunk over time....

Rockwell Raiders Charity Team 1990

Back Row: Kevin Woods, Bill Glover, Jim Northen, Paul Breeze, Andy Maile, Mick Ward, Derek Dancy, Carl Walker, Gary Stewart. Front Row: Ian Woods, Steve Brattan, Alan Thurston, John Tague, Phil Haselgrave, Paul Bright, Steve Grainger, Andy French.

So: particularly interesting people in the team photo on the previous page - apart from me – are:

John Tague (front row centre) former Pirates netminder who played as an outfield player

Andy French (front row, far right) - who was Pirates team manager at the time and went on to be the Team GB manager and then overall supremo. Here he was bench coach.

Bill Glover (back row, 2nd left) was the Pirates physio and also a champion road race cyclist.

Pirates defensive import for that season Gary Stewart (back row, far right).

There was a video taken of this game, although I have never been able to track down a copy.

Above: me in the charity match. My biggest claim to fame here is that I was wearing Todd Bidner's shirt and I played on the first line for change! (Photo by Francis Page)

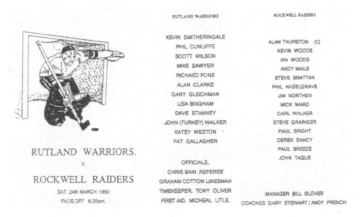

RUTLAND WARRIORS.

v.

ROCKWELL RAIDERS

SAT. 24th MARCH 1990
FACE OFF 6.00pm.

RUTLAND WARRIORS	ROCKWELL RAIDERS
KEVIN SMITHERINGALE	ALAN THURSTON (C)
PHIL CUNLIFFE	KEVIN WOODS
SCOTT WILSON	IAN WOODS
MIKE SAWYER	ANDY MAILE
RICHAED FONE	STEVE BRATTAN
ALAN CLARKE	PHIL HASELGRAVE
GARY GLEICHMAN	JIM NORTHEN
LISA BINGHAM	MICK WARD
DAVE STANNEY	CARL WALKER
JOHN (TURKEY) WALKER	STEVE GRAINGER
KATEY WESTON	PAUL BRIGHT
PAT GALLAGHER	DEREK DANCY
	PAUL BREEZE
	JOHN TAGUE

OFFICIALS,
CHRIS BAIN ,REFEREE
GRAHAM COTTON LINESMAN
TIMEKEEPER, TONY OLIVER
FIRST AID, MICHEAL LITLE.

MANAGER BILL GLOVER
COACHES GARY STEWART / ANDY FRENCH

Charity Match In Aid Of Peterborough Children's Hospital Appeal. Rockwell Raiders v Rutland Warriors

So, most of the foregoing – as you will have realised – actually took place BEFORE my Bachelor Pad period, and occurred in spite of - rather than because of - my complicated domestic arrangements... but my own crowning glory in terms of ice hockey as a player definitely came within the BP period - in March 1990.

I had no involvement in the organising of this game. That might be hard for people to imagine now – considering all the various things I have done in the meantime - but, back in 1990, I was still very much a follower rather than a mover and shaker.

On a walk around the factory floor at Baker Perkins one day, I noticed a poster hanging up advertising a charity ice hockey match.

It was to be between a works team called the Rockwell Raiders and a team of randomly assembled people from the Peterborough ice rink who were calling themselves the Rutland Warriors for the purposes of having an opposition for the match.

Having already played a bit in the past and having all my own gear, and - as far as I was concerned, being eligible to play by working for the company - I decided to find out who was behind this superb initiative and see if I could get involved. It turned out that it was being put together by Bill Glover - who worked in the cylinder section - and Alan Thurston - a fitting shop fitter, both of whom I knew already from my time working down in the office.

They were **DELIGHTED** have me on the Rockwell team - which was quite a first for me in itself – especially as most of the other guys had certainly never played properly before and, indeed, quite a few of them could hardly even skate!

Bill Glover was the Physio for the Pirates team and he had arranged ice time for the game and the loan of sticks, skates and equipment for the Rockwell players to use.

A lot of the guys had been going down to the ice rink on their own in the evenings to get some practice skating but, a week or so before the big game, we had a proper training session after work with full gear on so that they could all get the feel of it.

This was great fun for me as, for the one and only time in my life, I was one of the best players on the team!

There were also John Tague who was a netminder with the Peterborough Pirates for a number of years. Despite being a goalkeeper, he could obviously skate very well and had good puck handling skills - and Steve Brattan who was the union rep at Baker Perkins. He had played with the Pirates when they first started in the early 80s and had also run the Peterborough Ravens women's team.

Right – now. One "elephant in the room" needs addressing here, before we go any further talking about this charity game.

As we are talking turkey, getting down to brass tacks, telling like it is, facing our demons - and not beating about the bush, or any other sort of prevaricating or filibustering – I need to flag this up and get it out of the way.

At the time that it was played, this match was supposed to be a fundraiser for the new Jimmy Savile Children's Hospital that had been planned for Peterborough.

Now, I know that following all the revolting revelations about that man that have come out since his death, the idea of him having his own children's hospital is quite monstrous. But you have to remember that, back in 1990, the general public were completely unaware of these goings on and he was still a big media celebrity.

He had been a mainstay on BBC TV for many years and was famous for doing lots of good works for charity.

Cutting from the Peterborough Evening Telegraph, 26th March 1990

When the Jimmy Savile hospital plans were first unveiled, there was huge front page coverage in the Peterborough Evening Telegraph and lots of people in the city were very supportive of the idea.

Like him or loathe him – and I think everybody loathes him now that they know the truth about him – he made quite a name for himself running marathons for charity and he was also closely involved with the Peterborough 6 mile road race.

Savile reportedly had a luxury riverside apartment overlooking the Nene for a while and I actually saw him once when he was out on a training run when I was driving home from work.

He was running around the Queensgate Roundabout and heading towards Crescent Bridge and all the traffic had stopped for him to get across. He had a sweatband around his head, dark glasses on and a cigar in his mouth and was waving to people as he went past.

At the time I was quite chuffed to have seen him – what with him being a famous TV celebrity – but, knowing what we all do now, I wish my clutch might have just slipped, by accident...

Anyway, the good thing is that Savile never attended our ice hockey match and the proposed children's hospital was never built. All the funds that were raised by the city wide appeal were used instead for other children's health facilities around the area instead.

*****

On the day of the game I did myself an injury and almost didn't take part at all. I had gone into town in the morning – mainly for something to do to take my mind off being nervous about playing - and on the way home, in slow moving traffic, I managed to fall off my motorbike. Have you ever heard anything so daft? In the middle of a traffic jam?

Anyway, I must have lost my footing or my balance as I was edging along somehow and the bike tipped over and I went with it. I was hardly moving so there was no damage done – except to my pride. A long queue of traffic had built up behind me as I got up and got going again and I headed home for a cup of tea and a lay down.

I had a doze on the settee in front of the TV – which is most unlike me to sleep during the day – so the motorbike spill must have affected me more than I had realised.

As I went to get up, I noticed that my right leg was a bit stiff - which I could have done without with an ice hockey match coming up in a few hours – but, worse than that, my right hand was sore and I was having trouble moving my thumb and forefinger.

I was determined to play in the game, however, and got to the rink in plenty of time to join the others and get changed but the whole of my right side was sore by this time and this made things more difficult.

The worst thing was that I couldn't grip my laces tightly enough to be able to do my skates up properly and this left them fitting more loosely on my feet than I would have liked.

But I didn't want to tell anybody about my footling embarrassing injury in case somebody suggested I didn't ought to be playing.

So I got all my gear on, one way or another, and out we went for the game. The other team were wearing shirts borrowed from the Northamptonshire army regiment's Steelbacks ice hockey team team and we were wearing the old Pirates shirts from the 88/89 season when they had the orange Silver Spoon logos.

I had the number 20 shirt which Canadian import – and later GB international - Todd Bidner used to play in and I had the "A" for Alternate Captain on my chest, so I was quite chuffed although I am not sure whether any of his aura rubbed off on me.

There was a pretty good crowd in attendance – 300 or so for a charity game with a load of recreational players – and, with it being a works event, there were a lot of people there who had never been to an ice hockey match before – so the good thing was that they wouldn't have known if we were actually any good or not.

My mum and Dad were there. So far as I can recall that was the only time that my dad ever watched me doing anything sports-wise. My mum had previously come on the coach – along with my then girlfriend - to watch my first Spartans game away at Medway, although she generally found it too cold in the ice rink.

My friend and colleague from the office Anne Castellano was there and she took a few photos for me. Paul Hornsby and Zahlia were there – plus a lot of other people who I didn't see on the afternoon but who commented to me afterwards when we were all back at work, so it was a very nice occasion all round with a lively, cheery atmosphere.

Our Rockwell Raiders team came onto the ice to the sound of the "Eye Of The Tiger" from the Rocky film, which the Pirates team used to skate out to at that time as well and it all went on from there.

I don't remember much about the game, to be honest.

The "modern day me" would have insisted on grabbing a copy of the game sheet and writing a match report straight afterwards – but I wasn't that kind of bear in those days.

I remember being on the bench and joking with Andy French. I remember being on the ice when Taguey scored with a slapshot from a long way out that the referee disallowed because he was a professional guest player and it was unfair on everybody else – and I remember having lots of ice time and thoroughly enjoying myself .

But I couldn't possibly tell you what the score was or who did what in terms of goals and assists.

I didn't score myself but I was far more used in my previous games to playing in defence and trying to clear the puck away, rather than necessarily doing anything useful with it. So, in this game, when I was suddenly expected to take it forward and try to pass to a team-mate or shoot on goal, I was rather out of practice.

I THINK it might have finished something like 4-5 to the opposition but couldn't really swear to that.

I know there was a little jiggery pokery at the end when the clock was about to reach zero and the timekeeper added an extra minute on because we were attacking, in the hope that we might draw level. And when that didn't work, the referee awarded us a highly controversial penalty shot - and that didn't work either! But it was just a bit of fun and everybody seemed to enjoy themselves.

The odd thing was – and I think this is common with lots of sportspeople people and certainly ice hockey players who I have spoken to in the past – I didn't feel any pain or discomfort from my fall during the game but was in absolute agony and could hardly move by the time I got home, especially with any other additional knocks and bangs I might have picked up in the heat of the action.

Still, it got me plenty of sympathy from the girls at work the following week!

Well – here it is. Young free & single in Preston in May 1992. Got the car, got the house – all ready for another year of Bachelor Pad fun!

1992-93: The Bachelor Pad Mk2 - Preston

I actually had a "Bachelor Pad Mk2" for a year when I first moved to Preston for work.

Because I was on the "transition team" as part of the factory move from Peterborough, we all got hotel accommodation and travel expenses paid for by the company. After a while, I got fed up with staying in hotels and having to cart my stuff back and forth every week and, as I was going to be there for at least a year, I rented a house near to work and the company paid for that instead.

It belonged to one of my new workmates, Neil, in the contracts office at the Preston factory where I was now based and he rented it out to students at the nearby university.

Once the current batch of students had moved out at the end of May for the summer, I moved in and he worked out a monthly price that included the rent and all the bills so that I could present it as a single accommodation cost to be refunded by the company.

It was cheaper for them than paying out for 4 or 5 nights' hotel accommodation every week for a year and it gave me a base where I could relax and leave all my stuff - so everybody was happy with this arrangement.

It was a traditional terrace house on Henderson Street – which was a quiet residential street but was just a few minutes' walk from the Plungington shops and the main road.

There was plenty of room for me as it had a living room, dining room & kitchen downstairs and three bedrooms of varying sizes – and a bathroom - upstairs.

Because I got my travel time and costs paid for during this period and had a company car for the year – a nice spacious Citroen BX estate – I went home to Peterborough every weekend and was able to carry on with my usual leisure activities there.

It was about 180 miles door to door and usually took about 3 hours depending on traffic.

As I wasn't a formal Preston employee at this time, I had quite a bit of leeway and could arrange things to suit myself.

For example, I could leave off work at Friday lunchtime and drive home to Peterborough during working hours in the afternoon. Or I could finish at knocking off time on Friday, drive home in the evening and claim 3 hours overtime.

I also got my travelling time paid coming back on the Monday so I could travel back Monday morning – or come on the Sunday night and claim for it.

This meant that a typical weekend for me during 1992 and early 1993 consisted of:

- driving down to Peterborough on Friday afternoon or evening
- Friday night drinks with the lads around Stanground or elsewhere
- Football on a Saturday
- Sunday lunchtime squash with Simon
- Peterborough Pirates ice hockey on a Sunday evening
- A late drive back to Preston on Sunday night when the traffic was quieter

Sometimes I would be able to contrive some meeting or other reason why I needed to stay down at the Peterborough office and could thus have an extra day at home on a Monday or a Friday and travel back and forth to Preston accordingly.

Once I had the house in Plungington, I also had the option of staying in Preston on the Friday night and driving to Peterborough on the Saturday instead. I still got paid for my 3 hours travelling time and, if I chose to do it on a Saturday instead of a Friday, then that was entirely up to me.

By doing this, I was able to go and see Peterborough United away matches on the Saturday which were nominally "on the way" - and then carry on home to Peterborough afterwards.

I did this on a number of occasions and went to places that I might not ever have managed to go to otherwise – like:

Wolverhampton (5th September 1992),

Barnsley (twice - 19th Sept 1992 & 11th December 1993),

Grimsby (3rd October 1992),

Leicester (18th October 1992),

Derby (twice: 6th February 1993 & 11th September 1993),

Oxford (20th April 1993 & 12th March 1994)

& West Bromwich (16th October 1993).

I also remember doing this the other way round once and went to a Posh match at Notts County on a Sunday (21st February 1993) and drove straight up to Preston afterwards.

The 1992/93 season was Peterborough's first ever up in Division 1 (which is now called "The Championship") so it was quite an adventure. They achieved their highest ever season position of 10th in the second tier that season so I was very lucky to have been a part of it.

Steve Garratt was studying something postgraduate at Manchester University around the time that I moved to Preston so we often used to meet up for football trips.

We went to Friday night games at Tranmere (30th Oct 1992) and Birmingham (22nd January 1993) and also had a couple of epic weekends away to see games at

Newcastle (16th January 1993) &

Sunderland (13th March 1993),

where we stayed with a Geordie friend of his.

We also saw the Bjorn Again Abba tribute (impersonation) group in concert at Leeds Polytechnic Student Union together once and The Men They Couldn't Hang in Manchester.

I also went and saw the rather bizarre yet fun Japanese all-girl rock band Shonen Knife at Liverpool University with Neil Cook (24th October 1992).

There were quite a few other Peterborough colleagues up at Preston – either semi-permanent like me or regular visitors - so we also arranged to go to see some Peterborough away matches when they were played on midweek evenings in the vicinity.

When the mighty Posh qualified for the Play Offs in May 1992, I managed to be in Peterborough so that I could see the home leg game on the evening of Monday 11th May.

I then got a ticket for the away leg that was played in Huddersfield on the Thursday 14th.

Huddersfield is only about an hour's drive from Preston so a group of 7 or 8 of us from the hotel went in two cars.

The first leg saw a 2-2 draw in the home game and then Peterborough snatched a dramatic 1-2 victory in the second leg with just 4 minutes left to play. We all went home happy being able to look forward to a trip to Wembley for the final but the disappointed Huddersfield fans rioted on the pitch after the game and had to be cleared away by mounted police.

We got back OK but one of the guys in the other car was a Huddersfield fan who had come along for the lift and he got arrested after the game. The others had to go and wait outside the police station until he was released before they could drive back to Preston, which must have made it a long night for them!

A Few Sensible Things

During the period April 1992 to April 1993 when I was getting most of my living expenses paid by the company, I took advantage of the opportunity to get my personal finances on an even keel.

I had two credit cards with balances on that I was never going to be able to pay off in the normal course of events.

I also had an HP agreement for a stereo CD system that I had bought from Currys in 1986 and which had somehow morphed from the reasonable fixed easy payment plan that I had thought I had taken out into some sort of "store card" with snowballing interest payments that I had never asked for and never seemed to reduce.

So I went to the main Preston branch of the TSB – which had been my bank ever since I had started off saving 10p a week via the school a very long time ago - and explained my predicament to a very helpful Assistant Manager.

He very kindly arranged me a loan for £7.000 (or whatever amount it was) that I could pay off over the 12 months while I was in a better financial position.

This allowed me in one fell swoop to pay off the two credit cards and cut them up – and also to get rid of the stereo finance which I must have already paid for about three times over, so I was very much relieved.

In May 1993, Neil announced that he was planning to sell off the house that I was renting and would I like to buy it...?

At the time I didn't really take the matter as seriously as I might have done and, looking back now, it's one of the few things in my life that I regret not having done when I had the chance.

Back then with my newly increased Preston salary I could probably have got a mortgage to cover the full selling price and it would have been a great investment.

I seem to think that he wanted £41.000 for it – and that included all the contents which I was already using. By the time that Lucy and I were back in Preston, looking to buy a house in that same area in 1998, prices had gone up considerably and a similar terraced house was selling for £80.000!

However, it wasn't that straight forward at the time as I didn't have a deposit to put down. Even finding the relatively small sum of 5% of 41.000, ie £2000, was going to be difficult because I had no savings to speak of – having just shelled out £1200 on a car - and was still in the throes of paying off the TSB loan.

I didn't even bother enquiring at the bank as to how I might get on with a mortgage application and ways to get around the deposit - which I realise now was possibly the wrong decision.

The other thing that you need to bear in mind was that I wasn't by any means fully "settled" in Preston in 1993.

I still went back to Peterborough most weekends as my friends and family were all there.

I had also embarked on a new romance which necessitated me travelling back and forth to Germany quite a lot – but more about all that in another volume...

So, saddling myself with a £40.000 mortgage in a place that I wasn't sure I would be staying long term in wasn't the most prominent thought in my head at the time.

Of course, it's great being able to look back now with hindsight. Had I known for a fact back in May 1993 that I was definitely going to remain in Preston until June / July 1997, I would have probably figured that the money I would be paying out on rent during that period – effectively helping to pay off somebody else's mortgage - would be better invested in buying somewhere myself.

I could have rented the place out for the academic year 1997/98 when it turned out that I would be spending a year abroad for university (although I didn't know any of that back in 1993).

Plus, it would have been somewhere secure to go and live when Lucy and I returned to England during a frustrating period when we ended up paying out huge amounts for rented accommodation from June 1998 to November 1999.

But I couldn't foresee any of that back then – so I chose a different path and started looking for suitable rented properties to move to.

I eventually found a pleasant modern flat on the outskirts of Preston and Neil helped me move my stuff there over the Bank Holiday weekend at the end of May.

I chose this place with half an eye on the fact that Hanja would be coming to share it from September 1993.

Haighton Court was in a quiet leafy residential estate with lots of air and greenery around. It was handy for the ring road and, therefore, the motorway for getting to places.

The Last Throes of Bachelor Pad-ism - Haighton Court in Preston. Mine was the middle flat on the left.

It wasn't handy for walking to the University like the house on Henderson Street had been but, as I would be driving into work in Preston every day, just up the road from the Uni building, that didn't really matter quite so much.

It was on the main bus route into town, with the bus stop being about 2 minutes walk from the front door.

Also just a few minutes' walk was the Sherwood pub – which was very pleasant for a drink from time to time and a very handy venue for watching England football matches during that ridiculous period when they were only available to watch on Sky Sports.

I actually watched the live boxing on the TV there on the night of 2nd September 1995 when Frank Bruno beat Oliver McCall to win the world title in a huge double header at Wembley Stadium when Nigel Benn also beat Danny Perez in a thrilling spectacle.

There was also a big playing field within sight of the living room window – not so close as to be annoying if anything was happening there, but easy to walk across to for a bit of fresh air and leisure time if desired.

The large Asda superstore at Fulwood was just a bit further along the ring road and that was handy for shopping - and I actually went on to work there for a bit in later years.

About a year or so into my tenancy of the flat, I actually had the opportunity to buy it off the owners. Here again, looking back, this might have been an ideal investment opportunity - but I still wasn't very mature at that stage in my mortgage taking on outlook.

I think that the selling price was something like £25.000 – and similar properties today are on the market for 80 to 90k.

But I still didn't have a deposit – constant weekend trips to Peterborough and regular ferries and flights to Germany were taking their toll on my finances – plus RGS were in the middle of large scale redundancies and the word was that banks were reluctant to give out mortgages to remaining employees under those circumstances.

Also, the flat was leasehold in a building that was run by some distantly located management company to which monthly service charges had to be paid – so that was an unknown variable that could store up problems for the future.

So, I didn't buy that property either and ended up waiting until October 1999 before I eventually got a foot on the property ladder.

26th September 1992: Peterborough United were playing Newcastle United in the First Division in front of a huge crowd at London Road - and I was stuck at Mark Eastwood's wedding! At least I was asked to be an usher...

Above left: Out sightseeing with Jola, Summer 1992 (photo by Jola)
Above right: PB away at Sunderland, 13th March 1993 (Photo by Steven Garratt).

Not Jola in England - this is actually a photo of Jola in her flat in Warsaw but is taken from a birthday card that she sent to me in April 1993

1992 & 93: Jola In England

Jola came to visit me in England in the summer of 1992. Well, technically she didn't specifically come just to see me but she did come and visit me while she was in England. She went to stay with some Polish friends who were living in Vauxhall in South London and she spent several weeks working at an Aberdeen Angus Steak house.

I never fully understood the attraction of this but it would appear that, due to the wide difference between national economies at that time, she could make more money doing that for a few weeks in London than she would get for a few months in her main job in Warsaw – and she thought it well worth her using up her holiday entitlement to do it.

But because, at the time, the Eastern Bloc had only just opened up after the fall of the wall and immigration restrictions were still in place, I had to act as Jola's sponsor so that she could get a visa to come to England.

I had to fill out an official invitation form with my personal details on it and her personal details. I had to give my address where she would be staying while she was in England, give an assurance that I would support her during her visit and that she would leave again at the end of it!

Now, had anybody in authority checked up on her whereabouts – apart from the week or 10 days that she was actually with me – and discovered that she was working in London without the correct paperwork, my arse would have been toast. But, luckily, that never happened and the visa restrictions were later abandoned.

I was in quite a good financial position at this time as I had the company car, travel expenses and I also got a daily food allowance. This meant that I got something like £19.50 for every day that I worked, whether I spent it or not, and when Jola came to visit, I found a clever way of making the most of it.

Rather than taking a full day off, I worked in the morning and then took the afternoon off to go out and do things with her. This meant that I received my food allowance money for the day and also did not have to try and think of things to do all day long.

I had given her the front door key and pointed her how to get into town, which was quite easy from where I was living. It was a 15/20 minute walk along a straight road so you couldn't really get lost and she was used to walking a lot back in Warsaw so it wasn't a great hardship – plus the weather was nice all the time she was there.

There were also plenty of buses in case she got tired on the way back.

During the week or so that Jola was in Preston, we went out and saw somewhere different every afternoon and probably ate out in the evenings. I don't really remember all the specific details – but I can tell you that we:

- We went to the Lake District one day and took the boat across from Bowness to Ambleside
- Went to Blackpool on a very hot and sunny afternoon and she was thrilled by the various illuminations displays that were in place (as they didn't used to get taken down in between the lights seasons)
- Went to Beacon Fell Country Park up in the hills above Preston
- Went to Clitheroe
- Went to Ribchester to see the remains of the Roman settlement and the views across the river Ribble
- Walked around the Preston docks area which was being developed with expensive flats, a marina and leisure facilities.
- Probably ate at Owd Nells a lot as they had a good varied menu and it was a nice setting alongside the canal.

At the end of the week, we drove back to Peterborough and I seem to think that we went to visit Graham in Cambridge on the Saturday. On the Sunday I drove Jola back to London and then had the long drive all the way back to Preston ready for work on the Monday.

*****

Jola came to England again in the summer of the following year (1993). She stayed with her friends in London again and this time she worked in a Deep Pan pizza outlet.

I can't really fathom out the chronology of this but I distinctly remember that I went down once and met her for the evening and we had deep pan pizzas before going out somewhere on the Docklands Light Railway.

I am convinced that this was a completely separate occasion to when I picked her up and brought her back to Preston, but can't for the life of me work out how it might have fitted in.

Anyway, the particular week that Jola wanted to visit me in Preston this time wasn't overly convenient for me.

I was a full time employee at RGS Preston by then so didn't have the same flexibility that I'd had when I had been a Peterborough employee on transition and could more or less do what I wanted. This made it more difficult for me to get time off work – as I had to fit in with other people's holidays - so we weren't able to go out and have wall-to-wall fun all the time like we had the time before.

Also, I was living in the flat in Sherwood by this time and it wasn't just a quick walk into town, although the bus did go right past, so it wasn't quite so easy to merely pop out and do things.

My flat only had one bedroom. In fact, it had two bedrooms but the smaller second bedroom had a load of junk in it and wasn't easily accessible. It was almost completely filled up by the ¾ size bed that had been in the flat when I moved in and which I had shoved in there when I had bought a bigger, more comfortable, king size bed for myself.

So the irony was that I had a spare bedroom with a spare bed in it but the bed was in pieces and it was impossible to put it together so that it fitted in the room properly.

This meant that Jola had to sleep in my bed and I slept on the air bed in the living room, so I slept badly all week.

Anyway, I think I did manage to get a few days off in the end so we went out and did some things - and I dropped her in town on other occasions and picked her up later, so it wasn't too bad.

I was paying all my own bills by now - and had to cover my own petrol costs - so I wasn't able to drive up and down to London on a whim like I could before.

I couldn't really afford to drive her back down to London, having only just been the week before, so I went for the cheaper option and plonked her on the National Express coach –which didn't go down very well.

That was the last time I saw Jola. We carried on writing and telephoning for a while afterwards but I think she got married some time after that. Also Hanja came over and started at University in September 1993 so it wasn't really feasible for me to get nocturnal phone calls from exotic women any more.

So that brings us well and truly to the end of my Bachelor Pad years!

PB at Beacon Fell Country Park near Preston, June 1992

NORTH / SOUTH DIVIDE
WHY NOT COLLECT THE SET?

North / South Divide: The Original

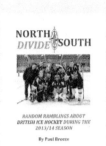

The 2013/14 season was a watershed year for me ice hockey wise. The Fylde Flyers team finished, leaving me with only recreational hockey to write about in Blackpool so I decided to branch out and cover the English National League in a more general manner.

What you will find in this book is a mixture of opinion columns written for Blueliner.com and round-ups and news items that started off on bestkeptsecrets and, after January 2014, ended up on icehockeyreview.co.uk. I hope that makes sense – it shouldn't be boring, anyway…!

ISBN: 9798563183759

Volume 2: Ice Hockey And Me

Mainly autobiographical and featuring random and bizarre topics such as:

How I came to be at the World Championships in Luxembourg,
The day I met Stewart Roberts,
Which Sims twin is which and
The story behind Lucy's "French And Ormes" poem...

ISBN: 9781909643451

Volume 3: Cricket & Baseball

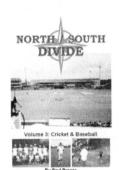

More autobiography - mainly about my involvement in cricket and baseball – plus a few other things as well.

So, just to whet your appetite, in this volume you can read all about:
Why I wasn't any good at cricket at school
The Cricket World Cup in 1999
The Preston Bobcats league baseball team
The Preston University student team of 1996/97
And my experiences of baseball coaching at Summer Camps in the Czech Republic.

ISBN: 9781909643468

North / South Divide – Volume 4

Volume 4: France Actually

Featuring all things France and French related, including:

- school trips to Quiberville-sur-Mer and Barneville-Carteret
- the French Exchange to Montpellier in 1984/85
- stories from the G14 printing press installations at IGPM and Sima Torcy
- Phoebe Cates And The McDonald's Milkshake Incident
- and how I almost came to live in Nantes ....

ISBN: 9781909643475

North / South Divide - Volume 5
by Paul Breeze

COMING SOON

Volume 6: Germany Calling

Yes - this volume is about trips to Germany plus other places in that general direction, including Belgium, Luxembourg, Czech Republic and Austria.

There's a bit of work related content including the DRUPA exhibitions in Düsseldorf in 1990 and 1995 and the year I spent in Luxembourg working for a radio station and a media agency.

So, if you are interested in travel trivia, this book may well be for you – when it comes out, anyway...

All books listed on these pages are available by mail order from Amazon, Posh Up North, Waterstones, Book Depository and all other quality outlets.

ICE HOCKEY BOOKS BY PAUL BREEZE

Ice Hockey (1936) by Major BM Patton - Annotated & Illustrated 2020: A facsimile reprint of the original 1936 edition with new introduction, author biography and appendices.

ED2n 11/12: A Review of the 2011/12 Ice Hockey Season In English Division 2 North

Ice Hockey Review 12/13 North: A Review of the 2012/13 Ice Hockey Season in NIHL North Divisions 1 & 2

Ice Hockey Review NIHL Yearbook 2014: The 2013/14 Season in NIHL N&S Divisions 1 & 2

Ice Hockey Review NIHL Yearbook 2015: The 2014/15 Season In NIHL North & South

Ice Hockey Review NIHL Yearbook 2016

Ice Hockey Review UK Hockey Yearbook 2017

Ice Hockey Review UK Hockey Yearbook 2018

Fylde Flyers - A Complete Record: Seasons 2011/12 & 2012/13

The Seagull Has Landed: A Light-Hearted Review Of the First 12 Months Back Together Of the Blackpool Seagulls Ice Hockey Team

A Year In The Wild: The 2016/17 season following Widnes Wild

Widnes Wild – Lockdown Lookback

North / South Divide: Random Ramblings About British Ice Hockey During the 2013/14 Season

I have also made contributions to:
The History Of Ice Hockey In Peterborough by Stuart Latham
60 Years Of The Altrincham Aces by Stuart Latham
The Deeside Dragons by Stuart Latham
From Vikings To Devils by Stuart Latham
Wightlink Raiders – Simply The Best by Chris Randall
UK Ice Hockey by Michael A Chambers

And I also produced commemorative match programmes for:
Blackpool Seagulls v UK Firefighters Charity Game (February 2012)
Blackpool Seagulls Bruce Sims Visit (April 2013)
Deeside Dragons v Liverpool Leopards Legends Match (July 2013)
Bob Kenyon Memorial Shield Game (June 2016)

I also provided weekly league round up columns for the Blackburn Hawks Match programmes for 3 seasons and series of "Rewind" nostalgia articles for 1 season.

Also numerous contributions to various play off and cup end of season programmes.

In addition, Paul Breeze has co-written, edited, or helped to publish all of the following:

Nov 2000: The History of Rot Weiss Erfurt: Forgotten Champions of DDR Football (Edition out of print)

Dec 2001: Darwen Football Club: Memories

Dec 2002: Colne Giants: Tales from the Forgotten World of Knur and Spell

Mar 2007: Blackpool to Bond Street!: The Fascinating Story of Amy Blackburn - Pioneer of the Makeover

May 2012: Guns & Pencils: An Anthology Of War Poems

Sep 2012: Twilight: A Single Act Stage Drama Written with Mature Actors in Mind...

Oct 2012: Bullets & Daffodils: The Wilfred Owen Story (Edition out of print)

Oct 2012: Selected Poems: Over 50 of the Best Entries for the 2012 Pendle War Poetry Competition

Oct 2012: A Tale Of Two Sisters: An Original Screenplay Suitable For TV or Film

Jan 2013: ED2n 11/12: A Review of the 2011/12 Ice Hockey Season in English Division 2 North

Feb 2013: Purple Patches: A Collection of Poems, Songs and Short Stories from the Fountain Pen of Lucy London

Apr 2013: The Seagull Has Landed!: A Light Hearted Review of the First 12 Months Back Together of the Blackpool Seagulls Ice Hockey Team

Jul 2013: Female Poets of the First World War: Part of an Ongoing International Centenary Research Project: Volume 1

Sep 2013: Ice Hockey Review 12/13 North: A Review of the 2012/13 Ice Hockey Season in NIHL North Divisions 1 & 2

Nov 2013: Pendle War Poetry Competition - Selected Poems: An Anthology of Over 100 of the Best Poems Submitted for the 2013 Pendle War Poetry Competition: 2013

Sep 2014: No Woman's Land: A Centenary Tribute to Inspirational Women of World War One

Oct 2014: Ice Hockey Review - NIHL Yearbook 2014: The 2013/14 Season in NIHL North & South

Nov 2014: Hearts in Unison: A New Collection of Poems by Natasha Walker

Nov 2014: Respect The 88: A collection of verse about - or inspired by - the Ingleborough Road Memorial Playing Field

Aug 2015: Love & War - 2015 Reprint: A Collection of Poems by "Nadja" - Later Marchesa Nadja Malacrida - Originally Published in 1915

Oct 2015: Ice Hockey Review NIHL Yearbook 2015 Sponsored by Red Hockey: The 2014/15 Season in NIHL North & South

Dec 2015: Faith Finds Out: A Short Story About The First World War (Kindle only - short story)

Dec 2015: Magical Mystery Christmas (Kindle only - short story)

Apr 2016: Fylde Flyers - A Complete Record: Seasons 2011/12 & 2012/13

Apr 2016: Women Casualties of the Great War in Military Cemeteries: (In Support of) Wenches in Trenches - Roses of No Man's Land: Volume 1: Belgium & France – limited charity edition

Jun 2016: The Somme - 1916: A Centenary Collection of Poets, Writers & Artists Involved in the 1916 Offensive

Sep 2016: Female Poets of the First World War: Volume 2

Sep 2016: Women Casualties of the Great War in Military Cemeteries: Volume 1: Belgium & France

Oct 2016: Ice Hockey Review NIHL Yearbook 2016

Jun 2017: A Year In the Wild: The 2016/17 season following Widnes Wild in the NIHL North Laidler Conference

Oct 2017: Ice Hockey Review UK Hockey Yearbook 2017

Apr 2018: Arras, Messines, Passchendaele And More: Poets, Writers, Artists & Nurses in 1917

Jul 2018: Aviator Poets & Writers Of WW1: with a special section on women pilots

Aug 2018: Poets' Corners In Foreign Fields: A Guide to Literary Graves in Military Cemeteries

Oct 2018: Ice Hockey Review UK Hockey Yearbook 2018

Oct 2018: Pendle War Poetry - Selected Poems 2018: Under 18 & Overseas Entries

Oct 2018: Pendle War Poetry Competition - Selected Poems 2018: United Kingdon & Ireland Entries

Oct 2018: Post 1945 German Cinema - Two DEFA Films: Comparing "Die Legende von Paul und Paula" & "Solo Sunny"

Oct 2018: Francois Mitterrand & Margaret Thatcher: A Comparison Of Leadership Styles

Oct 2018: The BBC And Radio Luxembourg: A Comparison Of Broadcasting Styles and Attitudes

Nov 2018: Merseyside Poets, Writers & Artists Of The First World War

Jan 2019: White Feather: An original song by Lucy London - arranged for a 7-Piece Band.

Jun 2019: Great War Memorial Birthday Book: Birthdates of Poets, Writers, Artists & Nurses From the First World War With Space To Keep A Note Of Your Own Memorable Dates

Nov 2019: The Adventures Of Bunny, Archie, Alice & Friends

Feb 2020: Wilfred Owen: Centenary: Featuring Brief Owen Biography, Wilfred Owen And Me, Wilfred Owen In Print & Birkenhead Centenary Commemorations.

Oct 2020: Ice Hockey (1936) by Major BM Patton - Annotated & Illustrated 2020: A facsimile reprint of the original 1936 edition with new introduction, author biography and appendices

Nov 2020: Nadja - The Complete Poems

Nov 2020: Widnes Wild - Lockdown Lookback

Nov 2020: North / South Divide: Random Ramblings About British Ice Hockey During the 2013/14 Season

Dec 2020: Artists Of The First World War: Volume 1

May 2021: The Lucy London Songbook

Aug 2021: Wightlink Raiders - Simply The Best: The 25 Year History of Ice Hockey on the Isle Of Wight

Sep 2021: North / South Divide – Volume 2: Ice Hockey And Me

Nov 2021: North / South Divide - Volume 3: Cricket & Baseball

Feb 2022: North South Divide – Volume 4: France Actually

Copies of most publications are available via Amazon, PoshUpNorth.com, Waterstones, Book Depositary and many other quality outlets.

Certain titles are also available as Kindle download.

PB TRANSLATING

Over 30 years' experience of translation & interpreting in industry & commerce - specialising in English / French /German.

Also involvement with Italian, Spanish, Dutch, Russian, Czech & Polish.

For enquiries, please e-mail to pbtranslating@gmail.com

INTERESTING WEBSITES

If you have found any of this in the least bit interesting, you might like to have the occasional look at some of these various websites which, as of March 2022, I am currently involved with:

Check out our audio and video archive in our dedicated "Paul & Lucy's Best Kept Secrets" YouTube channel at www.youtube.com.

IF YOU HAVE ENJOYED THIS BOOK, YOU WILL ABSOLUTELY <u>LOVE</u>
"FRANCE ACTUALLY"

North / South Divide – Volume 4

ISBN-13: 978-1-909643-47-5

Available now by mail order from Amazon, Posh Up North, Waterstones, Book Depository and all other quality outlets.

Full Contents List:
1950s: Early Family Voyages
From Rhodesia to Ramsey!
Saskatchewan, Canada
1970s & 80s: Staycating
A Wet Week In Hunstanton
Cub Camp
1978: Forest Of Dean
1979: Butlin's
1981: Auntie Sadie's
1983 and after...: Foxhills, Sheringham
1979: Abroad At Last!
1982: Barneville – Carteret
1983/84/85: French Exchange To Montpellier
Summer 1983
May 1984: Montpellier
July 1984: Peterborough
April / May 1985: Montpellier
June 1985: Peterborough
1984: Port Grimaud
1987: Italy...? France Actually!
1987/88: A French Connection
March 1988: St Etienne
Summer 1988: Paris
November 1988 to March 1989: Sima Torcy
1990: French Visitors
1991: Nantes or Frankfurt?
1995: French With Some Poles
Easter 1998: Paris
Phoebe Cates And The McDonald's Milkshake Incident
May 1998: Strasbourg
Travelling Across France But Not Actually Going There.